UNIVERSITY OF NOTTINGHAM
10 0647416 2
HOW SCIENCE WORKS
WITHDRAWN
FROM THE LIBRARY

How Science Works provides student and practising teachers with a comprehensive introduction to one of the most dramatic changes to the secondary science curriculum. Underpinned by the latest research in the field, this book explores the origins and meaning of How Science Works and reviews major developments in policy and practice.

With chapters structured around three key questions — *why* teach How Science Works, *what* it is and *how* to teach it — expert contributors discuss and debate the need for curriculum change, arguments for scientific literacy for all, school students' views about science, what we understand about scientific methods, types of scientific enquiry and, importantly, effective pedagogies and their implications for practice. Aiming to promote discussion and reflection on the ways forward for this new and emerging area of the school science curriculum, it considers:

- teaching controversial issues in science
- argumentation and questioning for effective teaching
- enhancing investigative science and developing reasoned scientific judgments
- the role of ICT in exploring How Science Works
- teaching science outside the classroom.

How Science Works is a source of guidance for all student, new and experienced teachers of secondary science interested in investigating how the curriculum can provide creativity and engagement for all school students.

Rob Toplis is Senior Lecturer in Secondary Science Education at Brunel University, UK.

D0120595

HOW SCIENCE WORKS

Exploring effective pedagogy and practice

Edited by
Rob Toplis

JUBILEE
CAMPUS
LRC

Routledge
Taylor & Francis Group

LONDON AND NEW YORK

This first edition published 2011
by Routledge
2 Park Square, Milton Park, Abingdon, Oxon OX14 4RN

Simultaneously published in the USA and Canada
by Routledge
270 Madison Avenue, New York, NY 10016

Routledge is an imprint of the Taylor & Francis Group, an informa business

© 2011 Selection and editorial matter, Rob Toplis;
individual chapters, the contributors

Typeset in Times and Helvetica by
GreenGate Publishing Services, Tonbridge, Kent

Printed and bound in Great Britain by
TJ International Ltd, Padstow, Cornwall

1006474162

All rights reserved. No part of this book may be reprinted or reproduced or utilized in
any form or by any electronic, mechanical, or other means, now known or hereafter
invented, including photocopying and recording, or in any information storage or
retrieval system, without permission in writing from the publishers.

The right of Rob Toplis to be identified as author of this work has been asserted by
him in accordance with sections 77 and 78 of the Copyright, Designs and Patents
Act 1988.

British Library Cataloguing in Publication Data
A catalogue record for this book is available from the British Library

Library of Congress Cataloging in Publication Data
How science works : exploring effective pedagogy and practice / edited by Rob
Toplis.
        p. cm.
1. Science—Study and teaching (Secondary)—England. 2. Critical pedagogy—
England. I. Toplis, Rob.
Q184.4.G7H69 2011
507.1'242—dc22
                        2010021479

ISBN13: 978-0-415-56279-9 (hbk)
ISBN13: 978-0-415-56280-5 (pbk)
ISBN13: 978-0-203-83826-6 (ebk)

CONTENTS

CONTENTS ▪ ▪ ▪ ■

10 Teaching science outside the classroom 134
JUSTIN DILLON

Final thoughts 148

Index 149

ILLUSTRATIONS

FIGURES

TABLES

NOTES ON CONTRIBUTORS

Michael Allen lectures in science education at Brunel University, west London, mainly to postgraduate trainee teachers. He is primarily interested in children's learning as they carry out practical work during science lessons. Other areas of interest include the influence of confirmation bias in science, how the philosophy of science impacts on science teachers' work and hypothesis formation in the context of experimentation. Michael worked as a science teacher and head of department in the state sector for 12 years in Berkshire middle and secondary schools.

Sue Collins is a Senior Lecturer in Education at Brunel University, west London. After a number of years as a primary/middle school teacher, specializing in science education, she now teaches on Initial Teacher Education programmes and master's and doctoral courses. Her main research interests are in pupils' attitudes towards science and models of assessment in science education.

Justin Dillon is Professor of Science and Environmental Education at King's College London. Prior to joining King's, he taught science in London secondary schools for 10 years. He is President of the European Science Education Research Association (ESERA) and an editor of the *International Journal of Science Education*.

Ralph Levinson is Senior Lecturer in Education at the Institute of Education University of London. He taught in comprehensive schools in inner London for 12 years before moving to the Open University, where he wrote the first distance learning science PGCE. His research interests include teaching of socio-scientific issues and risk, science and citizenship, teaching and learning chemistry, and the history, philosophy and ethics of science.

Helena Pedrosa de Jesus is Associate Professor at the Department of Didactic and Education Technology of the University of Aveiro, Portugal. Before joining the university, Helena was a schoolteacher for 20 years, where she was involved in teacher training and the supervision of trainee teachers. Her main research interests are in learners' questioning in education and training activities, with special emphasis on the role of questions in reflecting on learning and teaching.

Shirley Simon is Professor of Education at the Institute of Education, University of London, where she is head of department and supervises master's and doctoral students. She has taught in schools and on PGCE programmes over many years and has undertaken research into science investigations, argumentation, attitudes to science and teachers' professional learning.

Rob Toplis is Senior Lecturer in Secondary Science Education at Brunel University, west London, where he teaches and supervises on doctoral, master's and postgraduate certificate courses. He taught secondary science for 25 years and has research interests in the science curriculum, concept development and modelling in chemistry education, and science teacher education.

Mike Watts is Chair in Education in the School of Sport and Education at Brunel University, west London. He is Head of the Department for Education and responsible for developing teaching, research and consultancy in education at Brunel, with a special emphasis on STEM (science, technology, engineering and mathematics) research. His own areas of research interest lie in the learning and teaching of science, in schools and beyond.

Alan West is an experienced science teacher with wide knowledge of business education links gleaned through the development and implementation of the National CREST Awards, and a wide range of STEM education consultancy activities through his company Exscitec. He was a core contributor to the Gifted and Talented Education Arm of London Challenge and the STEM summer school programme at Imperial College London, where he is Director of the Reach Out Lab facility.

James Williams is a lecturer in science education at the University of Sussex, where he teaches on secondary science PGCE programmes. He was a science teacher and head of science in a variety of state schools before entering teacher education. His research interests include science teachers and their understanding of the nature of science and the evolution/creationism issue in science education.

Jocelyn Wishart is a Senior Lecturer in Science Education with the Graduate School of Education at the University of Bristol. She has taught science, psychology and ICT in secondary schools and directed PGCE programmes in both physics and ICT. Her research interests lie primarily in the psychology of learning via ICT and in the corresponding pedagogy of using new technologies for teaching.

PREFACE

The aim of this book is to provide a background to one of the most dramatic changes to the secondary science curriculum since the National Curriculum was introduced in England and Wales in 1989: that of How Science Works. It traces the historical moves behind the curriculum, reviews some of the reasons for this change and discusses the ways that scientists work. In particular, the book looks at some of the pedagogies involved in implementing this new curriculum. One important feature of this book is that it is research-informed; the chapters draw on a variety of research studies, many conducted by the chapter authors themselves, from policy, pedagogy and perceptions.

This book provides three themes for How Science Works. The first is about *why* How Science Works has been included in the science National Curriculum, its background, the need for a curriculum change and the arguments for a level of scientific literacy for all. The second theme is about *what* How Science Works is, in particular in terms of understanding the scientific method, its history, the things that scientists do and the types and role of scientific inquiry. The third theme is about the *how* of How Science Works, the implications for teaching and the pedagogies required.

If the curriculum sets out *what* is taught, pedagogy informs us about *how* it is taught. This important area of science education – and how it translates into practice in secondary schools – is covered by the majority of chapters in this book. Some of the pedagogies, such as scientific inquiry, are all too familiar to science teachers. Other pedagogies may lie outside the science teacher's 'comfort zone'; pedagogies that involve discussion, argument, controversy or out-of-school experiences may not appear to be within the traditional domain of the science teacher. However, it is these pedagogies that can engage young people and make science relevant to their lives by relating it to the world around them. It is creativity with these approaches that is an essential part of the craft of teaching, one of the features that sets science teaching as a profession apart from mere soulless delivery of a science curriculum or scheme of work.

This is not a 'how to do it' book; it is not one that provides a set of prescriptive schemes or 'tips for science teaching'. To follow such a line would fail to address the different and complex demands that teaching How Science Works places on teachers. It would also fail to recognize that every teacher, every class and every individual in that class is different, that these differences can change over time and that there are complex relationships between them and the subject or topic being taught. This book aims to provide some ideas, some background and some areas for thought and discussion which recognize that science teachers possess professional and situated knowledge at whatever stage of their careers and that they reflect on this knowledge and practice.

Although How Science Works is an explicit strand of the curriculum in England, other countries within the United Kingdom have their own curricula that reflect some of the themes found in this strand. For example, Scotland, which has always had a tradition of independence in its education system, includes in its curriculum such statements as 'express opinions and make decisions on social, moral, ethical, economic and environmental issues informed by their knowledge and understanding of science' in its introduction to the guidance for science (Learning and Teaching Scotland 2006); Wales since devolution has determined its own priorities in education with a science curriculum that, at Key Stage 4 (ages 14–16), includes activities that 'should promote peer discussion and reflection when thinking about tasks and problems' (Department for Children, Education, Lifelong Learning and Skills 2008). Over on the other side of the world, the curriculum statement on the Nature of Science from New Zealand has a familiar ring to it:

> The Nature of Science strand is the overarching, unifying strand. Through it, students learn what science is and how scientists work. They develop the skills, attitudes, and values to build a foundation for understanding the world. They come to appreciate that while scientific knowledge is durable, it is also constantly re-evaluated in the light of new evidence. They learn how scientists carry out investigations, and they come to see science as a socially valuable knowledge system. They learn how science ideas are communicated and to make links between scientific knowledge and everyday decisions and actions.
>
> (New Zealand Ministry of Education 2007: 28)

When a new curriculum initiative is announced, there are often comments that are variations on the theme of 'we've been here before'. At first sight the How Science Works strand of a new National Curriculum may appear like that. But appearances can be deceptive. At last How Science Works has managed to start to bring together a number of different ideas, movements, thinking and research work that have informed developments over the last two or three decades in science education, developments influenced by work in the international science education arena. Large-scale international surveys such as the Relevance of Science Education (ROSE) (Sjøberg and Schreiner 2005) and PISA (OECD 2007) attest to the importance of science in the lives of young people, but also to their attitudes to the science education they receive. The phrase 'important but not for me' (Jenkins and Nelson 2005) summarizes this attitude, particularly for school students in Northern Europe, North America, Japan, Australia and New Zealand.

How Science Works is an attempt to provide a curriculum that enhances scientific literacy and at the same time provide interest and engagement. It integrates science subject knowledge with how science is seen in the real lives of students, in their interest, their engagement and their thinking about and thinking through contemporary science as it affects their lives in society. As Alan West points out in Chapter 8, it is about providing a wonderful opportunity for pupils to develop as critical and creative thinkers and to become flexible problem-solvers.

Curriculum change has been the result of a number of factors and influences that are discussed in Chapters 1 and 2, which provide some historical background to the theme of *why* How Science Works has been incorporated into the National Curriculum. There were, however, many other influences for the inclusion of the range of topics in this book. Chapter 3 discusses the realization that science is based firmly on a body of evidence and theory and how this has developed over time. Chapters 4 and 8 discuss the move away from an algorithmic and contrived approach to practical inquiry to encompass more varied and authentic approaches. Chapter 5 covers the theme that science is not without controversy. Science impacts on all our lives and its results may have important implications for our existence – and future – on the planet. Chapters 3, 6 and 9 cover the fact that communication is an important part of science and the way that scientists work, and report and support their findings. Finally, an overarching theme of the book is that all these parts of the new school science curriculum have an impact on not only *what* we teach but *how* we teach it: the pedagogy. These pedagogies are needed for engagement, creativity and motivation. This is not a question of 'dumbing down' but a genuine effort to engage all students in order to make their science diet engaging, up to date and relevant to their lives as opposed to a diet where science is transmitted as a collection of bland, stodgy facts without variety and spice.

Finally, a word about the terminology used. With an increasingly international perspective on science education, a number of different words may be used. The terms 'enquiry' and 'inquiry' may be used synonymously to mean the same thing, reflecting their use in the literature and in line with US and European conventions. Similarly, the terms 'pupil', 'student', 'learner' and 'child' or 'children' may be used to refer to a secondary school student up to the age of 16 years; different chapter contributors use different terms, and although this is an edited book, it is important that their own voices be retained.

REFERENCES

Department for Children, Education, Lifelong Learning and Skills (2008) *Science in the National Curriculum for Wales*, Cardiff: Welsh Assembly Government.

Jenkins, E. W. and Nelson, N. W. (2005) Important but not for me: students' attitudes towards secondary school science in England, *Research in Science and Technological Education* 23(1), 41–57.

Learning and Teaching Scotland (2006) A curriculum for excellence. The guidance. Building the Curriculum 1: Science. Introduction. Online. Available HTTP: <http://www.ltscotland.org.uk/curriculumforexcellence/buildingthecurriculum/guidance/btc1/scn/intro.asp> (accessed 20 February 2010).

New Zealand Ministry of Education (2007) *The New Zealand Curriculum* Wellington, New Zealand: Learning Media.

OECD (2007) PISA 2006: Science Competencies for Tomorrow's World. Executive Summary. Online. Available HTTP: <http://www.pisa.oecd.org/dataoecd/15/13/39725224.pdf> (accessed 23 August 2010).

Sjøberg, S. and Schreiner, C. (2005) How do learners in different cultures relate to science and technology? *Asia-Pacific Forum on Science Learning and Teaching* 1–17.

ACKNOWLEDGEMENTS

I should like to thank all colleagues in the science education community who have provided their thoughts and encouragement for this book. Particular thanks of course go to the contributors for their patience with all my questions and emails, to the commissioning editor at Routledge, Helen Pritt, for her initial encouragement to publish, to Jerry Wellington for his guidance at the early stages of the book and to Kat Richmond for comments and suggestions on my drafts.

Finally, I should like to acknowledge the publishers who have given permission to reproduce illustrations from other works. Figure 2.1 is based on the Planet Science report, 'Student Review of the Science Curriculum. Major Findings', Fig 1.20, page 14, reproduced with permission from Planet Science. Figure 3.1 is taken from Williams, J. (2008) Science now and then: discovering *How science works*, *School Science Review* 90(330), p45, kindly reproduced with permission from the Association for Science Education. Figure 7.1 is from Barlex, D. (2007) Assessing capability in design & technology. The case for a minimally invasive approach, *Design and Technology Education: An International Journal*, 12, 2, p. 5 with kind permission from the author and the Design & Technology Association. Figure 9.1 is taken from McFarlane, A. (2000) The impact of education technology. In Warwick, P. and Sparks Linfield, R. (Eds) *Science 3–13: The Past, The Present and Possible Futures*, reproduced with permission from Routledge-Falmer.

HOW DID WE GET HERE?

SOME BACKGROUND
TO HOW SCIENCE
WORKS IN THE
SCHOOL CURRICULUM

Rob Toplis

INTRODUCTION

The background to the inclusion of How Science Works in the science curriculum is a chequered one. As with many curriculum initiatives, it has resulted from a mixture of historical events, initiatives and a not inconsiderable degree of political influence. This chapter examines the developments – and sometimes competing factors – that have brought secondary science education to where it is today. Of necessity it raises a number of questions. These may be about the history of science education in schools – what has happened before; philosophical questions about what sort of science education we want in schools and why; and what school science students really need to learn and why they need learn it. This chapter reviews some of the enduring debates in science education concerning teaching science through contexts, scientific literacy, content and process, key curriculum events and a critical evaluation of the National Curriculum over a twenty-year period since its introduction in 1989 and its revised versions in 1991, 1995, 2000 and now 2004.

ACTING LIKE REAL SCIENTISTS? PRACTICAL WORK IN SCHOOL SCIENCE

Wellington (1998) has identified three important phases in science education since the 1960s. He terms them the discovery phase, the process approach and a third phase that came with National Curriculum legislation which he terms (after Jenkins) investigations by order. A review of these phases provides some insight into the way that practical 'inquiry' in science education has evolved.

The Nuffield Projects exemplified the discovery approach, based on the late-nineteenth-century ideas of heurism, promoted by Armstrong (Jenkins 1979), that pupils should discover things for themselves by enabling them to practise scientific methods. The Nuffield Projects provided new laboratory equipment and brought new and well-resourced science into secondary school classrooms. The projects had professed additional advantages of providing a more active approach to learning, of increasing motivation and recall, and of providing an understanding of the nature of inquiry and the nature of science (Wellington 1981). However, the discovery approach was open to criticism. For a school curriculum previously content-laden and reliant upon the transmission of a body of knowledge, the transition to a new approach was unclear. 'What's supposed to happen, sir?' (ibid.: 167) succinctly summarizes the problem faced by pupils expected to 'discover' knowledge, resulting in contrivances to obtain a 'right' answer. Indeed, the tension of discovering knowledge in isolation from science content, as opposed to interpreting new knowledge with a prior understanding of scientific content, has been discussed by Driver (1975), who noted that pupils may bring in alternative frameworks consistent with their observations but not with acceptable theory.

The process approach placed emphasis on scientific processes or methods, such as classifying, observing and inferring, rather than science content such as facts, laws and principles (Gott and Duggan 1995). Millar and Driver (1987) have discussed some of the problems with a process approach to learning science. They point out that there is not necessarily a dichotomy between process and content; rather, the two are integral to learning science. They highlight the fact that learning content is an active process and not mere rote learning and recall of facts. They also note that processes, for example observation and evaluation, may be generic and not unique to science. Although they may be part of the skill base of pupils, there is some question about their transferability in practice between school subjects. They also argue that although scientists may have characteristic ways of working, the 'scientific method' (ibid.: 41) cannot be portrayed as a set of rules of procedures of science; that there are no general algorithms of the way that science is carried out.

The methods of science may vary between different branches of science. Physiologists may rely more on experimental approaches whereas astronomers or animal behaviourists may adopt detailed observation and suggested explanations of phenomena in their work. One other thing that scientists do – and do so increasingly on an international scale – is communicate with each other. Scientists meet their colleagues, discuss ideas, argue, debate, email and attend conferences all over the world. A flavour of this interactive aspect of science is richly conveyed with the story of the structure of DNA (Watson 1968) but is a frequently overlooked part of scientists' work, certainly in school science, where the image of a scientist as a lone figure in a laboratory still remains in the minds of many pupils.

Since 1989, Attainment Target 1 – later to be called Sc1 – has included the experimental and investigative requirements of the National Curriculum. This was the first time investigative work in school science was enshrined in a statutory curriculum. Students now had to predict, carry out, analyse and evaluate investigative science. Although these skills were an integral part of the process science schemes prior to the National Curriculum, they were neither a requirement nor adopted in every school; investigative science was a noticeable departure from the 'cookery book' type of practical work that was carried out across the country and which was designed to illustrate scientific phenomena and explanations. What students and teachers did when the practical work failed to illustrate their intended outcomes can only be guessed at, although Nott and Wellington (1997) have reported a number of ploys used to get the 'correct' answer.

Research into Sc1 investigations highlighted a number of criticisms. A major survey (Nott *et al.* 1998) reported the opinions of local education authority personnel, teachers and students about Key Stage 3 (ages 11–14 years) and Key Stage 4 (ages 14–16 years) science. Part of this report included data from questionnaires and interviews about practical work and Sc1 investigations. The student comments were retrospective in nature as the students were in Year 12 (age 17 years) but they paint a picture of assessment-driven and contrived investigations at KS4. The survey revealed that just over half of the pupils felt there was less practical work at Key Stage 4 than earlier; a clear majority felt they should be allowed to repeat to improve marks and most felt sure that they knew how to get good marks in Sc1 for the final General Certificate in Secondary Education (GCSE) examinations at the end of Key Stage 4. A clear majority felt that Sc1 work was more about 'getting a good mark' than learning or understanding some science (Nott *et al.* 1998: 30). Students realized they had to do practical work in the 'correct manner' and several of them complained that practicals were really 'pretend' since they knew the answers and had done similar things before (Nott *et al.* 1998: 33). These responses lend support to the following comment about attainment levels and investigations: 'Sc1 investigations are generally routines that teachers know will provide access to all the levels and can be organized and completed quickly in small 'windows' of time' (Nott and Wellington 1999: 17).

In a study of investigations at Key Stage 4 in Northern Ireland, Jones *et al.* (2000) interviewed over 100 pupils at the start and towards the end of Key Stage 4 from thirty different schools. They found that the major response from pupils about practical work was one of enjoyment, valuing independence as a feature of the activity, appealing to pupils' spirit of inquiry and providing a sense of achievement. However, twelve of the pupils indicated that they did not enjoy doing investigations, with common reasons being the requirement to write and submit a report for GCSE coursework, and associated exam pressure and shortage of time. Some found the experience too intellectually challenging while others found it boring. Keiler and Woolnough's (2002) report of research carried out in one school highlighted six major categories of motivational behaviours during practical coursework: implementing correct procedures; following instructions; doing what is easy; acting automatically; working within limits; and earning marks. It shows that pupils 'were all very clear about the supreme importance of the assessment system in creating and curtailing their choices and behaviours during the two years leading up to the GCSE examinations' (Keiler and Woolnough 2002: 84).

Research reported by Toplis and Cleaves (2006) identified pupils' concerns about the limited time available when investigations were carried out during the two-year GCSE course, lack of familiarity with apparatus and the association of investigations almost exclusively with assessment. Pupils perceived the teacher's role in investigations as one of trainer and supporter of strategies to maximize performance for assessment. Furthermore, there is a need to fit investigative work and its attendant demands, in terms of apparatus, technician time and resources, into what is often perceived by teachers as an overburdened curriculum (Donnelly *et al.* 1996). To yield good marks within the full range of possible scores, teachers often select certain set-piece investigations as they seem to be sufficiently flexible to allow pupils of different abilities to achieve their potential. The demands made by examination boards to both internally moderate within schools and externally moderate between schools may make tried and tested investigations more attractive than new and novel approaches that need to be trialled and accepted. They concluded that the tendency to train pupils to do investigations may be viewed as a response to the 1988 Education Reform Act, where the comparison of school with school, the so-called 'league tables', has given rise to a culture of high-stakes assessment that seems to have had the widespread effect of conflating the teaching and assessment of investigations.

SCIENCE FOR ALL?

The argument for a 'science for all' hinges on a desire of scientific literacy for all pupils. Prior to a National Curriculum, it was theoretically possible for pupils to leave school having received no science in their curriculum diet. In practice this was generally unlikely, as schools tried to provide a degree of balance across the whole curriculum. However, many pupils left school with a limited knowledge of science as a whole, or knowledge of only one of the sciences. This begs the question about why pupils should study science and what sort of science they should study.

The Association for Science Education (ASE) was active in providing a focus on the science curriculum itself. In publishing the consultative document *Alternatives for Science Education* in 1979, the ASE noted, among other things, the problem of an imbalance between boys and girls studying science and proposed a broad coverage of science education for all pupils. This, then, was one of the first attempts to highlight some of the problems, propose a broadening of science and open a debate within science education itself. This 1979 document was followed two years later by the Association's *Education through Science* policy statement in 1981. The preface commented on the educational debate and on the direction of science education, noting that 'Social, political and economic pressures are such that changes in our educational provision are inevitable' (ASE 1979: 1). This is important, as this statement represented the realization from a professional organization that a certain level of scientific literacy is essential for all school pupils in order to make sense of the world, and not only for the elite minority who will go on to careers in science or the health professions. *Education through Science* was an important foundation for future developments as it made a number of recommendations and proposals about science *in* the school curriculum and the development *of* the school science curriculum. Some of these, such as effective provision of science education in the early years and broad general courses at the lower secondary level, are familiar in today's National Curriculum. Other recommendations about, for example, class sizes for practical work and the provision of physical science teachers are problems that are still with us today.

Why is science for all necessary? Questions remain about why pupils need to make sense of the world and what science they need to do so. Despite problems with definitions, answers to these questions are often referred to as scientific literacy, citizen science or the public understanding of science. We live in a society which is reliant on science and technology. It is therefore desirable, if not essential, for everyone in the society to have an understanding about the science and, importantly, an understanding of the impact that science has on society, in order to make informed judgements. School science contributes to public understanding by developing pupils' understanding of the scientific enterprise itself, its aims and purposes and the knowledge produced. This understanding is needed in order to develop an appreciation of the power and limitations of scientific claims and to produce informed citizens who can participate in a modern democracy. As the 2003 PISA report notes:

> An important life skill for young people is the capacity to draw appropriate and guarded conclusions from evidence and information given to them, to criticise claims made by others on the basis of evidence put forward, and to distinguish opinion from evidence-based statements.
>
> (OECD 2003: 132)

This does not mean that the 'big ideas' of science are ignored: concepts and explanatory frameworks are important in order to understand science in society. Some knowledge of topics such as particles, forces and the relationships between living things and their environments are still needed – clearly, an understanding of climate change would not be easy to acquire without some understanding of combustion and photosynthesis. However, engaging with the issues of the world around them is important for pupils. Just as driving a car and appreciating its impact on health, safety and the environment are important, a detailed knowledge of the precise working of each component in the car may not be required although *some* understanding of the general ways a car works is an advantage. People need to be in a position to review the impact of the car on the environment and on the safety of its occupants, pedestrians and other road users, as well as to assess critically the car salesman's claims for performance and to measure these against the car's specifications. This somewhat superficial analogy illustrates some of the important components of scientific literacy that involve weighing evidence, reaching conclusions, making decisions and supporting or rejecting arguments about controversial issues. The way that school science can help is to teach these skills as well as the knowledge and understanding about the big ideas of science.

A number of authors (for example Driver *et al.* 1996; Jenkins 1999; Millar 1996) have discussed reasons for the importance of promoting a public understanding of science. The first of these is an economic argument which puts forward a direct connection between a public understanding of science and a nation's wealth, a point highlighted by Prime Minister Tony Blair's speech to the Royal Society in London, where he stated that science was crucial to the United Kingdom's economic success (BBC News, 23 May 2002). A second argument is the democratic one which claims that understanding science is a necessary part of an individual's participation in the decision-making processes of society. Jenkins (1999) notes that many countries are revising or reforming school science to the end of developing an informed citizenry, although the impulse for doing so is often principally economic rather than democratic. Third, the utilitarian argument suggests the practical usefulness of science for living in a modern society where decisions are needed about health and welfare. The fourth argument concerns social considerations about maintaining cohesive links between science and a wider culture in order that science is not seen as a remote discipline alienated from the social world.

One essential part of scientific literacy is an understanding of the nature of science itself – that is to say, how scientists arrive at scientific knowledge, as opposed to scientific knowledge per se. It is about the process of how scientific knowledge is built up, the means used to develop ideas in terms of the ways of observing, thinking and experimenting and validating, and the wider social aspects of science. A detailed definition of the nature of science has been offered by the American Association for the Advancement of Science (1990). This definition is based around three principal subjects: a scientific worldview, scientific inquiry and scientific enterprise.

The scientific worldview is based on a systematic study of the patterns within the universe, on scientific ideas being subject to change with changing knowledge, on producing scientific knowledge which, although not attaining absolute truth, is nonetheless mostly durable, and the belief that science cannot always provide answers to all questions.

Although there is no fixed method or approach that scientists always follow, scientific inquiry demands evidence that may be obtained in different ways. It blends logical thought and imagination to explain and predict phenomena; it attempts to identify and remove sources of bias; and its findings are open to scrutiny, criticism and debate.

The scientific enterprise itself is not one of the lone scientist at the bench but is a complex social activity that may be conducted across subject disciplines and in different institutions. Scientists follow accepted – and changing – ethical principles and procedures and are able to participate as both specialists and citizens in the public domain.

The nature of science appears to have played a relatively small part in the school curriculum. Although in the past it may have been included in teachers' own practice, it became part of the 1989 National Curriculum in Attainment Target (AT) 17. This AT introduced the nature of science as a topic within which pupils should develop their knowledge and understanding of the ways in which scientific ideas change through time and how the nature of these ideas and the uses to which they are put are affected by moral, social, spiritual and cultural contexts. For example, at a lower level, level 4, pupils were expected to be able to give an account of a scientific advance and describe the ideas and the life of the scientist involved. At the upper level, level 10, pupils were expected to be able to understand the uses of evidence and the tentative nature of proof. The expectation here was that all teachers of secondary science should be able to teach the nature of science, a situation for which they had little time to prepare and which they had to balance against the preparation time for the other twenty-one ATs. A study by Lakin and Wellington (1994) found AT 17 (the nature of science) to be problematic. In particular, teachers' lack of knowledge about the nature and history of science emerged during their discussions. Lederman's (1992) review of research on teachers' conceptions of the nature of science reports that they lack a view of the tentative nature of science or that they have inadequate conceptions.

AT17, covering the nature of science in the 1989 curriculum, was subsumed into AT1 in the 1991 National Curriculum in an attempt to make the National Curriculum look less daunting. However, AT1 – later to become Sc1 – had a primary focus on practical inquiry and investigation, and the nature of science aspects were no longer assessed. As a result, this was not explicitly addressed in schools despite it being an important part of scientific literacy.

WHY DO YOU NEED TO KNOW? SCIENCE IN CONTEXT, SCIENCE IN SOCIETY

There is a longstanding tension in science education between studying topics of relevance in students' everyday and future lives, and formal courses structured for progressive development of key concepts and knowledge. It applies to some degree at all stages of school education, but more starkly at the secondary level, where it has surfaced most recently with the applications and implications section of How Science Works. In context-based approaches to science teaching, contexts and applications of science are used as the starting points for the development of scientific ideas. This contrasts with more traditional approaches to secondary science that cover scientific ideas first, before looking at applications. The example of the context-based *Salters Advanced Chemistry* illustrates this point. In a questionnaire survey, teachers reported that although they found the course more demanding to teach, they found it more motivating and that their students were more interested in chemistry, in both their responses in lessons and an increased likelihood of an interest manifested in them deciding to study chemistry at university. Interviews with students revealed that student interest and motivation were maintained at a higher level across the two-year Salters course than in the more conventional, non-context-based course (Bennett and Lubben 2006).

The Science and Technology in Society (SATIS) materials of the 1980s and 1990s, and the adapted, updated and revitalized SATIS Revisited materials, are testimony to previous work to bring science into the lives of school students. Through SATIS and *Science in a Social Context* (SISCON) (Solomon and Aikenhead 1994), aspects of science and society and environmental education have been framed by contexts with which pupils can engage in a variety of ways in order to provide relevance and authenticity through links to industry and science in practice. These include current debates about social-scientific issues and controversies, and use the process of argument that concerns the role and use of evidence; these are discussed in later chapters of this book.

TOWARDS A NATIONAL CURRICULUM FOR SCIENCE

Developments prior to the National Curriculum provide a context for the lead-up to the statutory orders of 1989 and for the political climate of the time. As with most initiatives, the National Curriculum did not appear out of the blue; there were a number of previous documents that give an insight into some of the thinking behind this major curriculum change, a change which removed curriculum power from teachers and placed it firmly in the hands of politicians. Teachers would no longer be allowed into the secret garden of the curriculum.

Following the then Prime Minister James Callaghan's Ruskin College speech in 1976, calling for a great debate on schooling, there had been growing pressure for change in terms of efficiency, value for money, relevance and a curriculum that could be rigorously assessed and reported. Alongside documents from the ASE and debates about the future of science education, work emerged from the Assessment of Performance Unit (APU). Following political debates about standards in the new comprehensive schools in the 1970s, the APU was set up by the Department of Education and Science (DES) to monitor pupils' capabilities and to provide greater accountability for the resources education consumed. With sites in Leeds and London, it was collecting data and disseminating its findings to the teaching profession during the 1980s. The APU is mentioned here because of its contribution to science education and for its role in the establishment of the teaching of process science, which included measurement, observations, interpretation and planning and performing investigations.

A number of the ASE proposals, and some of the APU approaches, emerged again in the document *Science 5–16: A Statement of Policy* (DES 1985). This was produced following a recognition of the need to improve science education and consideration of aims and the ways change could be brought about. This document came at a time of great change and debate. The new General Certificate of Secondary Education (GCSE) examinations were being developed, the Royal Society had published papers about school science, there was an interest in primary school science and there were new curriculum developments under way such as the Technical and Vocational Educational Initiative and the Secondary Science Curriculum Review. In contrast to the later National Curriculum in 1989, the *Science 5–16* document had less of a prescriptive 'flavour' to its wording. However, *Science 5–16* was important, as it served as a blueprint for the curriculum working group which would submit proposals to the Secretary of State for the new National Curriculum for Science.

■ **Table 1.1** Changes to the Science National Curriculum

Date	Major changes
1988 Proposals	Twenty-two Attainment Targets (ATs), of which sixteen were Knowledge and Understanding; two for Exploration and Investigation; two for Communication; and two for Science in Action
1989	Seventeen ATs formed by merging communication and the applications of science to form two profile components, 'Exploration of science' and 'Knowledge and understanding of science'
1991	ATs reduced to four: Sc1, Scientific investigation; Sc2, Life and living processes; Sc3, Materials and their properties; and Sc4, Physical processes
1995	Simplified and reduced Science National Curriculum but still using the four 1991 ATs. Reduction in level descriptions for pupil attainment from 10 to 8
2000	Little change except Sc1, Scientific enquiry (including ideas and evidence), and links to other subjects, the use of language, ICT and inclusion
2004	Two major strands, Knowledge and Understanding and How Science Works

CURRICULUM BY ORDER: A CRITICAL VIEW OF THE SCIENCE CURRICULUM SINCE 1989

There have now been five versions of the National Curriculum: 1989, 1991, 1995, 2000 and 2004 – quite a series of changes. What does this indicate? Changing criteria for the science curriculum? Different political agendas? Or the realization that previous versions of the curriculum were in need of change? Table 1.1 summarizes the changes to the science National Curriculum.

Two areas of the National Curriculum were open to general criticism as far as teachers are concerned: its manageability in practice and its assessment. A third criticism relates to scientific literacy and the question 'Who is the science curriculum for?'

Reports of events in 1988 (Black 1995) point to the conclusion that the 1989 National Curriculum was 'a rushed job'. The Task Group on Assessment and Testing, chaired by Professor Paul Black, carried out its work in only a few months; Black himself, reflecting on the events leading up to the National Curriculum, comments that 'Much of what has been described has been driven by the need of the politicians responsible in Britain to produce results quickly, and to react with equal haste when the media reported difficulties' (1995: 183). This rapid level of curriculum reform led to 'mass reading activities' (Wellington 1994: 3–4) where teachers and other educational professionals would attempt to interpret the new requirements. This was one of the major difficulties for a group of teachers with a degree of professional autonomy, more used to *controlling* aspects of the curriculum (certainly below the examination years) than *delivering* a centralized and prescribed format over which they had no control whatsoever. In trying to interpret the statements and programmes, teachers needed to learn the words of the new vocabulary and then to speculate on the meanings and intentions of those words. Teachers then had to write complex schemes of work to accommodate all of these factors. The 1991 version of the National Curriculum attempted to address some of the problems and simplify them. It reduced the number of ATs to a more manageable four and the Statements of Attainment from 409 to 176. Black (1995: 174) notes that '[T]eachers were very angry, for they had been working to alter completely their teaching to fit the schemes which came into operation in 1989, and in 1992 they had to start planning again'. The 1995 and 2000 versions retained the four ATs but attempted to simplify levels further by relying more on the professional judgement of teachers in their interpretation and implementation. Despite these attempts, the burdens of changes within the science curriculum have been onerous. The authors of *Beyond 2000* (Millar and Osborne) summarized this succinctly:

> Science teachers and schools have had to contend with the introduction of a National Curriculum which has been revised twice, and a new system of inspection and monitoring which many have found alienating and threatening. In addition, the introduction of competitive league tables, greater parental choice and, more recently, benchmarking and target-setting have been an additional burden.
>
> (1998: 28)

The assessment of the science National Curriculum has involved a tension between formative assessment, the methods that inform teaching and learning, and summative assessment, those methods that provide raw data about achievement. With this tension it appears that summative assessment, by means of Key Stage tests or SATs, has won out completely for nearly twenty years. This does not appear to have been the original intention. Gott and Duggan (1995: 127) note that the 'National Curriculum was originally intended for formative as well as summative assessment purposes'. The attainment targets from the 1989 National Curriculum contained detailed performance criteria which were appropriate for formative assessment (Gott and Duggan 1995; Black 1995). One problem of a criterion-referenced approach is that every statement would have to be separately assessed; Black (1995: 174) refers to this as 'the well known trap, in criterion-referencing, death by drowning'. Earlier recommendations (Black 1995) included one that national assessment should be based on a combination of teacher assessment and externally set tasks (SATs). This only partially occurred, with teacher assessments being limited to AT1 and published alongside the SATs results. These assessments were then used in a summative way because they were to be published for the 'league tables' where schools could be compared.

A third criticism is related to the wider area of science education policy and scientific literacy: what is science education for? Is the National Curriculum, in all its versions, aimed at educating pupils to be future science specialists or to be scientifically literate citizens? The report *Beyond 2000* (Millar and Osborne 1998) notes a growing disparity between the science education provided in schools and the needs and interests of pupils for the future. Although, with successive versions of the National Curriculum, content may have been reduced, there has still been a tendency to retain those aspects that were considered important for providing a grounding for post-16 study and to eliminate those areas more related to social and technological applications. Millar and Osborne (1998: 9–10) point out that 'For only a minority of young people, school science from 5–16 is the first stage of their training as scientists.'

A NEW DAWN? THE SCIENCE CURRICULUM SINCE 2004

Within the last ten years there have been international concerns about school science education, in particular the uptake of the physical sciences beyond the age of 16, gender differences, and pupils' attitudes towards and motivation for studying science. The Relevance of Science Education (ROSE) study of pupils' attitudes to science shows that in over twenty countries, pupils' response to the statement 'I like school science better than other subjects' is increasingly negative the more developed the country (Osborne and Dillon 2008: 13). Taken with other findings from the ROSE study, this points to pupils' views that although they may regard science as important, it may not be what they want to study further (Jenkins and Nelson 2005).

Alongside concerns about pupils' views about science education and the uptake of the physical sciences are concerns about what sort of science education needs to be taught in schools. Changes that resulted in the 2004 curriculum originated at the instigation of prominent science educators with a series of open meetings in 1997 and 1998 that culminated in the document *Beyond 2000: Science Education for the Future* (Millar and Osborne 1998). This seminal document was the product of a desire to provide a vision of science education that addressed the needs and interests of young people as future citizens at the end of the twentieth century. One important outcome from *Beyond 2000* was the inception of the Twenty-First Century Science project, which was the first attempt to develop and pilot a major curriculum initiative and to use evaluations of the pilot to inform further development (Millar 2006). Further criticisms of the previous versions of the Key Stage 4 National Curriculum included its prescriptive and assessment-driven nature, an overload of factual content, little contemporary science content, and coursework that was restricted to a few tried and tested investigations that were divorced from day-to-day science teaching (House of Commons Science and Technology Committee 2002; Keiler and Woolnough 2002; Nott and Wellington 1999; Toplis and Cleaves 2006).

These developments, and criticisms of a curriculum that was content-laden and seen to be lacking relevance to the lives of youngsters, resulted in the introduction of a new National Curriculum in 2004 and the adoption by the various examinations boards of new specifications for the examination at the end of Key Stage 4, the GCSE. The four main sections of the How Science Works strand of the National Curriculum are detailed in Box 1.1.

Box 1.1 **How Science Works**

Data, evidence, theories and explanations, where pupils should be taught:

- how scientific data can be collected and analysed;
- how interpretation of data, using creative thought, provides evidence to test ideas and develop theories;
- how explanations of many phenomena can be developed using scientific theories, models and ideas;
- that there are some questions that science cannot currently answer, and some that science cannot address.

Practical and inquiry skills, where pupils should be taught to:

■ plan to test a scientific idea, answer a scientific question, or solve a scientific problem;

■ collect data from primary or secondary sources, including using ICT sources and tools;

■ work accurately and safely, individually and with others, when collecting first-hand data;

■ evaluate methods of collection of data and consider their validity and reliability as evidence.

Communication skills, where pupils should:

■ recall, analyse, interpret, apply and question scientific information or ideas;

■ use both qualitative and quantitative approaches;

■ present information, develop an argument and draw a conclusion, using scientific, technical and mathematical language, conventions and symbols and ICT tools.

Applications and implications of science, where pupils should be taught:

■ about the use of contemporary scientific and technological developments and their benefits, drawbacks and risks;

■ to consider how and why decisions about science and technology are made, including those that raise ethical issues, and about the social, economic and environmental effects of such decisions;

■ how uncertainties in scientific knowledge and scientific ideas change over time and about the role of the scientific community in validating these changes.

(DfES/QCA 2004)

CONCLUSION

This chapter has reviewed some of the major arguments and historical developments that resulted in shifts and turns in the school science curriculum over a forty-year period – moves that culminated in the How Science Works strand of the National Curriculum. In doing so, it has highlighted some of the main criticisms in the National Curriculum story that has got us to where we are today. A challenge remains: that of developing the pedagogies necessary for fully integrating How Science Works into the school science curriculum – pedagogies that, for example, are designed to prepare students for evidence-based argument and discussion about the implications of science; pedagogies that can introduce the skills needed to discuss and debate controversial or ethical issues. These pedagogies will require particular proficiencies and structures that may not necessarily be in the current repertoire of science teachers' skills. To build these proficiencies requires training, exemplars and confidence, as well as time and resources.

Despite changes that have contributed to How Science Works and that have now produced a curriculum for all pupils that is relevant, up to date and engaging, there is still the nagging issue that this new curriculum remains dominated by assessment. With the very recent suspension of the SATs tests at Key Stage 3, projected changes at Key Stage 2 (ages 7–11 years) and an impression that politicians are thinking that it may now be time to start trusting teachers again, it remains to be seen if central government will dare to relinquish its hold on the school curriculum.

FURTHER READING

Millar, R. and Osborne, J. (eds) (1998) *Beyond 2000,* London: King's College.

Osborne, J. and Dillon, J. (2010) *Good Practice in Science Teaching: What Research Has to Say,* second edition. Maidenhead: Open University Press.

Roberts, R. (2009) Can teaching about evidence encourage a creative approach in open-ended investigations? *School Science Review* 90(332): 31–38.

REFERENCES

American Association for the Advancement of Science (1990) *Project 2061. Science for All Americans Online.* Chapter 1: The nature of science. Online. Available HTTP: <http://www.project2061.org/publications/sfaa/online/chap1.htm> (accessed 29 October 2009).

Association for Science Education (ASE) (1979) *Alternatives for Science Education*, Hatfield: ASE.

Association for Science Education (ASE) (1981) *Education through Science*, Hatfield: ASE.

BBC News, Thursday 23 May 2002 Science must not be stifled – Blair. Online. Available HTTP: <http://news.bbc.co.uk/1/hi/uk_politics/2003596.stm> (accessed 13 November 2009).

Bennett, J. and Lubben, F. (2006) Context-based chemistry: the Salters approach, *International Journal of Science Education* 28 (9), 999–1015.

Black, P. (1995) 1987–1995: The struggle to formulate a national curriculum for science in England and Wales, *Studies in Science Education* 26, 159–188.

Department for Education and Skills (DfES) and Qualifications and Curriculum Authority (QCA) (2004) *Science, the National Curriculum for England*, London: DfES.

Department of Education and Science (DES) (1985) *Science 5–16: A Statement of Policy*, London: HMSO.

Donnelly, J., Buchan, A., Jenkins, E., Laws, P. and Welford, G. (1996) *Investigations by Order*, Nafferton: Studies in Education).

Driver, R. (1975) The name of the game, *School Science Review* 56(197), 800–804.

Driver, R., Leach, J., Millar, R. and Scott, P. (1996) *Young People's Images of Science*, Buckingham: Open University Press.

Gott, R. and Duggan, S. (1995) *Investigative Work in the Science Curriculum*, Buckingham: Open University Press.

House of Commons Select Committee on Science and Technology (2002) *Science Education from 14–19:Third Report of Session 2001–02*, Vol. *1: Report and Proceedings of the Committee*, London: The Stationery Office.

Jenkins, E. W. (1979) *From Armstrong to Nuffield*, London: John Murray.

Jenkins, E. W. (1999) School science, citizenship and the public understanding of science, *International Journal of Science Education* 21(7), 703–710.

Jenkins, E. W. and Nelson, N. W. (2005) Important but not for me: students' attitudes towards secondary school science in England, *Research in Science and Technological Education* 23(1), 41–57.

Jones, M. E., Gott, R. and Jarman, R. (2000) Investigations as part of the Key Stage 4 science curriculum in Northern Ireland, *Evaluation and Research in Education* 14(1), 23–37.

Keiler, L. S. and Woolnough, B. E. (2002) Practical work in school science: the dominance of assessment, *School Science Review* 83(304), 83–88.

Lakin, S. and Wellington, J. J. (1994) Who will teach the 'nature of science'? Teachers' views of science and their implications for science education, *International Journal of Science Education* 16, 175–190.

Lederman, N. G. (1992) Students' and teachers' conceptions of the nature of science: a review of the research, *Journal of Research in Science Teaching* 29(4), 331–359.

Millar, R. (1996) Towards a science curriculum for public understanding, *School Science Review* 77(280), 7–18.

Millar, R. (2006) *Twenty First Century Science*: insights from the design and implementation of a scientific literacy approach in school science, *International Journal of Science Education* 28(13), 1499–1521.

Millar, R. and Driver, R. (1987) Beyond processes, *Studies in Science Education* 14, 33–62.

Millar, R. and Osborne, J. (1998) *Beyond 2000: Science Education for the Future*, London: King's College London School of Education.

Nott, M. and Wellington, J. (1997) Producing the evidence: science teachers' initiations into practical work, *Research in Science Education* 27 (285), 61–66.

Nott, M. and Wellington, J. (1999) The state we're in: issues in Key Stage 3 and 4 science, *School Science Review* 81(294), 13–18.

Nott, M., Peacock, G., Smith, R., Wardle, J., Wellington, J. and Wilson, P. (1998) *Investigations into KS3 and KS4 Science*, a report prepared for the Qualifications and Curriculum Authority, Projects 10905 and 10906, Sheffield: Sheffield Hallam University.

OECD (2003) *The PISA 2003 Assessment Framework – Mathematics, Reading, Science and Problem Solving Knowledge and Skills.* Online. Available HTTP: <http://www.oecd.org/dataoecd/38/29/33707226.pdf> (accessed 24 October 2009).

Osborne, J. and Dillon, J. (2008) *Science Education in Europe: Critical Reflections*, London: Nuffield Foundation.

Relevance of Science Education (ROSE). Online. Available HTTP: <http://www.ils.uio.no/english/rose/> (accessed 15 March 2010).

SATIS Revisited. Online. Available HTTP: <http://www.satisrevisited.co.uk/> (accessed 22 June 2009).

Solomon, J. and Aikenhead, G. (1994) *STS Education: International Perspectives on Reform*, New York: Teachers College Press.

Toplis, R. and Cleaves, A. (2006) Science investigation: the views of 14 to 16 year old pupils, *Research in Science and Technological Education* 24(1), 69–84.

Watson, J. D. (1968) *The Double Helix. A Personal Account of the Discovery of the Structure of DNA,* Harmondsworth: Penguin.

Wellington, J. J. (1981) What's supposed to happen, sir? *School Science Review* 63(222), 167–173.

Wellington, J. (1994) *Secondary Science. Contemporary Issues and Practical Approaches*, London: Routledge.

Wellington, J. (1998) *Practical Work in School Science: Which Way Now?* London: Routledge.

WHAT DO STUDENTS THINK ABOUT SCIENCE?

Sue Collins

INTRODUCTION

> The most important thing we have discussed? Well, I think the most important thing today has been that someone has been prepared to listen to what we have to say. No one ever, like, asks us our opinion, it's like we don't have one, or that what we think isn't, like, relevant.
>
> (Marlon: Year 11 pupil. Osborne and Collins 2000)

Over the past twenty years or so in England, attempts have been made to broaden the school science curriculum to address the needs of the population while retaining sight both of the requirements of the post-compulsory science curriculum and of the perceived need to maintain the supply of well-qualified scientists. A number of educationalists had long expressed the view that the existing school science curriculum served neither purpose well, leading to calls for further reforms to science education (e.g. Millar 1996; Donnelly and Jenkins 1999).

Almost entirely absent from this debate were the voices of students, perhaps reflecting an assumption that they had little to contribute to issues of such import as the teaching and learning of science, which needed to be decided by scientists and science educators. The Education Act of 1993 and the *Special Educational Needs Code of Practice* (DfES 2001) reflected Article 12 of the United Nations Convention on the Rights of the Child (1989), which provided that

> State Parties shall assure that the child is capable of forming his or her own views, the right to express those views freely in all matters affecting the child, the views of the child being given due weight in accordance with the age and maturity of the child.

This signalled a right for students to be heard, leading to an understanding among researchers of the importance of students' views of their own education. Since that time, researchers have focused on the importance of students' views to establish conditions conducive to learning and, by implication, raising levels of attainment. One other very important reason, postulated by Sinclair Taylor (2000), was the need to recognize that student perceptions of experiences of learning may differ markedly from those of teachers and curriculum designers. It is vital to encourage students to articulate their experiences, views and opinions; as Cook-Sather put it, 'There is something fundamentally amiss about building an entire system without consulting at any point those it is ostensibly designed to serve' (2005: 1).

Research conducted in recent years has focused on a range of aspects about students' views of science education. Haste's (2004) UK study explored the beliefs and values held by young people aged between 11 and 21 years in relation to scientific inquiry, while Cerini *et al.* (2003) collected students' views of science education in England through the use of online questionnaires designed by students with findings analysed and written by students with support from the Planet Science team. The Relevance of Science Education (ROSE) project (Schreiner and Sjøberg 2004) is an international survey designed to compare attitudes towards learning science and technology among 15-year-olds. The focus is on young people's attitudes, interests and out-of-school experiences that are relevant to science and technology. ROSE relies on the use of questionnaires to gain insight into students' views; as a result, we have a considerable amount of data about *what* views students hold about science and science education, but we know less about *why* they hold these views.

In an attempt to gather more in-depth information about students' views, studies conducted by Reiss (2000) and Osborne and Collins (2000) collected qualitative data about students' experiences and opinions of school science in England. Reiss conducted a five-year longitudinal study into students' learning in science, following a group of mixed-ability students throughout their science education from age 11 to 16 years, using a combination of observation and in-depth interviews with students and their parents. Osborne and Collins utilized focus group discussions involving 144 students aged 16 years to elicit views and experiences of their education in science. These two studies demonstrated that students were able to make informed judgements about what was important in education, regardless of whether they found it interesting or whether it was likely to inform further study and future career choices.

The purpose of this chapter is to explore some of those views, focusing on aspects of science that are interesting to students and valuable in their lives. While it is recognized that students' views cannot be the sole determining factor in decisions concerning the content, teaching and learning of science in secondary schools, nevertheless it is essential to articulate their contribution to this ongoing debate.

IS SCIENCE IMPORTANT TO STUDENTS?

Over the past ten years or so a number of studies have shown that students think scientific knowledge is an important part of their education and should be a compulsory component of the curriculum for all (Reiss 2000; Schreiner and Sjøberg 2004). Osborne and Collins (2000) encouraged focus groups of Year 11 (aged 16 years) students to discuss the extent to which school science was important to them and students in general (Box 2.1). What is clear from students' statements is the recognition that *learning science is important* and that *scientific knowledge* is an important part of contemporary life. However, studies have shown that students will only value their school science education if they are able to see that the science they are being taught is of personal worth to themselves (Reiss 2000). The Osborne and Collins (2000) study found that the most common argument for the importance of science among Year 11 pupils was its instrumental value for future careers. There were, however, two strands to this claim. First, occupations for which science was seen to be valuable were restricted to those with an overt science element, for example medicine, veterinary work and being an airline pilot. Second, students expressed the view that though it was important, science was not a core curriculum subject in the same sense as mathematics and English, which – unlike science – were considered crucial elements for all occupations.

Box 2.1 **Students' views of the importance of school science**

Students had little difficulty in articulating reasons why science was an important part of the education of every young person. In the broad sense, school science was important because:

COLIN: It has led to a lot of discoveries … if it wasn't for science we wouldn't be where we are today. Really, we'd still be living in caves.

HELEN: I think science is really important because, for example, now in present days we wouldn't be using washing machines because they were constructed by scientists, weren't they?

The controversial nature of some aspects of scientific research did not feature in students' comments and there was little recognition of the value of scientific knowledge to enable them to engage critically with contemporary scientific issues. Rather, what was emphasized was that scientific knowledge offered a point of entry into discussions:

LUCY: It's really important for me to learn about science to keep in line with everything else, because if you switch on the TV they're always talking about things that they've discovered and new ways they can do things. To understand what they are talking about you've got to know science. Like I was watching Children's Hospital the other night and they were talking about sickle cells, stuff like that, and I know about sickle cells so I could understand it.

There is a clear recognition of the importance of school science in these comments and recognition that science and scientific knowledge is an important part of contemporary life. For science educators this is a significant finding as it suggests that science has achieved such a level of significance in contemporary society that its place as a core subject of the curriculum is unquestioned.

On a personal level, students advanced the notion that science was a prestigious subject. Those who were good at science were seen to be intellectually able and enjoyed a higher academic status:

JULIE: In ten years' time when you meet these people and you ask, 'What GCSEs did you get?', if you sit there and say, 'I got a B in maths, a C in English, an A in art …', they'll sit there and go, 'Oh that's good, yes.' But if you come out with 'I've got two As in science and an A in maths … they'll sit there and think, 'Oh brilliant, this is someone who we want to know.'

However, there was disagreement among students concerning the extent to which science was important for future careers. Apart from the more overtly science-related occupations such as doctors, nurses and pilots, students were divided in their views:

PARESH: … for science you only use it in certain jobs, whereas IT you use it in almost every job.
CHARLIE: I think most careers … they've probably got science involved in them anyway, one way or another, even if it's not really in-depth.

Girls in particular had little difficulty in elaborating reasons for the importance of science in their everyday lives. The following comment illustrates the point that outside school is the context where the importance of learning science in school is realized:

JULIE: Like a little electric heater … I remember I was plugging it in and I felt the plug was warm and I remember learning that warm was faulty. I told my mum and she was so impressed. If I hadn't learned that warm was faulty I would have plugged it in and found out.

(Adapted from Osborne and Collins 2000: 17–20)

STUDENTS' INTEREST IN SCIENCE

In exploring students' views and interests in science a number of factors need to be considered. In addition to characteristics such as individual academic goals and career aspirations, a clear link has been established between attainment in science and students' level of interest in the subject. It follows that a student who lacks ability in science is likely to demonstrate a lack of motivation, which in turn leads to a lack of progress and poor attainment, with the inevitable loss of interest (Hidi and Harackiewicz 2000; Papanastasiou and Papanastasiou 2004).

In their *Student Review of the Science Curriculum* survey, Cerini *et al.* (2003) asked respondents to select from a list those adjectives that best described their view of learning science at GCSE level (Figure 2.1).

The most reassuring responses from the perspective of science educators were that science was thought to be '*interesting*', '*useful*', '*relevant*' and '*thought-provoking*'. This suggests that attempts over the past ten years to develop curriculum content for science that is more relevant to students' lives in the twenty-first century and appeals to their interests are beginning to show results. Whether or not this will be enough to encourage more young people to continue their studies of science beyond the age of compulsory education and to consider science-related careers remains to be seen.

While such studies provide useful insight into students' views of school science in general, they are somewhat broad, leading to the assumption that there is no clear distinction between students' views of biology, physics and chemistry. If research is to inform curriculum development in science and encourage pedagogical change to improve students' views of science, it is necessary to explore their responses to individual sciences. This assertion is confirmed by the findings of a number of studies undertaken in the last ten years that have revealed variations in students' views of the three sciences – girls demonstrating more positive attitudes towards biology while boys prefer the physical sciences (Osborne and Collins 2000; Reiss 2000; Spall *et al.* 2004; Murphy and Whitelegg 2006).

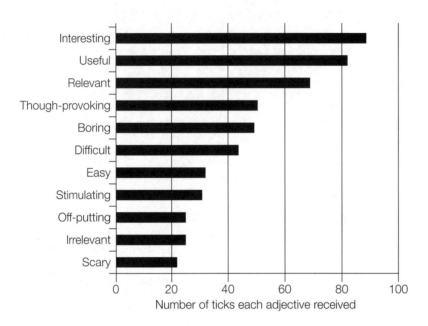

■ **Figure 2.1** Respondents' selection from a list of those adjectives that best described their view of learning science at GCSE level.
Source: Cerini *et al*. (2003 p. 14).

STUDENTS' VIEWS OF BIOLOGICAL SCIENCES

It is generally acknowledged that girls demonstrate keener interest in biological sciences than boys, particularly human biology. As the following comment shows, the attraction of human biology for some students is contingent on its relevance to themselves:

> The main thing is that people like to relate it back to themselves, like I think most people like learning about themselves, like you said – puberty and everything like that. I mean whereas electrons …
>
> (Sana: Year 11 student. Osborne and Collins 2000: 34)

Students in this study appreciated the importance of understanding how to achieve and maintain a healthy body through diet and exercise. These aspects of biology were said to be interesting, stimulating and relevant to students because they were '*more modern*' than many topics studied in science; they contained elements seen to be crucially important to young people such as the effects of drugs and alcohol on the body and the exploration of cures for a range of diseases.

Several studies conducted in recent years have highlighted students' interest in aspects of environmental science encountered outside the science classroom, for example the causes and effects of environmental pollution. Specific issues of interest among students include the effects of global warming and the greenhouse effect, demonstrating a real concern about the implications for the future – for example:

... the ice cap thing, where they're all melting down. It's important, like if it carries on doing that there might be no England left.

(Megan and Jane: Year 11 students. Osborne and Collins 2000: 43)

Students participating in this study showed considerable interest in events and natural disasters around the world that had an impact on the environment, including storms, hurricanes and tornadoes. These were seen to be increasingly common events, and not only a cause for concern but 'exciting' and 'fascinating' because they were current and had immediate relevance to the students' lives – as this exchange shows:

Rajan: It's because it's in the present and it's ...
Brendan: Because it's now and it's happening. It's not just theory, it's happening ...
Rajan: ... it's not A = B, it's things that are relevant to our lives, not like the Blast Furnace.

(Y11 students. Osborne and Collins 2000: 44)

Studies conducted elsewhere, for example Sternika's (1999) research among 11- to 14-year-old students in Poland, showed that 66–70% of boys and girls demonstrated high levels of interest in nature preservation and environmental protection. Factors endangering the environment that were rated highly by students were:

■ destruction of forest and the deterioration of climate;
■ pollution of rivers and lakes;
■ radioactive substances in the environment;
■ the ozone hole as a threat for humans.

Similarly, the PISA assessment of science competencies among 15-year-old students in fifty-seven countries (OECD 2006), reported that students across the world, including the United Kingdom, were taking a keen interest in environmental issues and demonstrating a desire to contribute to the improvement of the environment. The majority of students were said to be familiar with issues such as pollution, and a large number with more complex issues such as the impact of the clearing of rainforests and its implications for land use. The report concluded that student awareness of issues and a general desire to contribute to improvements to the environment reflected well on the science curricula of secondary schools across the world, thought to be the main source of students' information, knowledge and understanding of environmental issues.

However, it cannot be assumed that students hold common views concerning contemporary issues in environmental science. Findings from a recent ROSE survey (Shreiner and Sjøberg 2008) of 15-year-old students from forty countries suggested that boys considered environmental problems to be exaggerated and easily remedied by experts, while girls tended to take the issues more seriously, regarding the challenges as the responsibility of every citizen and demonstrating a belief that individuals were capable of bringing about change.

The National Curriculum How Science Works Programme of Study (QCA 2007) offers potentially rich opportunities to stimulate students' curiosity and develop understanding of phenomena that directly affect their lives and those of others across the world. Students' knowledge and understanding can be enhanced through participation in debates structured to explore contemporary and potentially contentious issues, utilizing evidence drawn from a range of sources, and through modelling and experimentation of relevant aspects of environmental science.

STUDENTS' VIEWS OF THE PHYSICAL SCIENCES

Physics

Studies conducted over many years have highlighted gender differences among secondary students in their responses to physics. It is acknowledged that in general girls demonstrate less interest in physics than boys, and levels of interest in both groups diminish over time in secondary school. Boys and girls demonstrate a preference for different physics topics: for example, Biklen and Pollard (2001) found that girls showed equal or less interest in topics related to *light*, *sound* and *heat* than boys and considerably less interest in *mechanics*, *electricity* and *radioactivity*. However, Osborne and Collins (2000) found that despite gender differences, students' interest was rooted in the concrete, observable features of physics. Boys' interest focused on an understanding of forces in relation to *cars* and *flight*, while girls expressed a keener interest in topics on *light* and *electricity*.

Despite these differences, *space* is one aspect of physics found to capture the interest of boys and girls in equal measure. Students have expressed a fascination with the Earth and the solar system, how they were formed, and particularly with the unexplored as this reinforced a view of science as something other than an existing body of knowledge to be learned. There are aspects of our galaxy that remain a mystery as well as those scientists understand only partially, and students find this exciting, as though they are sharing scientific experiences and discoveries with experts.

Osborne and Collins (2000) found that girls tended to relate their interest in *space* more closely to themselves and the way it made them feel. For example, in answer to the question *Why are you particularly interested in space?* two girls responded:

> … you think how small you are compared to everything in space. Because that affects you. You look up and then you know what they [stars] are and you feel good, you think, 'I learnt that at school'.
> (Hazel and Emma: Year 11 students. Osborne and Collins 2000: 35)

School science has the potential to offer exploration of fundamental questions concerning *who we are*, *what we are* and *where we came from*. Such knowledge has the potential to help students construct versions of self, identity, place and role within the cosmos.

Students' fascination with aspects of space is not restricted to the United Kingdom. Secondary students in Israel (Trumper 2004, 3) listed their top three favourite physics topics as:

- how it feels to be weightless;
- how meteors, comets or asteroids may cause disasters;
- black holes, supernovas and other spectacular objects.

Girls in Trumper's study also expressed interest in such topics as *how the eye can see light and colours*, while boys preferred *rockets, satellites and space travel*.

Focusing on the interests of Finnish students in the physical sciences, a recent ROSE survey (Lavonen *et al.* 2005) highlighted similar topics of interest among boys and girls, all relating to *astronomy*, *space*, *stars*, *planets*, *meteors*, *supernovas* and *the universe*.

Science educators keen to stimulate students' interest in the physical sciences should not underestimate the value of these findings in identifying how possible areas of engagement with physics arising from interest in other topics might be generated.

Chemistry

Features of chemistry favoured by students are liable to be those that are concrete, observable and manipulable, for example mixing chemicals, observing the colours and smells associated with chemical change and witnessing results for themselves. Students tend to be motivated by activities that encourage autonomy, such as selecting from a range of tests to be carried out and hands-on involvement in selecting appropriate equipment.

Students value activities in chemistry – and in science more generally – that provide opportunities for first-hand experience and physical involvement in their own learning. Inquiry-based topics appeal to students, particularly boys, as they welcome the autonomy associated with devising and conducting their own experiments (Wolf and Fraser 2008). However, stringent health and safety regulations governing practical science lessons often make it difficult for teachers to encourage autonomy, resorting instead to demonstrations with occasional input from selected students. In many ways this is an unfortunate development in school science, particularly as students' interest appears to be stimulated by an element of danger associated with aspects of chemistry, as the following exchange between a group of girls clearly illustrates:

> *Caroline*: I was thinking about that one when you put the metal in the water and that. You know when …
> *Hannah*: It went on fire.
> *Caroline*: The alkali metals went …
> *Asha*: Yeah, and the magnesium, or something …
> *Suzanne*: Put it in water, and the reaction, it was spinning round and it goes on fire, that was good (laughs).
> *Jenny*: And like, the first I saw, like, magnesium being lit and it was really bright…
> *Kim*: Yeah when the thing sparked …
> *Asha*: And they were saying, 'Don't look, don't look', it was like some sort of exciting moment.
>
> (Year 11 students. Osborne and Collins 2000: 34)

As with other areas of science, gender differences have been shown in the specific topics that appeal to boys and girls. Perhaps not surprisingly, girls show a keener interest in aspects of chemistry related to human biology and health education, for instance the effects of narcotics and alcohol on the body and effects of radiation from sunbeds on the skin. Boys have also demonstrated an interest in the effect of chemicals on the human body, though topics tend to focus on the effects of poisons, explosive objects, electric shocks and lightning on the human body. Lavonen *et al.* (2005) revealed that topics in chemistry that were of interest to girls were often found to be of at least some interest to boys, but the reverse was not the case.

One positive response to this finding might be to offer topics in chemistry with a more humanistic element to stimulate the interest of girls in chemistry. It has been suggested that topics such as 'kitchen chemistry' might appeal to girls, for example the titration of sodium chloride solutions to see if vegetables absorb salt when cooked; enzymes and jellies; chemistry of flavour; and many more (Lister 2005).

STUDENTS' VIEWS OF PRACTICAL SCIENCE

> In our view, practical work, including fieldwork, is a vital part of science education. It helps students to develop their understanding of science, appreciate that science is based on evidence and acquire hands-on skills that are essential if students are to progress in science. Students should be given the opportunity to do exciting and varied experimental and investigative work.
>
> (House of Commons Science and Technology Committee 2002: para. 40)

Many researchers and science educators support this view of the importance of high-quality practical work in school science. In addition to developing scientific skills, knowledge and understanding, practical work in science lessons has the potential to stimulate and engage students (Lunetta *et al*. 2007). There is evidence to show that practical work is a feature of school science for many students in the United Kingdom and elsewhere, though questions have been raised recently about the quality of practical science lessons offered to students in secondary science (SCORE 2008).

The term 'practical work' in school science is often used as a catch-all phrase to encompass all aspects of science that involve students in some form of active inquiry. The Science Community Representing Education (SCORE) report (2008:9) made a useful distinction in separating practical work in science into three categories: *core activities* and *directly related activities* to encourage active participation in learning, and *complementary activities* designed to consolidate and develop students' conceptual understanding in science (Figure 2.2).

Core activities involve students in hands-on practical science such as investigations, laboratory procedures and techniques, and fieldwork. *Directly related activities* provide opportunities for students to design and plan investigations, observe teacher demonstrations, analyse data using ICT, analyse results of investigations, and record and report findings. *Complementary activities* utilize a range of contexts to enhance and develop science concepts – for example:

■ science-related visits
■ surveys

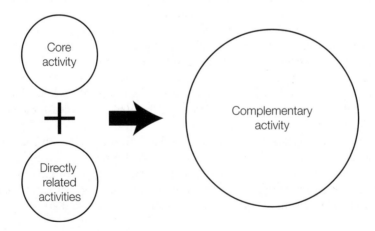

■ **Figure 2.2** Practical work in science

■   presentations and role play
■   simulations including use of ICT
■   models and modelling
■   group discussion
■   group text-based activities.

The SCORE (2008) study sought to elicit students' views of what constituted practical work in science. The results (Figure 2.3) indicated that almost all students surveyed associated practical work in science with *core* and *directly related activities* while only a very small percentage related *complementary activities* to their experiences of practical work in science.

   The findings of the SCORE study confirm those of Osborne and Collins (2000). Students participating in this research demonstrated higher levels of interest in science lessons that included opportunities for experimentation, investigation and discussion; they valued the autonomy afforded by such activities – of being in control of their own investigations, working independently and the absence of a 'right answer'. Well-planned and effectively taught practical activities in science have the potential to engage students both mentally and physically, making scientific concepts more accessible in ways not possible through less hands-on approaches to teaching and learning (Box 2.2).

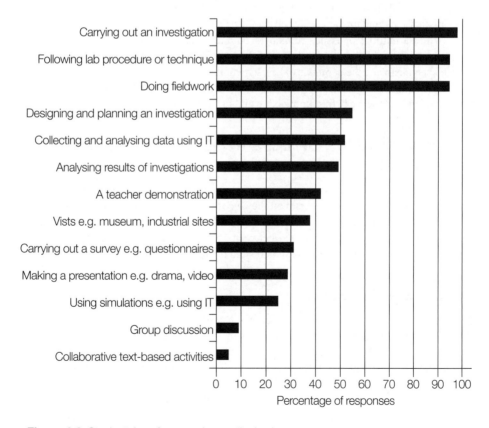

■ **Figure 2.3** Students' preferences in practical science
Source: adapted from SCORE (2008: 8)

However, a note of caution needs to be sounded here. It cannot be assumed that simply enabling students to engage in practical science activities will automatically lead to an understanding of underlying scientific concepts. Practical work in science may be effective in developing students' scientific skills, but ensuring that they utilize reliable scientific knowledge and understanding in conducting hands-on activities and reflecting on the data gathered is more problematic. Abrahams and Millar developed this point in stressing the need for a greater balance between 'doing' and 'learning' in science lessons, urging teachers to 'devote a greater proportion of the lesson time to helping students use ideas associated with the phenomena they have produced, rather than seeing the success-ful production of the phenomenon as an end in itself' (2008:1967).

While practical work is a feature of a great many science lessons in secondary schools in England, science teachers frequently complain about the level of facilities and resources available for practical science. The point was raised in the influential Roberts Report (2002) on the supply of science, technology, engineering and mathematics gradu-ates to the job market. The report questioned the quality of resources and equipment to support students' learning in maintaining that 'only just over a third of school science and D&T laboratories in secondary schools are estimated to be of a good standard or better; in general they are in a worse condition than the overall school estate' (p. 66). In an effort to address the standard of facilities for school science, the report went on to recommend that 'the Government and Local Education Authorities prioritize school science and D&T laboratories, and ensure that investment is made available to bring all such laboratories up to a satisfactory standard (as measured by OFSTED)' (p. 66).

While a number of issues remain to be addressed in relation to practical work in school science – for example, teacher confidence in leading practical sessions outside their area of specialism and the demands of assessment that tend to restrict opportunities for prac-tical work – students clearly value inquiry-based practical science that encourages them to utilize and extend their existing knowledge and understanding of scientific concepts.

STUDENTS' VIEWS OF LESS INTERESTING ASPECTS OF SCIENCE

A number of aspects of school science education have been found to be less appealing to students. However, much will depend on the age of those questioned, their attitudes towards science, and whether or not they intend to continue their studies of science or are considering a science-related career. Students aged between 15 and 16 years, approaching their GCSE examinations, have highlighted as less interesting the following aspects of school science.

Science is a difficult subject

Many students have reported finding science 'hard' or 'difficult to learn' and for some this will affect their level of interest in the subject (Osborne and Collins 2001; Jenkins and Nelson 2005). Many students will find such challenges stimulating and rewarding, but for others, sustained difficulty in understanding concepts can be demoralizing:

> … if it's something you want to understand and can't it just gets boring after a while.
> (Julie: Year 11 pupil. Osborne and Collins 2000: 22)

Box 2.2 **Students' views of practical science**

While students prefer work in science that includes opportunities for experimentation and investigation, as the following exchange shows, some also consider personal autonomy to be of paramount importance:

MARLON: You're in control of your own experiment …
JUSTIN: You're using your own initiative to do things, really, aren't you?
MARLON: Instead of being told where to put things …
JUSTIN: You're independent, really
MARLON: … you're told a baseline and then you can work from that. It just makes it a lot more interesting because you feel you're in control more.
STEVE: You know your own results as well.
JUSTIN: … and your outcome is not something that's processed; you feel like you have actually accomplished something instead of, like, doing the routine.

This finding is supported by the work of others, who pointed to the fact that tasks and activities assume greater relevance when students have at least some control over the planning and execution of the work (Rudduck et al. 1996).

Students made the point that scientific concepts were more accessible and more easily retained when supported by practical involvement, even when the practical work produced incorrect results:

SALLY: Say if you did an experiment and you got it wrong and then you came to the exam and you think, 'Oh I got this wrong because I did this, so this is what really should have happened.' It sort of makes you remember, it triggers what you did before.

There was widespread agreement that there were too few opportunities for students to engage in forms of practical work, including discussion. It was clear that students believed that there was an unrelenting decline in opportunities for them to engage on practical work of any kind in science as they moved from Key Stage 3 to Key Stage 4:

SUMIT: We all get a month when we all have to do practical stuff and, like, the teacher will bring a liver or something like that and that will be all right. But you only get that now and again and since we started Year 11 I don't think many of us have done a practical yet. [Interview conducted in the spring term]

For many students, the decline in opportunities to engage in practical work during Key Stage 4 meant that the subject matter became less accessible and interest waned – for example:

IRFAN: Before, when I was like sitting in English and, you know, thought you had science next lesson and you know you would learn something and do something. Now with science you're sitting on English and you think, 'Ooohh no not science'.

(Adapted from Osborne and Collins 2000: 36–37)

Points of particular difficulty mentioned by students included the language of science with its unfamiliar terms and words, and the fragmented nature of the subject that can seem to students to be a series of apparently unrelated topics in biology, chemistry and physics. The physical sciences have a history of being mathematical, obscure and difficult to learn. An understanding of physics is seen by students to require high-level mathematical skills, particularly at GCSE and A level. However, it is not only the perceived difficulty of the subject that turns some students away from science, but also the requirement to memorize and regurgitate half-understood facts for tests and examinations (Osborne and Collins 2001).

Rushed but repeated curriculum

An important finding emerging from studies of students' view of school science is the sense in which they feel themselves to be rushed through the curriculum with limited opportunity for reflection, or to absorb concepts, discuss their thoughts and understandings, or to ask questions. As one student put it:

> It's all crammed in, you either take it in or it goes in one ear and out the other. You catch bits of it, then it's confusing, then you put the wrong bits together and, if you don't understand it the teachers can't really understand why you haven't grasped it.
> (Keiran: Year 11 student. Osborne and Collins 2000: 23)

The basis for this and other similar comments was predominantly the students' experiences of examination courses from age 14 to 16 years in 2000. Certainly, the science syllabus at Key Stage 3 and Key Stage 4 at that time was broad, covering physics, chemistry and biology, earth science and basic astronomy; this, coupled with pressures of time and examination preparation, inevitably left little time for reflection.

It may seem surprising to learn that the same students who complained of a rushed curriculum also expressed frustration at the apparent repetition of science topics through Key Stage 3 and Key Stage 4. This is not the level of repetition frequently associated with students' transfer from primary to secondary school, but an apparent lack of recognition of the spiral nature of the National Curriculum for science in England – for example:

> Every year I've done science … I've learned about photosynthesis. It's not as if I learn it in more depth every year, I just do the literally the same thing. … When you get to secondary school it's not that more advanced and that's it, you learn the same things over and over again.
> (Alice: Year 11 student. Osborne and Collins 2000: 26)

Where students were able to see progression in their learning, this was often perceived to be in very small stages, with concepts gradually becoming 'more complex … but basically the same', and this leads to a growing disenchantment with the subject. While students acknowledged the need to revisit aspects of science, science educators need to take account of students' prior experiences and take time to explain how a topic will review and build on previous knowledge and understanding of key scientific concepts. The revised science curriculum for England (QCA 2007) is designed to encourage greater flexibility in the content and teaching of science at Key Stages 3 and 4 in England and therefore go some way towards alleviating this aspect of student dissatisfaction.

Approaches to teaching science

Students have complained that the final year of compulsory education (Year 11) is when considerable pressure is applied to revise a number of topics in haste – often despite a substantial amount of curriculum time being devoted to science teaching in England. The result of exam preparation, particularly for those students following double and triple award science courses, can be seen by students to be of little educational benefit, as they copy notes from textbooks, whiteboards or overhead projectors with little understanding:

> … you haven't time to read it when you're copying it down, it's only when you come back to revision that you think, 'I didn't understand that and I wished I'd asked him'. But then you remember that you didn't have a chance to ask because you were that busy trying to copy it down you weren't reading it.
>
> (Vishal: Year 11 student. Osborne and Collins 2000: 28)

As an educational tool to support learning in science there is little to recommend undemanding transcribing of notes. However, given the pressure of high-stakes testing in secondary education, it is not difficult to see why teachers feel driven to use this practice, in an educational system where students' examination scores are taken as a measure of the quality of teaching and the achievement of the school.

Students have indicated that they would welcome opportunities to express their ideas on scientific topics of particular interest during science lessons, to pursue topics of particular interest and/or relevance to themselves and their lives, and to engage in discussion to explore their own ideas in relation to those of their peers. Such opportunities would encourage students to explore their own understanding of scientific concepts. School science education presents opportunities to incorporate a range of activities such as role-play, group presentations, writing for a range of audiences, and debates and discussions. The adoption of such strategies would go some way towards dispelling students' views of school science as dealing only with well-established, consensual knowledge which is not open to critical scrutiny or reinterpretation.

CONCLUSION

The science curriculum in England at the present time offers opportunities for the exploration of aspects of contemporary science in a stimulating and practical way. From the student perspective, such an element is essential to provide a connection between school science and the outside world, giving much-needed relevance to secondary science courses. It is possible for students to understand the need for – and to positively respond to – school science that is underpinned by established scientific knowledge and received wisdom as long as this is supplemented with opportunities to explore contemporary issues, providing insight into the world of here and now as well as the world of the past.

The underlying aim of this chapter is to demonstrate the importance of the student voice in developing the content and teaching of science in secondary schools. The majority of research studies of students' views and attitudes towards school science have tended to utilize questionnaires to gather information. Although such methods are valuable in ascertaining *what* students think about their science education, they cannot tell us *why* students hold the views they express – and this is an important consideration for science educators if we are to stimulate and maintain students' interest in science. To achieve this depth of insight it is desirable to interact with students, ideally to track their progress, experiences and developing views of science education over the entire period of their secondary science education (Reiss 2000). However, shorter studies involving face-to-face interaction with students (Osborne and Collins 2000) are also capable of providing important insights into students' views, experience, concerns and opinions of schools science at particular points in their education. These two studies and others highlighted in this chapter help to show the importance of the student voice in decisions about the content and teaching of science in secondary school in England. It is acknowledged that the voice of students cannot be the sole arbiter of decisions about the future of science education in England, but taking account of their views should help us to identify the steps needed to enhance students' awareness of the importance of science, to stimulate their interest and convince them of the value of pursuing science beyond the age of compulsory schooling.

FURTHER READING

Braund, M. and Reiss, M. (eds) (2004) *Learning Science outside the Classroom*, London: Routledge.

Braund, M. (2008) *Starting Science Again: Making Progress in Science Learning.* London: Sage.

Frost, J. (ed.) (2010) *Learning to Teach Science in the Secondary School*, London: Routledge.

Lewis, A. (1999) *Researching Children's Perspectives,* Buckingham: Open University Press.

Parkinson, J. (2002) *Reflective Teaching in Science*, London: Continuum.

Parkinson, J. (2004) *Improving Secondary Science Teaching,* London: Routledge.

Peters-Wotherspoon, A. M. (2005) An exploration of young pupils' attitudes towards science: the influence of the laboratory, cultural stereotypes, the home, interaction with the teacher, the demands of the subject and internal/external pressures related to performance, Ed. thesis: University of East Anglia.

Reiss, M. J. (2000) *Understanding Science Lessons: Five Years of Science Teaching,* Buckingham: Open University Press.

Sharp, G. D. (2003) *A Longitudinal Study Investigating Pupil Attitudes towards Their school Science Learning Experiences from a Gender Perspective,* Buckingham: Open University Press.

Wellington, J. and Ireson, G. (2007) *Science Learning, Science Teaching: Contemporary Issues and Practical Approaches* (2nd Edition), London: Routledge.

Zohar, A. and Dori, Y. D. (2010) *Metacognition in Science Education: Trends in Current Research,* London: Springer.

REFERENCES

Abrahams, A. and Millar, R. (2008) Does practical work really work? A study of the effectiveness of practical work as a teaching and learning method in school science, *International Journal of Science Education* 30(14), 1945–1969.

Biklen, S. K. and Pollard, D. (2001) Feminist perspectives on gender in classrooms, in V. Richardson (ed.) *Handbook of Research on Teaching,* Washington, DC: AERA.

Cerini, B., Murray, I. and Reiss, M. (2003) *Student Review of the Science Curriculum: Major Findings*, London: Planet Science/Institute of Education University of London/Science Museum. Online. Available HTTP: <http://www.planet-science.com/sciteach/review> (accessed 16 December 2009).

Cook-Sather, A. (2005) *Authorizing Students' Perspectives: Toward Trust, Dialogue, and Change in Education.* Online. Available HTTP: <http://www.aera.net/uploadedFiles/Journals_and_Publications/Journals/Educational_Researcher/3104/3104_CookSather.pdf> (accessed 9 March 2010).

DfES (Department for Education and Skills) (2001) *Special Educational Needs Code of Practice.* Nottingham: DfES Publications. Online. Available HTTP: <http://www.teachernet.gov.uk/_doc/3724/SENCodeOfPractice.pdf> (accessed 9 March 2010).

Donnelly, J. F. and Jenkins, E. W. (1999) *Science Teaching in Secondary School under the National Curriculum*, Leeds: Centre for Studies in Science and Mathematics Education, University of Leeds.

Haste, H. (2004) *Science in My Future: A Study of Values and Beliefs in Relation to Science and Technology Amongst 11–21 Year Olds*, Nestlé Social Research Programme.

Hidi, S., and Harackiewicz, J. M. (2000). Motivating the academically unmotivated: A critical issue for the 21st Century, *Review of Educational Research* 70, 151–179.

House of Commons Select Committee on Science and Technology (2002) *Science Education from 14–19: Third Report of Session 2001–02*, Vol 1: *Report and Proceedings of the Committee,* London: The Stationery Office.

Jenkins, E. and Nelson, N. W. (2005) Important but not for me: students' attitudes towards secondary science, *Research in Science and Technology Education* 23(1), 41–57.

Lavonen, J., Jute, K., Uitto, A., Mensal, V. and Byman, R. (2005) *Attractiveness of Science Education in the Finnish Comprehensive School*, Helsinki: Department of Applied Sciences of Education, University of Helsinki.

Lister, T. (2005) *Kitchen Chemistry*, London: Royal Society of Chemistry.

Lunetta, V. N., Hofstein, A. and Clough, M. P. (2007) Teaching and learning in the school science laboratory, in S. K. Abell and N. G. Lederman (eds) *Handbook of Research in Science Education.* Mahwah, NJ: Lawrence Erlbaum Associates.

Millar, R. (1996) Towards a science curriculum for public understanding, *School Science Review* 77, 7–18.

Murphy, P., and Whitelegg, E. (2006) Girls and physics: continuing barriers to 'belonging', *The Curriculum Journal* 17(3), 281–305.

Osborne, J and Collins, S. (2000) *Pupils' and Parents' Views of the School Science Curriculum*, London: King's College London.

Osborne, J. and Collins, S. (2001) Pupils' views of the role and value of the science curriculum: a focus group study, *International Journal of Science Education* 23(5), 441–467.

OECD (2006) *Education at a Glance: OECD Indications 2006*, Paris: OECD.

Papanastasiou, C. and Papanastasiou, E. (2004) Major influences on attitudes toward science, *Educational Research and Evaluation* 10(3), 239–257.

QCA (2007) *National Curriculum for England at Key 3 and Key Stage 4*, London: QCA.

Roberts, Sir G. (2002) *SET for Success: The supply of people with science, technology, engineering and mathematics skills*, London: HM Treasury. Online. Available HTTP: <http:// www.hm-treasury.gov.uk/documents/enterprise_and_productivity/research_and_enterprise/ ent_res_roberts.cfm> (accessed 2 December 2009).

Roberts, Sir G. (2002) *The Research Career Initiative, Final Report 1999–2002*. London: DTI.

Rudduck, J., Chaplain, R. and Wallace, G. (eds) (1996) *School Improvement: What Can Pupils Tell Us?* London: David Fulton.

SCORE (2008) *Practical Work in Science: A Report and Proposal for a Strategic Framework.* London: SCORE. Online. Available HTTP: <www.score-education.org.uk/downloads/practical_work/report.pdf> (accessed 9 March 2009).

Schreiner, C. and Sjøberg, S. (2004) *ROSE: The Relevance of Science Education. Sowing the Seeds of ROSE. Background, Rationale, Questionnaire Development and Data Collection for ROSE – a Comparative Study of Students' Views of Science and Science Education*, Oslo: Department of Teacher Education and School Development, University of Oslo. Also online. Available HTTP: <http://www.ils.uio.no/english/rose/key-documents/key-docs/ad0404-sowing-rose.pdf> (accessed 9 March 2010).

Schreiner, C. and Sjøberg, S. (2008) *Concerns for the Environment: Data from ROSE*. Oslo: Department of Teacher Education and School Development, University of Oslo.

Sinclair Taylor, A. (2000) The UN Convention on the Rights of the Child: giving children a voice, in A. Lewis and G. Lindsay (eds) *Researching Children's Perspectives*, Buckingham: Open University Press.

Spall, K., Dickson, D. and Boyes, E. (2004). Development of school students' constructions of biology and physics, *International Journal of Science Education* 26(7), 787–803.

Sternika, A. (1999) *Pupils' Interest in Nature and Environmental Protection as a Feedback for the Science Subject Teachers*. Poland: University of Gdansk.

Trumper, R. (2004) *Israeli students' interest in physics and its relation to their attitudes towards science and technology and to their own science classes*, Haifa: Faculty of Science and Science Education, Haifa University.

United Nations (1989) *United Nations Convention on the Rights of the Child: Article 12*. New York: United Nations.

Wolf, S. J. and Fraser, B. J. (2008) Learning environment, attitudes and achievement among middle-school science students using inquiry-based laboratory activities, *Research in Science Education* 38, 321–341.

HOW DO SCIENTISTS WORK?

James Williams

> Ask a scientist what he conceives the scientific method to be and he will adopt an expression that is at once solemn and shifty-eyed: solemn, because he feels that he ought to declare an opinion; shifty-eyed, because he is wondering how to conceal the fact that he has no opinion to declare.
>
> (Medawar 1982: 40)

The word 'science' originates from the Latin *scientia*, meaning 'knowledge' and passed into the English language by way of the old French term *science*. Those who pursue any form of knowledge can be thought of as scientists, regardless of their field of work. Yet science has acquired a specific meaning for the general public and for children who come to study the subject in school. Historically, school science has been conceived of as the disciplines of biology, chemistry and physics. More recently, the addition of Earth sciences, astronomy and psychology has widened the remit of science in a school setting. While social scientists, political scientists, even library scientists may justifiably argue for the designation of the title 'scientist', children and the general public will not conceive of those who pursue knowledge in these fields as true 'scientists'.

For the purposes of this chapter, science and a scientist are defined as knowledge and understanding of the natural world and universe and those who pursue it. Even this simple definition will, no doubt, raise objections with some. Such a definition is needed, however, to provide meaningful parameters for looking at the work of science and scientists.

How scientists pursue knowledge is the subject of this chapter. What method or methods they utilize, what procedures they adopt and how they make sense of the data (evidence) they collect defines how scientists work. The problem for school science, is that, far from there being simple descriptions for how scientists work, there is no one agreed way of working, no one scientific method and often no agreed simple definitions for the key terminology used by scientists.

Exactly how a scientist works depends on what knowledge and explanations they are seeking as well as how they conceive of their own scientific discipline. The methods followed by the theoretical physicist to predict the existence of as yet undiscovered sub-atomic particles can be as different from the method followed by organic chemists intent on discovering the properties and structure of an intracellular protein as the difference between a mathematician and musician investigating the properties of an equation or a symphony.

To date, there has been little consensus on a model for How Science Works. In 2008 I proposed a simple model (Figure 3.1) which would help define aspects of the history, philosophy and processes of science such as argumentation, experimentation and investigation, within which teachers and pupils could locate various scientists and their approaches to their day-to-day work (Williams 2008).

The key to this model is not that it is a fixed idea about science, more that it is a guiding framework within which teachers and pupils can locate various science 'workers' to help guide their understanding of the nature of the job they are completing. For example, an organic chemist carrying out laboratory-based work may reside within the sphere E+I, with little to no consideration of the history and philosophy of science. A researcher dealing with embryonic stem cell research resides within spheres A and E+I, as their work must consider moral and ethical dimensions. A theoretical physicist may reside within the HPS and E+I spheres.

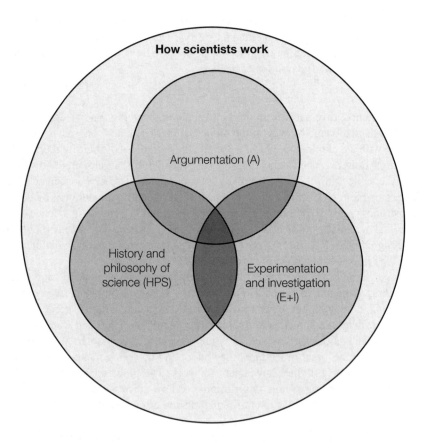

■ **Figure 3.1** A model for how science works
Source: Williams (2008)

CHILDREN'S CHARACTERIZATION OF A SCIENTIST

Studies of pupils' perceptions of science and scientists using a DAST (Draw-a-Scientist Test) activity have typically shown that they are often driven by stereotypical images consisting of white, male, middle-class characters, often grey-haired, balding and with glasses (Buldu 2006; Quita 2003). Yet it seems that while these images may contain references to the tools of science, such as the inclusion of scientific instruments to help reinforce the image of a scientist, for example a microscope or test tubes, the notion of how scientists work or operate and how they develop understanding of the phenomena they observe is absent. For most children, how scientists work is dominated by laboratory settings. This is reinforced by a pupil's own experience of science at secondary school level, where the activity of science or science lessons almost always takes place in a laboratory setting. There may even be resistance from science teachers to working outside the laboratory, even when the lesson itself requires no laboratory equipment or facilities. Moreover, the lack of practical opportunities for pupils and the declining quality of laboratory provision has been identified as contributing to the lack of uptake of science at post-16. In its evidence to the House of Lords Select Committee on Science and Technology, the Association for Science Education (ASE) stated that 'practical work has become routine and uninspiring so that, rather than engaging students with the excitement of science, such experiences contribute to students considering science as "boring"' (ASE 2006: 10). Furthermore, it paints a damning picture of the current state of school science laboratories as unfit for the purpose of teaching science in many cases. Even where some refurbishment and investment in upgrading facilities has taken place, the results do not always meet the demands of teaching science that will fulfil the programme of study requirements (ASE 2006: 11). The assumption from reading the ASE evidence is that the most effective science is taught in a laboratory setting and through a practical-based curriculum. This view is also endorsed by the National Science Teachers Association (NSTA) of North America: 'Laboratory experience is so integral to the nature of science that it must be included in every science program for every student' (NSTA 2006). This is not necessarily how science, or indeed how scientists, work day-to-day. Although the practical, laboratory-based, experimental basis of science cannot be denied, the degree to which all scientists undertake day-to-day practical and experimental work to further their knowledge and understanding is something that cannot be measured easily. The theoretical physicist spends much of their time developing mathematical models to explain known phenomena. The astronomer is a largely observational scientist, where the chance to set up and 'run' an experiment is limited by the nature of the phenomena under study, phenomena that happen vast distances away from Earth and on a huge scale, too big for conventional laboratory study. The ASE and NSTA acknowledge that the term 'laboratory' can be limiting. They include reference to working in the environment and working in the community as equally valid 'practical experiences'.

BREAKING THE STEREOTYPE

As stated, if you ask children what a scientist is, you will probably get a range of stereotypical depictions, including balding, middle-aged, spectacle-wearing, absent-minded professors; the mad professor bent on world domination; even the scientist as a saviour of mankind, who eliminates the virus threatening to kill all life on Earth. The scientist is at once the saviour and the destroyer of mankind. The scientist is also deemed to work mainly in the laboratory, with the tools of science being glassware, Bunsen burners and bubbling coloured liquids.

Many of these stereotypes originate from media portrayals of scientists. Such representations have been investigated by Haynes (1994: 3–4), who proposed the following categories for depictions of scientists:

■ *Alchemist*, a person who appears at critical times, an obsessed or maniacal scientist.

■ *Stupid virtuoso*, a person who is out of touch with the real world, who can be both comic and sinister, the absent-minded professor.

■ *Unfeeling*. This is one of the most enduring stereotypes: the scientist who has reneged on human relationships. Putting relationships to one side is often seen as the price a person must pay to achieve scientific prowess.

■ *Heroic adventurer*, who operates in the physical or intellectual world and emerges at times of scientific optimism.

■ *Scientist as helpless*, the person who has lost control over their discovery or over the direction of its implementation.

■ *Scientist as idealist or world saviour*, an acceptable scientist who sometimes holds out the possibility of a scientifically sustained utopia, but who often is engaged in conflict with a technology-based system that fails to provide for individual human values.

Haynes notes also that the depictions of scientists often represent societal attitudes to science at the time of depiction. The characterization of scientists as unable to control their discoveries – harmful mutated viruses that threaten human civilization, or technological developments that acquire an artificial intelligence and turn against their creators (the premise for the Terminator series of films and countless others) – is common and damaging to science today, even though the reality of what science can achieve and what damage science has actually done to society is far from the Hollywood creation. Science education needs to play its part in repairing this damage, but effecting such a major repair to an image that Haynes traces back to biblical texts and Scandinavian mythology will not be easy. As she states, 'from the Middle Ages to the twentieth century, scientists as depicted in literature have, with very few exceptions, been rated as "low" to "very low" on the moral scale' (Haynes 1994: 4). Print and newer forms of media – film, television, videogames, etc. – have the greatest influence on how science is communicated to children beyond the classroom (Cresswell *et al.* 2009) and for this reason alone, steps must be taken to combat the stereotypes such media present.

The notion of such a negative stereotype does not go unchallenged. Meredith (2010a, b) looked at the incidences of scientists in Hollywood films and recorded six times more 'hero' scientists than villainous ones. The popular demand for science led TV programmes, such as *CSI* and *Waking the Dead* also provides a positive view of the work of forensic scientists. The ever popular medical programmes such as *Casualty* and *Holby City* can positively promote science. While it is right to see such moves in the films and TV as positive, one has to wonder how realistic they are as portrayals of the day-to-day life of scientists. Do forensic pathologists interrogate witnesses and solve crimes with hardly any recourse to the police? Do patients recover as quickly from major surgery as the *Holby City* patients seem to do? Since Haynes published her work on scientists as villains, it is indeed possible to track changes in the positive portrayal of scientists and perhaps this is linked to the increasingly diverse scientific and technological developments that infiltrate our everyday lives from the internet to mobile phone technology and the advent of mammalian cloning and stem cell research, which promises so many positive developments in medical science.

If the stereotype does still exist, and in children it may well be more persistent than in adults – it needs to be challenged by providing alternative characterizations of scientists, in the form of real-life examples which are meaningful to children and which represent real science and scientists. Children must understand how science works in real life so that distinctions can be drawn easily between the fictional characterizations that abound in books, plays and films, etc. and how scientists really function. Understanding the work of scientists necessarily involves understanding the language of science and how science-related terminology, which may have a vernacular meaning, can also have a specific, yet different, meaning when used in a scientific context. Understanding the language of science, and the methods that scientists use to gain knowledge and understanding of nature also needs an appreciation of the history and philosophy of science. Science proceeds often by argument, by inference, by induction and by deduction. Understanding the process of science needs an appreciation of the roots of science and how science came to be the way it is today.

THE ROOTS OF SCIENCE

Three periods may be considered as defining in the history of science: the ancient Greek philosophers and their attempts to explain science from a naturalistic standpoint; the Baconian revolution in science and the development of inductive reasoning; and the major developments of the twentieth century with the work of Thomas Kuhn, Karl Popper and Paul Feyerabend.

The Greek naturalistic movement: Thales and Aristotle

The Greek philosopher Thales of Miletus (*c.* 624–546 BCE) is often credited as an originator of the scientific method (Ronan 1983: 67–68) and a founder of the school of natural philosophy. Rather than rely on a supernatural explanation of observed phenomena – the causal explanation for everything being 'the gods' – Thales and the Greek natural philosophers searched for naturalistic explanations. For Thales, there must have been a primary substance or primary principle from which all things originate. His conclusion was that this primary principle was water. His problem was to explain how everything originated from water and how, eventually, everything returns to water. His answer was that the Earth, as either a disc or a cylinder, 'floated' on a universal sea of water (Ronan 1983: 68). To explain how the Earth floats on this cosmic ocean, he hypothesized that it had properties similar to that of wood. Miletus, a Mediterranean coastal town, would have had a harbour and, most likely, wooden ships sailing in and out all the time. It is possible that seeing how 'heavier-than-water' wooden ships could float on the sea prompted Thales' ideas that the Earth, to which he gave properties similar to those of wood, could then float on a cosmic ocean. Indeed, the region is also well known for its volcanic activity, and the observation of lighter-than-water rocks, such as pumice stone, common in Mediterranean areas, may also have prompted Thales' notion of a lighter-than-water Earth.

Some 200 years after Thales, Aristotle (384–322 BCE) – one of history's most prolific natural philosophers – made countless observations of nature, especially the habits and attributes of plants and animals, and focused on categorizing things. He also made many observations on the large-scale workings of the universe, which led to the development of a comprehensive theory of physics. His method of working included the implementation of questions and answers in order to arrive at 'truths' or axioms. He applied this logical method at deriving 'truths' to the many and varied observations he made, and developed 'laws of reasoning' to arrive at conclusions about the nature of his observations and, more importantly, explanations for those observations. The aim of Aristotle's written works, known collectively as the *Organon* was to develop this universal method of reasoning by means of which it would be possible to learn everything there is to know about reality. Aristotle's book *Categories* produced the description of particular things in terms of their properties, states, and activities. His works *On Interpretation*, *Prior Analytics* and *Posterior Analytics* examine the nature of deductive inference, outlining the system of syllogistic reasoning from true propositions that later came to be known as categorical logic. His philosophical approach had a long-lasting influence on much of Western scientific thought and processes.

THE SCIENTIFIC REVOLUTION

Sir Francis Bacon (1561–1626) is often credited as one of the prime figures of the so-called scientific revolution (Ronan 1983; Marks 1983; Gribbin 2002). Alongside Newton and Galileo, he holds a position in the history of science that has been seen as an influential one on many generations of scientists (Gribbin 2002: 134). His position is not, it seems, due to his work as an experimental scientist, since this was one aspect of his work that was lacking, but in the arena of the development of a philosophical approach to science. Bacon performed few actual 'experiments', his influence being to promote the study of science from a position of gathering data and then, by inference or inductive reasoning, to come to conclusions. Bacon's method, while influential, did not secure his place as one of the great thinkers or philosophers of his time (Marks 1983: 81). His influence, though, stood the test of time until the early twentieth century.

Approaches to science

Bacon's inductive method was prevalent for over 300 years, but its application in certain areas was seen as limited by Sir Karl Popper (1902–1994). In thinking about the nature of science and the status of theories, he said:

> '*When should a theory be ranked as scientific?*' or '*Is there a criterion for the scientific character or status of a theory?*'
> The problem which troubled me at the time was neither, 'When is a theory true?' nor 'When is a theory acceptable?' My problem was different. *I wished to distinguish between science and pseudo-science*; knowing very well that science often errs, and that pseudoscience may happen to stumble on the truth.
> I knew, of course, the most widely accepted answer to my problem: that science is distinguished from pseudo-science—or from 'metaphysics'—by its *empirical method*, which is essentially *inductive*, proceeding from observation or experiment. But this did not satisfy me.
>
> (Popper 2002: 63; emphasis in original)

Popper believed in a creative force in scientific thinking and that everyone, including experimental and theoretical scientists, would have a bias. He stated that science advances by 'deductive falsification' through a process of 'conjectures and refutations' – the title of his 1963 book. He asserted that if a theory can be shown to be falsifiable then it is scientific; if it cannot, then it is pseudo-science. He went on to claim that experiment and observations test theories; they do not necessarily produce them.

By way of contrast, Thomas Kuhn, in his book *The Structure of Scientific Revolutions* (1996), promulgated the view that science proceeds or operates through 'revolutions'. He postulated that competing scientific workers initially generate a number of theoretical standpoints or frameworks, which are in direct competition. Over time, one of these becomes the dominant framework. The dominant framework is the one that explains the largest number of phenomena observed. Kuhn called this a durable 'paradigm'. Once this paradigm is accepted and used, during a period that Kuhn calls 'normal science', contradictory observations and accounts test the paradigm, undermining its dominant position. New frameworks are then developed to account for the anomalous observations and eventually a new 'paradigm' is adopted. This is the nature of what Kuhn terms his 'scientific revolution'. What is important here is that the new model or paradigm does not always completely replace the old paradigm and the two may coexist, e.g. Newtonian physics and Einsteinian physics.

A strict, but not wholly correct, interpretation of Popper is that any scientific theory, if falsified, should be abandoned. What Popper actually called for is explanation of the contradictory evidence and subsequent modification of the theory to account for the contradictions. Kuhn, on the other hand, stated that during periods of 'normal science', scientists hold on to their theories even in the face of contradictory evidence until such time as the contradictions prove overwhelming and a revolution replaces the old scientific paradigm with a new paradigm. Popper described what scientists *should* do: explain, accommodate and revise. Kuhn described what scientists *actually* do when faced with contradictions: defend their ideas and try to counteract criticism and contradictory evidence.

Feyerabend's anarchistic theory of science

Paul Feyerabend (1924–1994) countered the notion of any form of scientific method. In *Against Method* (1975), derived from a 1970 essay of the same title, he set out his argument against the notion of any scientific method. Feyerabend later conceded that he had merely introduced another rigid concept, perhaps even another form of scientific method.

> One of my motives for writing *Against Method* was to free people from the tyranny of philosophical obfuscators and abstract concepts such as 'truth', 'reality', or 'objectivity', which narrow people's vision and ways of being in the world. Formulating what I thought were my own attitude and convictions, I unfortunately ended up by introducing concepts of similar rigidity, such as 'democracy', 'tradition', or 'relative truth'. Now that I am aware of it, I wonder how it happened. The urge to explain one's own ideas, not simply, not in a story, but by means of a 'systematic account', is powerful indeed.
>
> (Feyerabend 1995: 179–80)

Science, for Feyerabend, was an anarchistic enterprise, his idea being that theoretical anarchism is more humanitarian and more likely to encourage progress than any 'law-and-order' alternative. This, he believed, was shown both by an examination of historical episodes and by an abstract analysis of the relation between ideas and actions. The only principle that did not inhibit progress for Feyerabend was 'anything goes'.

The 'scientific method' and school science

Bacon, Popper, Kuhn and Feyerabend do not provide us with an uncontroversial picture of what science is or, indeed, how it works. Scientists are not all Baconian observers; they may indeed 'become Baconian' when they describe their observations in their published work. Scientists are rigorous in how they present and finally publish their work. Data are the currency of science and they are always treated with great regard and respect. Should data have been found to have been improperly generated or reported, it rightly shocks the community and brings harsh penalties on those who perpetrate scientific fraud.

Scientists do not have to falsify their own theories; there are many others who will oblige and attempt to falsify a rival's theory. What the scientist wants is a theory that withstands falsification, as this would be considered a strong theory. Although Kuhn's notion of scientific revolutions may suggest wholesale step-changes in how we view the workings of the world around us, scientific progress is, perhaps, more incremental than revolutionary. The science of the twentieth century has undoubtedly provided more explanation and more detailed understanding of natural phenomena than the explanations for those same phenomena put forward in the seventeenth and eighteenth centuries. It is almost a foregone conclusion that as the twenty-first century progresses, so to, will our knowledge and understanding progress. The move from Newtonian physics to Einsteinian physics was a revolution, but science and, indeed, the physics textbooks have not thrown out all of Newton's 'laws', and neither should they.

The fundamental question of whether or not there is one agreed 'scientific method' and that this is indeed how science works appears to have no simple answer. Indeed, Chalmers, in describing the difficulties that science has in either proving or disproving theories, states that 'the reconstructions of philosophers bear little resemblance to what actually goes on in science' his reaction to this being that we should 'give up altogether the idea that science is a rational activity operating according to some special method or methods.' (Chalmers 1999: xvii). Neither Chalmers nor Feyerabend was the first to postulate that the 'scientific method' does not exist. The philosopher Cornelius Benjamin (1897–1968) stated that 'the strongest grounds for contending that there is no scientific method is the fact that science consists, in the final analysis, of scientific discovery, and that there are no rules by which this act takes place' (1956: 234).

Yet teaching that there is 'no method' is not satisfactory and would not achieve a greater scientific understanding for pupils. Teachers, and pupils, need to appreciate the variety of methods of 'doing science' and how these approaches may be used by different disciplines.

THE LANGUAGE OF SCIENCE

A study conducted by Cassels and Johnstone in 1985 (cited in Wellington and Osborne 2001) identified 'troublesome' words that confused pupils learning science. They concluded that it was not the technical language (which they determined formed only a small percentage of the vocabulary used in science education) but words which were more context-dependent on providing real understanding that were the most troublesome, e.g. 'excited'. This word will have a general everyday or vernacular meaning, for example in the context of a child being excited about a forthcoming birthday, which is different from the meaning in science, where a particle may be 'excited' in a chemical reaction. Definitions of words and consequent understanding relying on 'correct' definitions were not investigated. The Cassels and Johnstone study raised important questions about language and 'scientific literacy' in a pure sense. As Wellington and Osborne (2001) concluded in their study of language and literacy in science education, the technical language and vocabulary of science does pose problems for pupils. While Wellington and Osborne provide a useful grouping of the vocabulary of science as scientific, semi-technical and non-technical words, what is missing is discussion of the key scientific terms, i.e. fact, hypothesis, theory, principle, law. It is acknowledged in the study by Cassels and Johnstone and by Wellington and Osborne that many words in the vocabulary of science have dual (sometimes more) meanings. For example, the word 'conductor' will have a specific scientific meaning, but could also mean a person collecting money on a bus or a person leading an orchestra. What will specify for the reader or listener the correct interpretation or meaning is the context within which the word is used. For example, 'copper is a good conductor' would seem to be unambiguous and lead a person to determine a scientific definition of the word 'conductor'. It is not inconceivable, however, for there to be a bus conductor called Mrs Copper, and there is an American composer called William Copper who may well be a very good orchestral conductor. The everyday language of science teachers will include a wide range of technical, semi-technical and scientific words and, as Wellington and Osborne point out, we cannot assume that the correct meanings of these words will be 'acquired or caught'. There is also the possibility that teachers of science may also have confusion and misunderstandings over some of the scientific and technical language used when dealing with the newly introduced approach to teaching science from a process perspective, i.e. How Science Works. If teachers are themselves confusing the scientific meaning of, for example, the word 'theory' with a more general vernacular meaning, then there is even less chance that pupils will acquire an understanding of How Science Works.

SCIENTIFIC THEORIES

A common tactic for groups with an interest in casting into doubt sound scientific theory, such as the creationist movement, is to present a definition of a scientific theory as being only a 'guess' or a 'hunch'. For this type of pressure group, promoting this definition is crucial to discrediting the work of science and scientists.

> First, they play upon a vernacular misunderstanding of the word 'theory' to convey the false impression that we evolutionists are covering up the rotten core of our edifice. … In the American vernacular, 'theory' often means 'imperfect fact' – part of a hierarchy of confidence running downhill from fact to theory to hypothesis to guess. Thus creationists can (and do) argue: evolution is 'only' a theory, and intense debate now rages about many aspects of the theory. If evolution is less than a fact, and scientists can't even make up their minds about the theory, then what confidence can we have in it?
>
> (Gould 1983: 254)

FACTS AND SCIENCE

The notion of a 'fact' in science is also subject to misinterpretation. Many people equate a 'fact' with something that is either 'true', 'real' or 'proven', indicating a lack of understanding of facts in relation to science and scientific evidence. In the fields of philosophy, mathematics and law, it would indeed be correct to equate facts with proof and truth. In science, facts have a different characteristic. A scientific fact can be thought of as a repeated and verifiable observation, so much so that to not call that observation a fact would be illogical. The evolutionist Stephen Jay Gould's definition of a scientific fact is much the same: 'In science, "fact" can only mean "confirmed to such a degree that it would be perverse to withhold provisional assent"' (Gould 1983: 255). In science, it is recognized that as our understanding increases, so our theories will develop and change. Facts do not normally change, but science does not preclude facts that are counter to what we have known; for example, the force of gravity means that we can predict with almost unerring certainty that any object dropped would fall towards the Earth's surface. Yet we cannot state that in all known and unknown parts of the universe gravity will always behave in that fashion. The likelihood of gravity behaving counter-intuitively – that is, forcing a small object to move away from the surface of a large planetary mass – is so small that we dismiss this and call gravity a scientific fact. At no point do we assert that the laws of gravity as defined by us are 'true' and must hold 'true' in all situations.

Were we to chart the development of certain scientific theories over time, we would see how new evidence obtained from the gathering of data (facts) changes our interpretations. For example, the apparent 'fit' of the continents (e.g. the fit that could be obtained by juxtaposing South America and Africa) has been explained in the past using an 'expanding Earth' theory, with expansion accounting for the drift apart of two continents. When geophysical data gathered from the sea floor provided evidence that this 'continental drift' was not due to an expanding Earth, but due to the movement of crustal plates over the surface of the Earth, with new rock forming along mid-oceanic ridges, the theory of plate tectonics was born and the expanding Earth theory effectively killed off. The facts or data that showed that at one time South America and Africa were indeed joined in geological history. The similarity in fossil fauna and flora, and the chemical and stratigraphical similarity between the rocks, fitted both theories, but plate tectonics provided a better explanation than an 'expanding Earth' theory, which had a number of deficiencies. An expanding Earth may explain how land once covered by the sea is now remote from the shore, but it does not explain how seas can invade lands, a phenomenon clearly shown in our geological history. If our Earth is expanding, why don't electricity cables, telephone lines and transatlantic undersea cables break more often as they become stretched between continents that are moving apart? If the Earth is expanding, why do we have subduction zones which mean that continents move towards one another in some areas and constructive margins where new rock forces the Earth's surface apart in others, such as the Mid-Atlantic Ridge? Finally, how could we account for the necessary increase in the mass of the Earth needed to fill the internal 'void' created by expansion? If the void is filled by a collapse of the oceanic crust, then surely the ocean basins would accommodate more water and the seas would retreat further from the coasts.

HOW SCIENCE PROCEEDS

The two dominant 'methods' or ways of reaching conclusions in science are deductivism and inductivism. Both methods use reasoning as their modus operandi; both have strengths and weaknesses in their operation. What is unclear from the examination specifications and the approach to How Science Works currently being taken is whether the distinction between these two approaches has been made clear to teachers and pupils alike.

The structure of reasoning and argumentation within science is important and constitutes part of the 'method' followed by all scientists. Arguments begin with a proposition: the Earth is round; my cat has four legs; rain is composed of water; raspberries are red. Propositions can be true or false. Not all propositions, however, can be easily divided into true or false, for example, the proposition 'bacterial life once existed on Mars' may be true or false. The main point of a logical or reasoned argument is how one proposition may be connected to another, and the 'truth' of those propositions. When one is constructing a logical argument, the idea is for the propositions (the premises) to support the conclusion. The step between the premise(s) and the conclusion is the inference. A simple argument with a set of true premises and a valid conclusion could be: My cousin Richard is a medical doctor; all medical doctors attend medical school; therefore Richard went to medical school. A true premise does not always guarantee a valid outcome even if the logic or argument is itself correct: for example, a bat has wings, all birds have wings, therefore a bat is a bird. Both of the premises are true, but the conclusion is invalid. This is of course due to the way that science has decided which features are the ones that distinguish how we classify organisms. This serves to show some of the issues presented when reasoning in science from a deductive position only.

Deductive reasoning is most commonly found in the discipline of mathematics. Proofs of theorems have been the nightmare of many children over the years – less so in today's approach to mathematics, but utilizing a deductive approach in mathematics allows for proof and, with it, truth and certainty. While some scientists undoubtedly use deductive reasoning to arrive at answers to their problems, equating such scientific reasoning with absolute proof and truth in science cannot happen. No matter the degree of confirmation for a scientific explanation, it can only be held as provisional, as it is always possible for a scientific fact to be shown to be wrong or incorrect, as for example in the case of plate tectonics revolutionizing our understanding of the movement of continents over the Earth's surface.

As noted previously, much of science until the time of Francis Bacon was deductive in its reasoning. A strong deductive conclusion can be made when the information or data that supports such a conclusion is itself valid. With deductive reasoning in science, rather than talk of proof, we talk about conclusions being valid or invalid. It is possible, as we have already seen, to come to an invalid conclusion.

Inductive reasoning proceeds in a different way. The outcome of inductive reasoning does not necessarily lead to a valid or invalid conclusion. It is more a case of the probability of the conclusion being more or less valid. The strength of inductive reasoning is in the number of initial supporting instances for the conclusion. For example, driving to Wales I observe 200 sheep in a field. All the sheep are white, therefore I may infer that in the next farm I drive past which contains a flock of sheep, all are likely to be white. While the first premise may be true, and while I may have 200 data items, my conclusion cannot be said to be valid or true. The 200 sheep, which in data terms is a lot of data points or observations, is a very small sample of the total possible number of sheep alive today. I may say that it is likely or more probable that the sheep will be white, but I cannot rule out observing a black sheep. Inductive reasoning involves moving from a specific set of facts (data) to a general conclusion. The more representative your data are of the total possible data, the more valid will be the outcome.

Whether a scientist uses deductive and/or inductive reasoning will depend on whether or not the work that they are doing is theory building or theory confirming. With deductive reasoning, a general principle or established theory in science is the initial premise from which a valid conclusion can be deduced. Where scientists are seeking to develop explanations from their observations or data, then induction is the method followed. For science and the scientific method, then, it is not a case of either/or deduction/induction. Science can, and does, utilize both approaches to establish the validity of an argument or to test the established, prevailing explanations.

CONCLUSION

How a scientist works is a complex process. It is not about where the science takes place. It is not just about following a specific methodology agreed by all scientists – the method depends on the discipline, the nature of the experiment or investigation. It is not even about the type of reasoning scientists employ to come to conclusions. It is about the interplay between all these things and more. In determining how a scientist works, it would be useful to provide a model within which we could position different aspects of science. All too often in the past, school science has been defined mostly by a 'scientific method', and the work of scientists has been characterized by their location in the laboratory and the use of experimental methods. The approach of teaching the facts of science while ignoring the process of science has led to pupils who have knowledge of science but who display insufficient understanding. Important aspects of the discipline of science, such as argumentation or reasoning, history and philosophy, moral and ethical considerations, were not considered. How Science Works should seek to redress the balance. The key is getting the balance right of the need to understand basic concepts in science, learn key facts, acquire skills and training in experimental procedures, and apply that knowledge to novel situations.

FURTHER READING

Bryson, B. (2003) *A Short History of Nearly Everything*, London: Doubleday.

Gorham, G. (2009) *Philosophy of Science: A Beginner's Guide*, Oxford: Oneworld Publications.

REFERENCES

ASE (2006) *Science Teaching in Schools*, Hatfield: ASE.

Benjamin, A.C. (1956) Is there a scientific method? *Journal of Higher Education*, 27,5, 233–238.

Buldu, M. (2006) Young children's perceptions of scientists: a preliminary study, *Educational Research* 48, 121–132.

Chalmers, A. F. (1999) *What Is This Thing Called Science?* Milton Keynes: Open University Press.

Cresswell, J., Ikedo, M., Schleicher, A., Shewbridge, C. and Zoido, P. (2009) *Top of the Class: High Performers in Science in PISA 2006*, Paris: OECD.

Feyerabend, P. K. (1975) *Against Method*, London: Verso.

Feyerabend, P. K. (1995) *Killing Time: The Autobiography of Paul Feyerabend*, Chicago: University of Chicago Press

Gould, S. J. (1983) *Hen's Teeth and Horse's Toes*, New York: Norton.

Gribbin, J. (2002) *Science: A History 1543–2001*, London: Allen Lane.

Haynes, R. D. (1994) *From Faust to Strangelove: Representations of the Scientist in Western Literature*, Baltimore: Johns Hopkins University Press.

Kuhn, T. S. (1996) *The Structure of Scientific Revolutions*, Chicago: University of Chicago Press.

Marks, J. (1983) *Science and the Making of the Modern World*, Oxford: Heinemann Educational Publishers.

Medawar, P. (1982) *Pluto's Republic*, Oxford: Oxford University Press.

Meredith, D. (2010a) *Explaining Research*, Oxford: Oxford University Press.

Meredith, D. (2010b) Scientists are heroes. *The Scientist.* Available HTTP: <http://the-scientist.com/news/display/57142/>.

NSTA (2006) *Position Statement: The Integral Role of Laboratory Investigations in Science Instruction*, Arlington, VA: NSTA.

Popper, K. (2002) *Conjectures and Refutations: The Growth of Scientific Knowledge*, London, Routledge.

Quita, I. N. (2003) What is a scientist? Perspectives of teachers of color. *Multicultural Education*, 11, 29–31.

Ronan, C. A. (1983) *The Cambridge Illustrated History of the World's Science*, Cambridge: Cambridge University Press.

Wellington, J. and Osborne, J. (2001) *Language and Literacy in Science Education*, Buckingham: Open University Press.

Williams, J. D. (2008) Science now and then: discovering how science works, *School Science Review* 90, 45–46.

THE PLACE OF SCIENTIFIC INQUIRY IN THE HOW SCIENCE WORKS CURRICULUM

Michael Allen

School science curricula attempt to serve a dual purpose. First, science theories are presented for students to assimilate; second, a 'scientific attitude' is encouraged by teaching students how to think and act like professional scientists. It is proposed that these two long-established aims, while being on the face of things a sensible way to go about teaching science, sometimes conflict with each other and create considerable problems for students. The recently introduced How Science Works curriculum claims to offer students and teachers an authentic version of scientific inquiry, but to what degree, if any, have these problems been addressed?

PRACTICAL WORK IN THE SCHOOL SCIENCE CURRICULUM

Historically, science has taken a significant share of secondary school curriculum time in England and Wales (Gott and Duggan 1996). Traditionally, a large part of the science curriculum has focused on the transmission of 'facts', which has typically occupied one-half to two-thirds of teaching time (Beatty and Woolnough 1982; Thompson 1975). The remainder of curriculum time is spent doing 'experiments'. These two curricular elements are described in science education academic parlance as *content* and *process* respectively, although science teachers commonly refer to the dichotomy as *theory* and *practical work*.

The purposes of asking students to carry out experiments during science lessons are manifold. Practicals are perhaps most often used to endorse and consolidate the theory taught during previous lessons where students have completed written work, thus being illustrations of science phenomena as given in the textbook. Rationales for the inclusion of practical lessons within the curriculum include the belief that the learning of science concepts is enhanced if students are given an opportunity to do something hands-on (Millar 1991), that student motivation is improved by offering an alternative to writing (Hodson 1993) and that learners are given a greater degree of control over their experimenting, so imparting a sense of ownership, allowing them to proceed at their own pace (Atkinson 1990).

It must be noted that the literature has been equivocal about the efficacy of using practical work to improve the learning of science theory, with some writers advocating its usefulness (Atkinson 1990; Gott and Duggan 1995; Millar 1989) and others challenging whether a hands-on approach can actually be successful in this regard (Erickson 1994; Hodson 1993; Watson 2000). Another reason for doing experiments is to develop and practise skills by means of the physical manipulation of science apparatus. In the past, teacher assessment of students' laboratory handling skills has played a more notable role than it does at present, where currently the emphasis tends to be on the augmentation of science knowledge and an understanding of the process of science.

A separate, though related, reason for requiring students to take part in hands-on work is the encouragement of a 'scientific attitude' by teaching them to think and act as professional scientists do. This approach is not new; the Nuffield courses of the 1960s, influenced by Piaget, introduced the idea into English schools that students should be a 'scientist for a day', re-enacting experiments and investigations using actual scientific methods (Fairbrother and Hackling 1997). This approach endeavours to make students familiar with the accepted conventions of scientific experimentation, forms of good practice, termed *process skills* (Millar 1989). It has been suggested that once they have been learned, students might be able to transfer these process skills, which are rooted in reason and logic, to other areas of the school curriculum and even apply them when solving everyday problems (ibid.). Some writers have argued that an understanding of process skills fosters an appreciation of the general value of empirical evidence (e.g. Gott and Duggan 1996), with others going so far as to claim an acceleration of children's overall cognitive development (Shayer 1999). This historical encouragement of a scientific attitude lies behind the current adoption of How Science Works into the science curriculum in England. All of these elements that relate to how professional scientists approach their work have been called *scientific inquiry*.

The National Curriculum in England is structured according to four strands, or Attainment Targets (QCA 2007). The first Attainment Target (AT1) encompasses process skills and related knowledge, and teaching activities therein fall under the umbrella of scientific inquiry – indeed, AT1 is officially titled *Scientific Enquiry* at primary level (ages 5–11 years) and *How Science Works* at secondary level (ages 11–16 years). The other three (AT2, 3 and 4) comprise substantive content, or science 'facts'. With AT1, during their school careers students work their way through a hierarchical series of process skills, called levels, which become increasingly difficult the higher the level. For example, most students aged 5–6 years are expected to be able to carry out the level 1 skill of observing simple phenomena such as the behaviour of living things, and summarize their observations in drawings. At the opposite end of the ability scale, some older secondary students would be working at level 8 (at the top of the hierarchy) and be consistently using scientific knowledge and understanding during the planning, execution and conclusion phases of their experiments. In line with the rationale for practical work given in the previous paragraph, AT1 is intended to promote a scientific attitude among students. For instance, Goldsworthy *et al.* (2000) have determined types of scientific inquiry tasks that primary students undertake, aping the work of professional scientists. These include classifying scientific information by making sets, planning fair tests by controlling variables, exploration of physical phenomena by means of careful observation, collecting experimental data by using apparatus to take results/measurements, then looking for pattern in their results. At the later stages of ages 14 to 16 years, AT1 encompasses a wider range of skills under the heading *How Science Works*.

In summary, the science curriculum in England is geared towards the teaching of both science theory and the processes of science (scientific inquiry). This approach is well established, and on the surface appears to be a sensible way to present science to learners. However, there are some notable, though infrequently recognized, problems associated with teaching science as a dichotomous entity.

CHASING THE RIGHT ANSWER

As discussed, science curricula have always had as a major aim the presentation of a canon of science 'facts' that students are required to learn, and later be examined on in order to assess both the extent to which individuals have successfully assimilated those facts, and the effectiveness of the teaching programme experienced by those individuals. This process of feeding facts to learners gives the impression that science is a collection of 'right answers' that are irrefutable, and in England this body of right answers is delineated by Attainment Targets 2–4 of the National Curriculum (Osborne and Collins 2000). For instance, if a student provides a written answer to a question that is at odds with a science theory that the National Curriculum explicitly includes, then the student is wrong. As will be explained later in the chapter, this approach takes a stance that is at odds with real science, which is in actuality a pluralistic venture in the sense that it considers competing theories.

It has been argued by some writers that this presentation of science as irrefutable facts is unavoidable since students need to be examined and so there has to be a rock-solid foundation of 'correct' information available for study (Nott and Smith 1995). As stated, practical work in school science is frequently illustrative in the sense that experiments are intended to verify the textbook, and so are set for reproducing a right answer that reflects the orthodox scientific response (Kirschner 1992). When students fail to gain the expected results during their experiments, they may say, 'is this what ought to happen?' or 'have we got the right answer?' (Driver 1975; Wellington 1981), to which teachers typically reply, 'your results are incorrect, but don't worry, this is what you should have got' (Claxton 1986).

Chasing a right answer during an experiment but failing to gain that answer can lead students to ask 'if the answer was known anyway, and we always get the wrong result what is the point in doing the experiment?' (Claxton 1986). This situation is extremely common in school science, yet is problematic in two main ways. First, it has been recognized for many years that students can see data collection during illustrative practicals as a chore with a lack of real intellectual challenge (Roth 1994); indeed, the House of Commons Select Committee has commented that GCSE science coursework such as the familiar generation of data to illustrate Ohm's law is tedious and dull for both students and teachers, and has little educational value (Roberts and Gott 2006). This approach espouses science as a positivist pursuit that reflects a naïve-realist epistemology where 'facts', once discovered, are set in stone and cannot be challenged. The education system provides strong motivation that discourages students from getting the 'wrong answer', particularly during assessed practical work and examinations. This can lead to students undertaking activities that professional scientists would view as unethical, such as the unfair manipulation of apparatus and methods, the discarding of 'bad' results and the invention of 'good' ones to ensure that they hand in the right answer at the end of the lesson and gain high marks (e.g. Allen 2009). This behaviour is tolerated and perhaps even encouraged by teachers who are driven by external scrutiny, for example to obtain marks that produce the grades that augur well with examination league tables that compare schools locally and nationally (Hodson 1993; Toplis 2004).

The second problem with chasing right answers lies in that not all of school science reflects a naïve-realist epistemology. During true scientific inquiry exercises in the classroom – that is, activities that properly reflect how professional scientists work – at the outset any right or wrong answer is unknown (sometimes even by the teacher) and the student carries out experiments with an open mind as to the eventual outcome. In England and Wales such lessons are called 'investigations', and, compared with the illustrative practicals previously discussed, students typically have greater degrees of control and ownership, being free to formulate their own research questions, select apparatus and devise an experimental method. Sometimes they generate several competing hypotheses, with the purpose of the experiment being to ascertain which one is more supported by the evidence they collect. Even though they operate with an open mind as per the outcome, students are permitted to hypothesize – that is, align themselves with the theory that they think will correspond with their results, by making a prediction. However, they must attempt to bracket any expectations towards a favoured outcome by conducting the experiment objectively and fairly, so to avoid any bias. This type of scientific inquiry, albeit closer to how professional scientists work, is epistemologically constructivist, and worlds apart from the naïve-realist positivist epistemology that underpins illustrative practicals of there being a single unassailable right answer.

Although it can be argued that investigations correspond to the closest experience of authentic scientific inquiry offered to students, there are recognized problems with presenting science in this way in the classroom. As mentioned, policy-makers have acknowledged that tried and tested investigations utilized by schools because they produce reliable experimental data are often routine and tedious (Roberts and Gott 2006), a sentiment that has been echoed by students themselves (Nott *et al.* 1999). Some students believe that the whole point of carrying out an investigation is merely to gain good coursework marks and improve their final grades, instead of learning science concepts or process (ibid.). Students also complain about other facets that are peculiar to science investigations, such as a lack of time for proper reflection once results have been collected, being unsure of the learning aims, and jumping through various assessment hoops, such as the fact that if an outlier or anomalous result is collected, then higher marks can potentially be awarded by the marker (Toplis 2004). Another issue is that since students operate with a low degree of supervision during investigative work, during the chase for a right answer there would be a greater probability of unethical manipulations of apparatus, methods and results going unnoticed (see the case on page 48). This problem is exacerbated when their view of what constitutes the right answer is actually a science misconception (Allen 2006).

Driver (1975) writes about the problems of the dualistic structure of the science curriculum, which the current author believes compels teachers to send out mixed epistemological messages. Students are required on one day to only produce results that verify the textbook, and on another day to act as constructivist thinkers who fairly conduct an experiment in order to weigh opposing hypotheses and come to a tentative conclusion. The presentation of science as a blend of two disparate epistemological positions does not help students to see the subject as a holistic entity. For instance, students are taught a theory

Box 4.1 **Case study: Chasing the right answer**

A large-scale ($n = 1023$) study of students who chased what they thought was the 'right answer' while carrying out a distinct type of science practical work, found evidence of various behaviours that appeared to be governed by experimenter confirmation bias (Allen 2006). More than half of the students felt that they were taking part in a competition against their peers, with the prize being success in obtaining the right answer. The lengths that some were prepared to go to in order to produce the correct results involved ethically questionable behaviours that reflected a reduced feeling of worth as regards their own empirical data in favour of the textbook result. These behaviours included copying the answers of others in the class who were thought to be good at science, unthinkingly deleting their own data if they were thought to be anomalous (i.e. they produced the 'wrong answer'), blaming those anomalies on either the apparatus or their lab partner, adjusting experimental set-up or procedures until the right answer was finally generated, inventing 'good' results then pretending that they were obtained fairly, and others.

Although these types of confirmation bias are well known, teachers sometimes ignore them, turning a blind eye because they believe the important thing is that students produce the right answer during practical work whose aim is verification of the textbook. Disadvantages of permitting the continuance of scientifically unethical experimenting include encouragement of the view that pre-existing theory always takes precedence over empirical results, and the survival of confirmation-biased behaviours that become part of experimenters' repertoires, reappearing during post-compulsory and higher education science courses, with the potential of manifesting at a later time in individuals' careers as serious scientific fraud.

lesson where they learn that when different objects are in free fall, those with bigger surface areas will tend to fall more slowly due to the effect of air resistance. The following lesson they are required to carry out a scientific inquiry activity where they fairly 'investigate' how having card 'skydivers' of different sizes affects the speed of fall. Students are obliged to make a gestalt shift as they switch from already knowing a positivistic right answer, to suddenly having to work in an epistemologically constructivist-pluralistic mode in order to fairly consider all possible outcomes. This must perplex students, particularly the less able, only serving to reinforce learners' views of the difficulty of science, despite the fact that many older students recognize the dichotomy in the sense that the science they do at school comes under two types – normal science, and investigations – the latter of which in the 14–16 age group is nearly always associated with assessed coursework.

ADDRESSING THE PROBLEM THROUGH THE HOW SCIENCE WORKS CURRICULUM

In 2006, How Science Works was introduced into the Key Stage 4 (ages 14–16 years) curriculum in England. This new curriculum emphasized an authentic model of scientific inquiry by reflecting a contemporary view of how scientists work, and includes the validity and reliability of evidence, control of variables, hypothesis formation and refutation in the face of data collected, and how observation acts as a link between theory and phenomena. 'The new Criteria for GCSE Science ... place far greater emphasis on the skills, knowledge and understanding of how science works and much less emphasis on knowing scientific facts' (Edexcel 2007: 2). There are two general themes that incorporate these ideas.

Pluralism

Positivism promotes a view of science as the uncovering of natural 'facts' or 'laws' about the universe; once these have been discovered, they are irrefutable, set in stone. This is often understood by laypeople as being a fundamental quality of science, and is usually expressed in this form by the media.

Despite there being different ways that scientists do their science, these are really variations on a similar theme. The way that scientists work is antithetical to the positivist view of discovering hard facts that, once supported by strong evidence, can no longer be challenged. Real scientists do not pursue irrefutable facts, but instead seek to construct *provisional* theories. Typically these theories start off as an idea or a question within the scientist's mind that s/he thinks might be able to explain certain natural phenomena. To illustrate this, imagine a fungus, known to excrete chemical X in large amounts, that holds a successful niche in a particular habitat. The scientist then hypothesizes that chemical X might be responsible for the success of the fungus, although in science it is not merely enough to make this argument in the hope that others will accept it as 'truth'. Instead, the scientist needs to gather evidence with which to support the argument – that is, conduct an experiment. The experimental process has to be designed in such a way that it challenges the provisional hypothesis, attempting to falsify it using a fair methodology. If evidence is collected that does not falsify the hypothesis, but instead supports it – in the case of our successful fungus this might take the form of data that show chemical X to be a powerful antibiotic that is able to kill competitors – then the hypothesis becomes a tentative theory.

A naïve-realist view of science would assume that findings of the fungus experiment are natural 'laws' that have been uncovered, and so can no longer be challenged. The scientist has discovered a little bit about how the world works, with this new fact entering the canon of knowledge that we call 'science', perhaps finding its way into authoritative textbooks for the use of future generations. However, this commonly held model of the nature of science (Thoermer and Sodian 2002) does not reflect the actual status of a scientific theory, which is provisional, not absolute. A different scientist might conduct an experiment which finds that although chemical X is an effective antibiotic *in vitro*, it has little effect *in vivo* against competitors in the true habitat. Therefore, all scientific theory has to hold tentative status since in the light of subsequent data it may one day be falsified. Science is pluralistic in the sense that it allows the construction of several theories that explain the same phenomenon, and encourages debate as to which best reflects reality (Kuhn 1996).

Hence, theories are merely ideas that have been constructed by individuals who attempt to explain natural phenomena in the light of current evidence. Laypeople sometimes fail to appreciate that science is a creative and imaginative pursuit of human endeavour. That is not to say that scientists automatically hold a relativistic epistemological view where everyone's idea is valid; they are realists who acknowledge the existence of the world, and undertake to represent that reality by making theory statements. Ideally, science moves forward: as more experiments are carried out and evidence collected, then theory and reality converge. For instance, if the entire gamut of fungal secretions are analysed, then we may be nearer to explaining the success of our organism. Note that although convergence may take place, we could never be in the position to state that a theory *is* reality, which is positivistic. Since we rely on our senses to tell us what is really 'out there', and we know they are sometimes unreliable, we can never be sure exactly what reality is because we can never access it directly. This Cartesian duality exemplifies the essence of science.

The How Science Works curriculum explicitly acknowledges the pluralistic and constructivist nature of science, as the following extracts from GCSE specifications illustrate:

> Observing phenomena can lead to the start of an investigation, experiment or survey. Existing theories and models can be used creatively to suggest explanations for phenomena (hypotheses). Careful observation is necessary before deciding which are the most important variables. Hypotheses can then be used to make predictions that can be tested. An example is the observation that shrimp only occur in parts of a stream. Knowledge about shrimp and water flow leads to a hypothesis relating the distribution to the stream flow rate. A prediction leads to a survey that looks at both variables.
>
> (AQA 2009: 27)

> [How Science Works will help students to] consider scientific findings in a wider context – recognising their tentative nature.
>
> (Edexcel 2007: 7)

> An accurate measurement is one which is close to the true value.
>
> (AQA 2009: 29)

In the specifications there are acknowledgements, Kuhnian in tone, that science theories are more human constructions than irrefutable facts:

> Evidence can be accorded undue weight, or dismissed too lightly, simply because of its political significance. If the consequences of the evidence might provoke public or political disquiet, the evidence may be downplayed…. The status of the experimenter may influence the weight placed on evidence; for instance, academic or professional status, experience and authority. It is more likely that the advice of an eminent scientist will be sought to help provide a solution to a problem than that of a scientist with less experience.
>
> (AQA 2009: 31)

> … show understanding of how scientific knowledge and ideas change over time.
>
> (Edexcel 2007: 150)

One statement uses the issue of global warming in order to explain pluralism:

> We are still finding out about things and developing our scientific knowledge. There are some questions that we cannot answer, maybe because we do not have enough reliable and valid evidence. For example, it is generally accepted that the extra carbon dioxide in the air (from burning fossil fuels) is linked to global warming, but some scientists think there is not sufficient evidence and that there are other factors involved.
>
> (AQA 2009: 31)

However, most of the same documents comprise of sets of 'facts', presented as a secure positivistic canon of right answers to be transmitted by teachers and digested by students.

> A body of content has been identified which underpins the knowledge and understanding of 'How Science Works' at all levels. ... [An aim of the course is for pupils to] acquire and apply skills, knowledge and understanding...
>
> (AQA 2009: 12, 16)

How Science Works attempts to present an authentic picture of science that is pluralistic (despite positivistic comments and philosophy that otherwise permeate the GCSE specifications). Cultural factors that are external to the world of science oppose this view; for instance, the television news medium commonly reflects a naïve-realist epistemology. Taking the issue of global warming mentioned earlier, the tentative hypothesis that greenhouse gas build-up has acted as a trigger is currently offered by TV news programme makers as an positivistic absolute, with dissenters from the theory ridiculed as being irrational or having hidden agendas, and being labelled 'deniers'.

Selective data collection

As discussed, illustrative practicals whose purpose is to verify right answers found in the textbook carry with them a number of problems. Some writers have commented on the unfeasibility of rejecting this time-honoured approach, given that curricula compel science teachers to present a set body of examinable knowledge to their audience (Nott and Smith 1995). Right-answer chasing can spawn ethically questionable behaviours such as rejecting anomalous results out of hand merely because they fail to support that answer, and copying the work of peers who are judged to be good at doing science (see Box 4.1). The How Science Works specifications have acknowledged this tendency:

> The credibility of the evidence is increased if a balanced account of the data is used rather than a selection from it which supports a particular pre-determined stance.
>
> (AQA 2009: 31)

However, other writers have advocated that situations where no right answer is initially known create an atmosphere that is more conducive to the proper treatment of empirical data, and so represent more valid forms of scientific inquiry. Fairbrother and Hackling (1997) particularly mention the hothouse conditions associated with assessed coursework being a strong driver towards improper behaviour, and if a standardized answer is not known to students at the outset then they will concentrate more on the process of science involved in gaining *an* answe r that can be defended by checking, as one would a well-oiled machine, that the whole thing fits together and runs properly (ibid). There is some evidence to show that during more bona fide inquiry practicals, improper scientific behaviours are reduced (e.g. Rigano and Richie 1995). In contrast, Allen (2009) found that for practicals where the right answer was not communicated to students, and ethically unsound behaviours were implicitly, though positively, *encouraged* by the lesson design, learning was enhanced up to three years after the event when compared to a control group, in likelihood due to the stimulation of students' emotions.

Fairbrother and Hackling (1997) also suggest that if students collect anomalous results that do not align with the textbook, instead of automatically rejecting them, these data should be given a temporary label of being *uncertain*. The intention is not to present science as a right/wrong dichotomy, but instead to promote a situation where anomalies giving rise to an erroneous conclusion are not seen by students as their fault, and so requiring correction (how often are we as science teachers presented with a set of perfect results that give a straight-line graph that aligns with the textbook answer?). Students should be told that any experimental system carries within it chance fluctuations that are statistically inherent, and not the fault of the experimenter. The How Science Works curriculum has recognized that scientific data can have statistical variability:

> There will always be some variation in the actual value of a variable no matter how hard we try to repeat an event. For instance, if a ball is dropped and doesn't land on exactly the same point on its surface there will be a slight difference in the rebound height.
>
> (AQA 2009: 29)

Even so, it should be noted that anomalies are sometimes due to error in technique or apparatus failure. Further, repeat observations will reveal whether a datum is an anomalous outlier, or indeed part of an unexpected identifiable trend (Gunstone 1991). Premature closure should be avoided and any outliers rejected only at the completion of the experiment, with the *uncertain* data being considered only at this stage; even then, solid justification in the way of normal statistical variation or methodological error should be sought in the place of any out-of-hand rejection.

> Any anomalous values should be examined to try and identify the cause and, if a product of a poor measurement, ignored.
>
> (AQA 2009: 29)

CONCLUDING COMMENTS

Although the How Science Works curriculum promotes an overt encouragement of an authentic view of scientific inquiry, its simultaneous presentation of a canon of unassailable right answers skirts around the issue of epistemological clash and its attendant problems. One aim of school science education is to produce a population of scientifically literate individuals who are able to make informed choices on science-related issues of importance. This outcome could only occur if learners fully assimilate a model of authentic scientific inquiry, and appreciate that science theories are not set in stone, but merely the creative constructions of people's minds, so are imperfect and subject to human foibles.

A proper understanding of the interplay between theory and evidence would help people distinguish between scientific and pseudo-scientific enterprises (such as Intelligent Design), and nurture rationality and criticality generally, in a world still governed to some extent by superstition and unconditional, blind belief.

SUMMARY

Scientific inquiry is a cover-all term that represents how professional scientists conduct their work. In England and Wales, practical work has traditionally been taught to secondary school children for a variety of reasons, including as a conduit for the learning of science theory, pupil motivation and the practising of apparatus handling skills. A further reason is the exemplification of scientific inquiry, or encouraging students to think and act like scientists to develop process skills that are potentially transferable to other areas of their life.

There are problems associated with presenting school science as both a collection of positivistic right answers and a pluralistic pursuit. Chasing a right answer can result in students undertaking scientifically unethical behaviours during their experimenting, and the epistemological clash can give students an impression that science is too difficult. The overt recognition by the How Science Works curriculum that scientists are epistemologically constructivist-pluralists and not positivists is a step in the right direction. However, it is felt more may be needed for learners to fully appreciate an authentic model of scientific inquiry.

FURTHER READING

Atkin, J. M. and Karplus, R. (1962) Discovery or invention? *The Science Teacher* 29, 45–51.

Edmondson, K. M. and Novak, J. D. (1993) The interplay of scientific epistemological views, learning strategies, and attitudes of college students, *Journal of Research in Science Teaching* 30, 547–559.

Gobert, J. D. and Pallant, A. (2004) Fostering students' epistemologies of models via authentic model-based tasks, *Journal of Science Education and Technology* 13, 7–22.

Gott, R. and Duggan, S. (1995) *Investigative Work in the Science Curriculum*, Buckingham: Open University Press.

Greenwald, A., Pratkanis, A., Lieppe, M. and Baumgardner, M. (1986) Under what conditions does theory obstruct research progress? *Psychological Review* 93, 216–229.

Gunstone, R. F. and Champagne, A. B. (1990) Promoting conceptual change in the laboratory, in E. Hegarty-Hazel (ed.) *The Student Laboratory and the Science Curriculum*, London: Routledge.

Kuhn, T. S. (1996) *The Structure of Scientific Revolutions* (3rd edition), Chicago: University of Chicago Press.

Monk, M. and Osborne, J. (eds) (2000) *Good Practice in Science Teaching: What Research Has to Say*, Buckingham: Open University Press.

REFERENCES

Allen M. (2006) 'The phenomenon of expectation-related observation: an exploration of nature, associations and causes'. unpublished PhD dissertation, School of Sport and Education, Brunel University, Uxbridge.

Allen, M. (2009) Learner error, affectual stimulation, and conceptual change, *Journal of Research in Science Teaching* 47(2), 151–173.

AQA (2009) *General Certificate of Secondary Education: Science 4463*, London: Assessment and Qualifications Alliance.

Atkinson, E. P. (1990) Learning scientific knowledge in the student laboratory, in E. Hegarty-Hazel (ed.) *The student laboratory and the science curriculum*, pp. 119–131, London: Routledge.

Beatty, J. W. and Woolnough, B. E. (1982) Practical work in 11–13 science, *British Educational Research Journal* 8, 23–30.

Claxton, G. (1986) The alternative conceiver's conceptions, *Studies in Science Education* 13, 123–130.

Driver, R. (1975) The name of the game, *School Science Review* 56, 800–805.

Edexcel (2007) *GCSE in Science (2101)*, Mansfield: Edexcel Publications.

Erickson, G. (1994) Pupils' understanding of magnetism in a practical assessment context: the relationship between content, process and progression, in P. J. Fensham, R. F. Gunstone and R. White (eds) *The Content of Science: A Constructivist Approach to its Teaching and Learning*, London: Falmer Press.

Fairbrother, R. and Hackling, M. (1997) Is this the right answer? *International Journal of Science Education* 19, 887–894.

Goldsworthy, A., Watson, R. and Wood-Robinson, V. (2000) *Investigations: Developing Understanding*, Hatfield: Association for Science Education.

Gott, R. and Duggan, S. (1995) *Investigative Work in the Science Curriculum*, Buckingham: Open University Press.

Gott, R. and Duggan, S. (1996) Practical work: its role in the understanding of evidence in science, *International Journal of Science Education* 18, 791–806.

Gunstone. R. F. (1991) Reconstructing theory from practical experience, in B. Woolnough (ed.) *Practical Science*, Milton Keynes: Open University Press.

Hodson, D. (1993) Rethinking old ways: towards a more critical approach to practical work in school science, *Studies in Science Education* 22, 85–142.

Kirschner, P. (1992) Epistemology, practical work and academic skills in science education, *Skills in Science Education* 1, 273–299.

Kuhn, T. S. (1996) *The Structure of Scientific Revolutions* (3rd edition) Chicago: University of Chicago Press.

Millar, R. (1989) Bending the evidence: the relationship between theory and experiment in science education, in R. Millar (ed.), *Doing Science: Images of Science in Science Education*, London: Falmer Press.

Millar, R. (1991) A means to an end: the role of processes in science education, in B. Woolnough (ed.) *Practical Science*, Milton Keynes: Open University Press.

Nott, M. and Smith, R. (1995) Talking your way out of it, 'rigging' and 'conjuring': what science teachers do when practicals go wrong, *International Journal of Science Education* 17, 399–410.

Nott, M., Peacock, G., Smith, R., Wardle, J., Wellington, J. and Wilson, P. (1999) *Investigations into KS3 and KS4 science*, report prepared for the Qualifications and Curriculum Authority Projects 10905 and 10906, Sheffield: Sheffield Hallam University.

Osborne, J. and Collins, S. (2000) Pupils' and parents' views of the school science curriculum, *School Science Review* 82, 23–31.

QCA (2007) *The National Curriculum: Statutory Requirements for Key Stages 3 and 4*, London: Qualifications and Curriculum Authority.

Rigano, D. L. and Richie, S. M. (1995) Student disclosures of fraudulent practice in school laboratories, *Research in Science Education* 25, 353–363.

Roberts, R. and Gott, R. (2006) The role of evidence in the new KS4 National Curriculum for England and the AQA specifications, *School Science Review* 87, 29–39.

Roth, W.-M. (1994) Experimenting in a constructivist high school physics laboratory, *Journal of Research in Science Teaching* 31, 197–223.

Shayer, M. (1999) Cognitive acceleration through science education II: its effects and scope. *International Journal of Science Education* 21, 883–902.

Thoermer, C. and Sodian, B. (2002) Science undergraduates' and graduates' epistemologies of science: the notion of interpretive frameworks, *New Ideas in Psychology* 20, 263–283.

Thompson, J. J. (ed.) (1975) *Practical work in sixth form science*, Oxford: Department of Educational Studies, University of Oxford.

Toplis, R. (2004) What do Key Stage 4 pupils think about science investigations? *Science Teacher Education* 41, 8–9.

Watson, J. R. (2000) The role of practical work, in M. Monk and J. Osborne (eds) *Good Practice in Science Teaching: What Research Has to Say*, Buckingham: Open University Press.

Wellington, J. (1981) 'What's supposed to happen, sir?': some problems with discovery learning, *School Science Review* 63 167–173.

TEACHING CONTROVERSIAL ISSUES IN SCIENCE

Ralph Levinson

INTRODUCTION

Discussion of controversial issues is at the heart of responsible action in democratic socie-ties. It is how young people acquire the knowledge and skills for critical thinking which strengthens democratic deliberation. This chapter will therefore focus on what is meant by controversial issues in science, how How Science Works underpins the teaching of contro-versial issues and what kinds of pedagogy and resources can best support discussion.

In recent years there has been increasing emphasis on the teaching of controversial socio-scientific issues reflecting debates on matters such as GM crops, stem cell research, radiation from mobile phones, cloning and use of pesticides on crops. The report *Beyond 2000*, which was instrumental in setting the agenda for reforms in science education in England, reflects these shifts: 'For the majority of young people, the 5–16 science cur-riculum ... must provide both a good basis for lifelong learning and a preparation for life in a modern democracy, ' (Millar and Osborne 1998: 2009).

Democratic participation for the future citizen is therefore an important feature of the case made for including controversial issues in the science curriculum, reinforced through aspects of the programme of study in the citizenship curriculum.

In this chapter I will:

- examine what is meant by a controversial issue;
- discuss why the pedagogic demands for teaching socio-scientific issues are differ-ent from those in substantive school science;
- identify the kinds of knowledge and skills needed for discussing controversial socio-scientific issues;
- explore the classroom opportunities for examining socio-scientific issues (SSIs) within the context of How Science Works.

WHAT ARE CONTROVERSIAL ISSUES?

The straightforward answer to the question of what constitutes controversial issues is that they are matters which people disagree about, ranging from what to watch on television, whether the classification of the drug ecstasy should be downgraded, and whether Britain should have troops in Afghanistan. Almost everything people do and talk about can be considered controversial. So what are the characteristics of controversial issues that might be appropriate for teaching in the classroom? The depiction of what is a controversial issue through the advisory report on citizenship should be a helpful pointer. A controversial issue is one 'about which there is no one fixed or universally held point of view. Such issues are those which commonly divide society and for which significant groups offer conflicting explanations and solutions' (Crick 1998: 56).

Because controversial issues 'are those which commonly divide society', this takes any definition beyond local individual differences such as arguments in a family or between friends over what to watch on television. But there are many issues which commonly divide society such as which is the best football team in the United Kingdom, who should win TV shows such as *The X-Factor*, should taxes be raised to help reduce carbon emissions. It is likely that a greater number of people are more passionately divided, and can offer good justifications, about who wins TV game shows than about many local or national policy issues, but it would be difficult to make a case for them to constitute a significant portion of the school curriculum.

Teachers and curriculum designers need to know the skills and knowledge which would be helpful in justifying the place of controversial issues in the curriculum. Dearden proposes an epistemic criterion of a controversial issue: 'a matter is controversial if contrary views can be held on it without these views being contrary to reason' (1981: 38). Reason within this definition refers to criteria of truth, critical standards of verification which at any given time have been so far developed. 'What is controversial', argues Dearden, is 'precisely the truth, correctness or rightness of view, which presupposes that at least it makes sense to search for these things even if we do not attain them' (Ibid.: 40). Hence, not only are controversial issues matters over which large sectors of an open and democratic society disagree but they presuppose rigorous justifications supporting diverse points of view where there is no necessary agreement over the criteria for judging what is correct or not. The emphasis is not on content but on the reasoning and underpinning dispositions such as criticality, openness and willingness to listen which support rational discussion (Bridges 1979).

Given the diverse types of disagreement possible in society from those which might be easily resolved to those which divide people on deep-seated beliefs, McLaughlin (2003) devised a categorization based on the work of Dearden and other philosophers which Levinson (2006) formulated in terms of levels of disagreement and the role of evidence in socio-scientific issues. Selected features of this categorization are listed in Table 5.1.

Table 5.1 demonstrates that there are different ways in which disagreements can be formulated, and highlights the distinct role of evidence. Issues such as climate change, introduction of nanotechnologies and the effects of the new genetics are so complex and multifaceted that it would be far too demanding to cover them satisfactorily within the constraints of the curriculum, but it is possible to identify the specific social and epistemic nature of disagreements within the overall controversy. The teaching points to be gleaned from this table are to identify particular aspects of an issue, to explain why they are controversial and to develop an approach that seeks to investigate the controversy further.

■ Table 5.1 Levels of disagreement. Source: Adapted from Levinson (2006)

Level of disagreement	Formulation	Examples	Role of evidence
1	Where insufficient evidence is as yet available to settle a matter, but where such evidence could in principle be forthcoming at some point	Which will be the best soccer team this season? Explanation for death of the dinosaurs. Is X likely to develop Huntington's disease? Is xenotransplantation free from retroviral infection? Has there been a global rise in temperature since the Industrial Revolution? What are the best conditions for keeping a particular polar bear at the zoo? Predicting the change in the size of a current when the configuration of a circuit is changed.	Criteria for evidence to be met are set out beforehand and agreed by all parties. Evidence is usually unambiguous and is consistent with the terms of the criteria. The likelihood of developing Huntington's can be confirmed by an unambiguous genetic test.
2	Where evidence relevant to settling a matter is conflicting, complex and difficult to assess.	What is the acceptable risk of the transmission of disease as a result of the after-affects of xenotransplantation? Which shoe design will help a runner sprint fastest? What factors are responsible for the pollution of a local river? Which is the best medicine for reducing the risk of heart disease? Does the use of 'green' fuels reduce carbon dioxide emissions?	Criteria can be agreed but it is difficult to assess whether evidence meets the criteria. Evidence is conflicting when there are good sources of data that support opposing conclusions; it is complex when it is obtained through technically sophisticated processes or requires deep background specialist knowledge; and it is difficult to assess because it is not straightforward and linear, and contains uneven variables. Acceptable risk may be estimated differently depending on cultural and economic factors. One medicine might be effective for a certain group of people while another might be better for other groups. The evidence might also be too complex to be understood by non-specialists.

Level of disagreement	Formulation	Examples	Role of evidence
8	Where the differing 'total experiences' of people in the course of their lives shape their judgements in divergent ways	Someone who has seen a sibling die from a genetic disease might be more likely to draw on that experience in supporting pre-implantation genetic diagnosis than someone who opposes this technique. Someone who has suffered from flooding attributed to climate change brought about by carbon emissions differs in their interpretation of climate change from an oil company executive, who might point out the complexity and unreliability of the climate change models used (see also category 2).	Where evidence is available, parties incorporate the evidence into the worldviews that stem from their experiences.

In Level of Disagreement 1, parties on different sides of an argument will accept that a disagreement is settled one way or the other by evidence. Such an approach can be illustrated in making a prediction and seeing if the evidence does or does not support the prediction. A simple but effective example was illustrated by a beginning teacher I was observing who, in a lesson on healthy eating, asked the students in her class to pour into a beaker the estimated amount of daily intake of salt recommended without using balances. There was a lively discussion and disagreement about what might be the right amount, and groups differed by a factor of 100. When the amounts from the groups were weighed, there was considerable shock when most realized how small the daily intake really should be. The point is that the evidence was incontrovertible, and once it had been demonstrated, disagreements were resolved.

Similar activities can be carried out, for example, in predicting how current will be affected when changing a circuit, the rate of cooling of different liquids, the relative amounts of oxygen evolved by plants in different conditions and predicted rates of reaction. But few socio-scientific issues are resolved so definitively.

TEACHING SOCIO-SCIENTIFIC ISSUES

Particular demands are placed on teaching socio-scientific issues in science and it is not surprising that science teachers have found them stimulating but difficult to deal with (Bryce and Gray 2004; Levinson and Turner 2001). Science as learned and experienced in school presents quite different pedagogical challenges from those incorporated in controversial socio-scientific issues (see Table 5.2) because in the latter, knowledge is used to try to solve socio-political, ethical and economic problems, whereas much school science revolves around the core principles of authoritative science, which do not lend themselves to solving such problems (Layton 1986; Ryder 2001). Although science has been characterized as both progressive and provisional in nature (Chalmers 1999; Popper 1972), much of the science taught at school is authoritative and universally accepted. At secondary school level, knowledge of the periodic table of the elements, Newton's laws of motion, the laws of thermodynamics, the Krebs cycle and the processes of photosynthesis is beyond reasonable question, let alone the orbits of the planets around the Sun, and Earth as a spheroid (Flat Earth Society excepted!). It would be strange for a student to complete studying science at age 16 thinking that the atomic number of hydrogen still had to be determined, that the laws of motion were tentative statements and that it was only true today that green plants incorporate carbon dioxide and water to build up more complex organic molecules. But the science in many contemporary issues – climate change is an obvious case – has a very different basis. While there is some consensus among experts, much 'frontier science' is still disputed (Bauer 1997), with experts generate conflicting models; data are uncertain and interpretation of even agreed data differs. Knowledge in contemporary socio-scientific issues such as genetic technologies and nanotechnology as well as climate change is therefore emergent and tentative whereas substantive science knowledge is seen as authoritative and certain.

It follows that school science knowledge is broadly uncontentious whereas contemporary science in socio-scientific issues is often conflicting, both among scientists and among many non-scientists too. But this difference suggests a link that can be made between traditional school science and 'frontier' science. Scientific theories, such as the great cosmological theories, the oxygen theory of combustion, circulation of the blood and natural selection, were themselves strongly contested historically, and a study of the

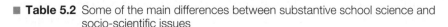

■ **Table 5.2** Some of the main differences between substantive school science and socio-scientific issues

Features of school science	Features of socio-scientific issues
Linear and straightforward	Complex and messy
Uncontentious	Contentious
Authoritative knowledge	Characterized by emergent knowledge
Teacher as authority figure in terms of knowledge	Teacher cannot claim to have solutions
Subject-specific	Interdisciplinary
Asocial or socially decontextualized	Framed by social interests/Socially contextualized
Apolitical	Political
Ethically neutral	Ethically charged
Driven by theory	Led by data and tentative theorizing
Hierarchical with scientist and teacher as experts	Dominated by groups with different types of expertise
Scientist as striver for objective knowledge	Scientists and others responsive to various socio-political interests
Closed	Open-ended
Non-emotive	Often affective

processes through which knowledge progresses from the tentative to the accepted can begin to give insights into disputed knowledge around the science behind contemporary socio-scientific issues. For example, students can readily appreciate why people might have believed the Earth was flat, that the Sun revolved around the Earth and that some indefinable substance escaped from fuels when they burned. Caution needs to be exerted here because the epistemic and social factors are historically contingent. To teach, for example, the conceptual basis of phlogiston theory or the complex mathematics in Newtonian mechanics, or the differences between the ways in which science is organized at a global level today compared with the seventeenth century, would be too demanding and unnecessary, but any study of change of status in scientific thought will help students to understand that ideas can be intellectually sound but also provisional.

As suggested above, the pedagogic implications are considerable. Science as learned and experienced in schools is predominantly deductive, involving the illustration and amplification of theory. Examples are experiments on pendulum motion, combustion of magnesium to demonstrate both gain in mass and combination of masses, pasteurization, and so on. Some of the examples in argumentation (see Chapter 6) help to provide evidence for dominant scientific concepts which contrast with classical and early medieval thought such that light scattered from a luminous source enters the eye rather than eyes actively emitting light rays to illuminate objects (Osborne *et al*. 2001). While secondary students are unlikely to formulate new hypotheses and theories, they can interpret and get beneath the skin of scientific ideas by trying to grapple with and explain original ideas (Sutton 1992). In fact, school science can generate new and exciting insights and problematize authoritative science. Erasto Mpemba, a Tanzanian schoolboy in the 1960s, is a wonderful example of how school science can provide convincing evidence to question even well-established laws. He showed how the cooling of an ice cream mix in a freezer can seemingly contradict the laws of thermodynamics through a phenomenon now known as the Mpemba effect (Jeng 1998).

Donnelly (2004) has argued that many of the core concepts in school science are reductionist and instrumental and free from the kinds of human considerations that feature in arts, humanities and even the social sciences. Entities such as electromagnetic fields and molecules behave very differently from the often serendipitous nature of humans. How they respond to certain stimuli is predictable and follows clear patterns and scientific laws; in other words, they are linear. Even then, in science causal relationships are predictable only to a certain level of complexity, as seen for example in chaos theory. In socio-scientific issues the science is often complex and bears little relationship to school science (Thomas 2000). Moreover, the science cannot be easily disentangled from its social effects. Where science has an impact on society, those involved have to take into account people's beliefs, experiences, cultural understandings, everyday practices and emotions. Values and human concerns feature predominantly in discussions of and decision-making in socio-scientific issues.

Such values might include ethical aspects of the introduction of a technology but also the kinds of values that support the introduction of a technology in the first place, for example why so many more medicines have been synthesized for coronary heart disease than in eradicating malaria. Or there are considerations which might affect one's everyday life such as whether it is acceptable to vaccinate a child given certain risks involved. How decision-making takes place around these issues also involves political skills, knowledge and understanding. Much contemporary R&D is initiated through corporations and government. How decisions are taken as to what is developed and regulated, and how people have a say in their impacts, are not straightforward: they depend on democratic processes, scientists' relationships with interested parties, how knowledge about the technical processes is communicated, trust in regulators and so forth (Irwin and Michael 2003).

WHAT DO STUDENTS NEED TO KNOW?

If what is learned in school science is so different from socio-scientific issues, what kind of knowledge and pedagogy is appropriate? Here are a few examples:

- A young couple who would like to have a baby suspect they are both genetic carriers for cystic fibrosis (CF), which is confirmed when they seek the advice of a genetic counsellor. What do they need to know about genetics to help make a decision? What kind of science ought the counsellor to tell the couple? Which other factors do they need to take into account to help make a decision?
- A group of residents in a village have been feeling unwell and displaying a range of symptoms since a mobile phone base station was erected nearby. Doctors are mystified as to the cause of the symptoms but they are sure that the incidence of ill health is much greater than expected from a similar population. A meeting is arranged with engineers from a mobile phone company.
- Recent surveys of global public opinion reveal that two-thirds of those surveyed saw climate change as a 'very serious problem'. This might seem a very promising statistic but is it of greater concern that nearly a third do not? Furthermore, even those who were concerned about climate change did not see a link between burning of fossil fuels and the effects on climate (BBC World Service 2009, online). Climate change activists consider a strategy to influence public opinion.

A number of points emerge from these three examples. First, the conceptual science content is very different. The first example involves a basic understanding of genetics and inheritance and the probability of two carriers having an affected child. But just as importantly, it involves questions about the rights and wrongs of having a child when there is a high chance it will have CF, the effects on other family members, the availability of care, the possibilities of cure, the increase in average longevity of CF sufferers, the costs of bringing up a child with genetic health problems, the psychological effects on child and parents, and of course the consequences of the couple deciding not to have children. In the second example some understanding is required of intensity of radiation, wavelength, frequency, whether radiation is ionizing or not, understanding of the differences between correlation and cause, sample size, cluster effects, as well as the ability to engage in dialogue with company representatives and to understand what political recourses might be available. The first example involved a couple and their immediate family, whereas the second example involves a group of concerned people and a range of social, political and environmental factors. The first two examples are relatively local; the third is global in range and the science will be derived from a number of specialisms: geoengineering, meteorology, physical chemistry. Rhetoric and political clout, knowing how to communicate research sensitively and compellingly, as well as distinguishing between science which is relatively certain and science which is highly uncertain, and an understanding of trust and the precautionary principle will be equally important.

While a basic knowledge of the underpinning scientific concepts is crucial to orient the issue, the predominant factors are personal, ethical, financial, medical, and include some understanding of risk.

Ryder (2002) carried out a survey of studies of a range of socio-scientific issues reported in the research literature and the substantive science needed to be able to act in these circumstances. His research revealed five different learning aims to support decision-making in the contexts of these issues. These are:

- an ability to assess the quality of data, for example to appreciate that measurements are inherently variable and that from a set of data students need to understand that there is no true value but a spread of measurements from which an estimate of variability can be obtained;
- a realization that the design of a study will influence the kind of data obtained, for example whether double-blind studies have been carried out and placebos administered in medical interventions, the sample size studied, and the differences between correlations and causal relationships;
- scientific explanations and the role of models;
- uncertainty in that many socio-scientific questions are complex, consisting of uneven and interdependent variables, and do not yield unequivocal answers;
- an understanding of the media through which science is communicated and that aspects of the reliability and validity of measurements are often excluded from media reports.

Ryder suggests teaching strategies arising from these aims which are more suited to decision-making in socio-scientific activities. One of these is an understanding of the use and interpretation of secondary data, the kind of complex data which it would be impossible to collect in science lessons. A problem, however, in interpreting secondary data is that these data themselves, as reported in specialized journals, often use complex sampling frames and statistical techniques which most teachers, let alone students, would understandably lack the knowledge and experience to interpret. While some data will be accessible to students at this level, another way of approaching the use of data is to incorporate data such as narratives of experience and ask students what kind of data would be helpful in trying to resolve a particular issue. In the next sections I will try to exemplify how students might construct informed arguments through two examples.

SUNBEDS: 'AS LONG AS YOU DON'T USE THE SUNBED TOO MUCH I'M SURE YOU'LL BE FINE'

In this example, in terms of How Science Works I will be drawing on how scientific data can be collected and analysed, the limitations of data, the benefits, drawbacks and risks of scientific and technological developments, and the social impacts of decision-making.

One of the main health concerns for young people is the risk of skin cancer from ultra-violet radiation, although there are benefits from tanned skin and the production of vitamin D. Deficiency of vitamin D can result in bone-softening conditions and rickets in young children, and can lead to osteoporosis in later life. But lack of vitamin D can be made up through food supplements as well as through exposure to sunlight and artificial sources of UV radiation.

In less sunny climates such as those of northern Europe and North America, many young people resort to tanning parlours and sunbeds as a way of producing 'healthy tans' that give a feelgood factor. Everyone is exposed to ultraviolet radiation because it is among the spectrum of electromagnetic wavelengths emitted by the Sun. Wavelengths of ultraviolet radiation are between 100 and 400nm: there are three types of ultraviolet radiation, UV-A, UV-B and UV-C, where UV-A has the longest wavelength and is least damaging to the skin and UV-C has the lowest wavelength and is most penetrating to the skin. Most UV-C radiation is absorbed by the ozone layer before it can enter the Earth's atmosphere. UV radiation can damage DNA in the cells, resulting in skin cancer. People with fair skin are most susceptible to skin damage from UV radiation whereas people with dark or black skin are at much lower risk and can withstand much higher levels of intensity of exposure.

Until 2009, health authorities suggested that there was only a probable link between the use of sunbeds and cases of malignant melanoma, one of the deadliest forms of skin cancer, but now the International Agency for Research on Cancer says that use of sunbeds is definitely 'carcinogenic to humans' (BBC News 2009, online). The risk of malignant melanoma is increased by 75 per cent for people who start using sunbeds regularly under the age of 30. Cancer Research UK states that 'Using a sunbed once a month or more can increase your risk of skin cancer by more than half. So when the tan fades, the damage remains' (Cancer Research UK 2010, online). Not only does Cancer Research UK claim it is a cultural myth that tanned people have a healthy appearance but it emphasizes that tanning is a sign of damaged skin which will wrinkle and become unsightly with increasing age. The problem seems to have become worse in recent years because high-power sunlamps are now available in tanning parlours which exceed the legal safe dose for UV radiation and, in mimicking effects from the Sun, emit UV-B as well as UV-A. From December 2009 it became illegal for under-18s to use sunbeds in Scotland.

Unsurprisingly, these findings, conclusions and warnings are strongly disputed by the Sunbed Association. They argue that scientific research shows that people exposed to UV-B have a *lower* risk of contracting malignant melanoma, provided sunbeds are used moderately. Moderate use of sunbeds appears to have health benefits: it promotes a feeling of well-being; it protects against too much exposure to the sun because pre-tanned people are unlikely to lie for prolonged periods in the sun to generate a tan; tanned skin in fact protects against sunburn and has a benefit in the production of vitamin D. The Sunbed Association further claims that by far the largest number of users of sunbeds do not exceed the European standards on maximum numbers of sessions per year, hence people using properly regulated tanning salons, or using their own sunbeds within pre-scribed limits, should be exposed to minimum risk. No amount of legislation can stop people using unregulated salons (Sunbed Association 2010, online).

The sunbed industry argues that medical and health authorities such as Cancer Research UK, through its Sunsmart campaign, would do better to lobby for safe and moderate use of sunbeds, and that there should be much more emphasis on safe outdoor exposure. Moreover, it questioned both the validity and the reliability of the studies in that they made no reference to scientific research that indicates there is *no* link between sunbed tanning and melanoma. It argues that rise in melanomas is a result not of increased use of sunbeds but of better diagno-sis, so while there is a correlation, it would be wrong to assume there is a causal relationship, and this is further evidenced by the fact that there has been no corresponding increase in mor-tality – that is, the number of deaths in a population sample – from skin cancer.

Whether sunbeds should be banned or not is therefore a controversial issue because there are reasons both in support of banning the use of sunbeds for under-18s and in opposing this type of regulation.

Does the evidence support or refute the decision to ban the use of sunbeds for under-18s?

In starting to answer this question it becomes clear that the evidence is complex, conflicting and difficult to assess, but that does not mean students cannot make a decision based on the evidence. The evidence is complex because these studies are sophisticated, often involving difficult statistics, and on their own the data are likely to be too com-plex for Key Stage 4 students to interpret. The evidence is conflicting because data have been gathered on both sides of the question which support opposite points of view and these data are difficult to assess because the sunbed industry claims that selection of research is partial and does not present the whole picture. A report on the British Medical Association's website, dated 22 November 2007, says:

> Westerdahl found that regular exposure to sunbeds significantly increased the risk of developing malignant melanoma. However, a recent large-scale study has found that there was little or no increased melanoma risk associated with sunbed use. A review of the epidemiological evidence shows that 16 out of 19 case-control studies found no association between tanning lamps and melanoma. Three found a sig-nificant positive association and consistent but not strong evidence suggesting that exposure at a younger age may give rise to a greater risk. The authors concluded that methodological limitations of the studies preclude reaching a firm conclusion regarding causation. Therefore new studies collecting precise exposure data are urgently needed.

How, then, are young people able to glean the knowledge and skills necessary to make sense of the arguments so they can make a reasoned decision based on a consideration of different points of view? One way forward is to identify the claims by organizations on opposing sides of the argument and subject them to critical analysis. While students are likely to attain different levels of critical analysis, depending on their background knowledge and level of attainment, both the reported data and the media presentation lend themselves to How Science Works skills.

A first consideration is to help students understand the statement from Cancer Research UK that 'Using a sunbed once a month or more can increase your risk of skin cancer by more than half.' 'Risk' is now a concept incorporated in Ideas about Science and in How Science Works. But unlike many scientific terms such as 'force' or 'potential difference', its meaning is imprecise and it can be interpreted even among scientific organizations in many different ways. Risk is commonly understood to refer to the probability of an event combined with its impact. So what does the statement from Cancer Research UK mean?

Does it mean that if you have a 50 per cent chance of getting skin cancer without using a sunbed more than once a month you will have a 75 per cent chance of getting skin cancer if you do use a sunbed more than once a month? Or if you have, say, a 0.01 per cent chance of getting skin cancer without using a sunbed your chance will rise to at least 0.015 per cent if you do?

If 200 people out of a population of 50 million die from skin cancer in a certain period of time, then if all those people were using sunbeds the figure would rise to 300 people?

Does an increase of risk of 50 per cent mean increases in numbers of deaths of 1 person per year out of a million people or 100 or 1,000 deaths?

How would people react if the statement said that your risk of developing skin cancer would be reduced by 25 per cent in relation to those who do use sunbeds more than once a month?

If 9,000 new cases of melanoma are reported each year and we assume that 5 per cent of the population of 50 million use sunbeds more than once a month, how many of these cases might be due to sunbed use?

How might the stated risks compare with those whose life expectancy is shortened by consuming three pints of beer every week?

How, for example, do estimates of relative risk compare with those of absolute risk? If the numbers affected are small to begin with then a 50 per cent rise might not seem very serious; if they are large, then the seriousness will be much greater. One way to approach this problem is to encourage students to experiment with these data in different ways: how might they represent the data visually? Students could experiment using pictograms or bar charts, or represent information in percentages. Asking students to represent information as in, say, a popular newspaper would help to reinforce understanding of how information can be interpreted differently depending on context (Jarman and McClune 2007).

A further way of analysing the arguments is for students to read relevant extracts from the websites of Cancer Research UK and from the Sunbed Association, where they can pick out sentences that support or challenge the case for a ban on using sunbeds for under-18s. A format for doing this, derived from Wellington and Osborne (2001), is:

■ Extract sentences that contain statements containing evidence for or against the banning of sunbeds.
■ Identify the *source* of the evidence used to justify the claim (as well as any raw data; this might include references to authoritative sources and why the students might trust or distrust those sources).
■ Justify to what extent the evidence supports or fails to support a ban.
■ Weigh the evidence on both sides: would you support or challenge a ban?

If, as may be likely, students felt there was not enough information to make a decision, what kind of information would be required and how might it be gathered?

BIOINFORMATION AND PERSONAL PRIVACY: 'IF YOU'RE INNOCENT, WHAT HAVE YOU GOT TO WORRY ABOUT?'

In the scenario on sunbeds the focus of the activity was on interpreting and weighing evidence. In the scenario on bioinformation, the focus is on the application and implications of science and accompanying ethical issues, i.e. levels of disagreement 8 and 9.

Bioinformation is a means of identifying a person from an analysis of unique characteristics such as fingerprints or DNA. With huge advances in the last twenty years in DNA technology, it is now possible to identify people from traces of DNA left, for example, at a crime scene. DNA can be extracted from blood (although not red blood cells), layers of skin and semen left behind at a crime scene. This has been made possible by the development of new techniques for rapidly amplifying DNA and separating small fragments to give unique identifiers.

Forensic use of DNA has very clear benefits. In 2009 a man who had served nearly thirty years in jail for the murder of Teresa de Simone was released because DNA evidence showed that he could not have been the murderer. A DNA sample taken from the body of a suspected man who had killed himself twenty years previously showed a clear match to DNA found on the body of the murder victim. There are many instances of people being convicted – and cleared – of crimes when no other type of evidence is available, and therefore DNA evidence has become a valuable technique.

There is now a national DNA database in which DNA information is held for all people who have been convicted of a crime, or who have had DNA samples taken when they have been arrested or suspected of a crime even if they have been found not guilty, or not even charged. The application of this technology therefore raises a number of ethical questions. First, while the technology is highly developed, it does depend on correct samples being taken and not contaminated with other DNA which might incriminate perfectly innocent people. Second, it has raised a more general question about civil liberties. If everyone contributed DNA samples to a national database, it would make it possible to eliminate suspects from a crime very quickly and identify the perpetrator. While DNA profiling is very reliable, there is the chance that the DNA at a crime scene might be collected incorrectly and tarnish the reputation of an innocent person. There is also the possibility that DNA from the database could be misused, given away without the individual's consent and possibly be very dangerous evidence against innocent people when in the wrong hands. For example, research has been done on correlating DNA with ethnic identity.

One argument has been 'If you're innocent, what have you got to worry about?' But there is some uncertainty in identifying people from DNA and there have been occasions when experts have disagreed about whether the DNA profile constitutes sufficient evidence. There is a core argument about the importance of civil liberties. For some people, protection of civil liberties takes priority over catching some criminals, whereas for others, personal and national safety are more important. There are, therefore, questions on the applications of science and technology about which people's judgements might differ based on their core values.

Once students have some understanding that DNA is unique (except in identical twins), and of how it might be amplified and profiled, they will have sufficient background to engage with the question as to whether a national database should include all people (possibly even children).

One popular approach is to take a 'vox pop' or estimate of agreement or disagreement before any discussion takes place. This can be done by a quick hand count, or asking students to arrange themselves from one end of the room to another depending on how far they agree or disagree with the question. Sometimes, the problem with this approach is that students haven't really thought about the issue at all and so any response can be arbitrary. The question can be put in a more focused and immediate way so that it has personal relevance – for example, would you be happy for your DNA to be put on a national database, given that it might be misused in the future and used against you?

Another way to present the question is through a range of differing opinions or concept cartoons (Keogh and Naylor 1999). For example:

■   'I think people's rights to protection against crime are more important than their rights to privacy.'
■   'Having a national database might turn us into a police state.'
■   'My biological information should be my property and nobody else's.'
■   'DNA evidence isn't 100 per cent safe, so we shouldn't use it.'

For the statement 'My biological information should be my property and nobody else's', an opposing argument is to cite cases where bioinformation is kept for perfectly good reasons such as doctors keeping medical records. There is also a more fundamental question as to why an individual should have any more right to their bioinformation than anyone else. On the other hand, supporting evidence could provide evidence where use of bioinformation has been mishandled.

Another strategy to support critical thinking in a discussion is to ask a group of students (group A) who are very committed to a point of view to state their viewpoint as clearly as possible in three minutes. They are not allowed to be interrupted and must not overrun their time. When they have finished, a group of students (group B) with opposing points of view must then repeat the same argument and, if anything, provide a stronger case than group A. After that, group B give their point of view and group A similarly have to repeat their argument. This shows that students have listened carefully to each other and understand the arguments. After that, the topic can be opened to questioning.

In discussing issues where there is no clear answer, students often resort to a tactic of 'that's just my opinion, take it or leave it', which simply ends a discussion. To make the discussion more fruitful it is important that the teacher can prompt the student to reason and explain their point of view without influencing the argument. This means understanding, and being prepared, with a range of different arguments. Useful resources for this are the reports on DNA profiling from Gene Watch UK and Nuffield Council on Bioethics.

In many controversial issues of this kind there is no unequivocal answer. There are always further questions that can be raised. For example, students might be willing to allow some constraints on their liberty if they know how reliable DNA technology is, how it is stored, how information is accessed and who can use it. The point here is not necessarily to resolve the issue but to help students think more deeply about it.

CONCLUSION

In this chapter I have argued that controversial issues are usually complex and need to be broken down into different levels of controversy if there is to be productive discussion and students enabled to engage and deepen their understanding of how science works. For science teachers, and for teachers generally, this is a tough task because controversial issues in science look very different from much of the science done on a day-to-day basis. Students can therefore be inducted gradually into the more open and messy area of controversial issues, for example by looking at the role of evidence in making simple predictions, then exploring areas in which the evidence is much more complicated and finally looking into the kinds of arguments that cannot be decided on evidence alone, or where evidence consists of more than numerical measurements, such as narrative accounts and experiences. Even in relatively simple ways of using evidence, students can begin to appreciate its complexity. There are intrinsic errors involved in reading even familiar instruments like temperature on a thermometer, length with a measuring tape and volume with a measuring cylinder. Asking students to measure the temperature of a beaker of water at room temperature will generate a range of values and offer opportunities for discussion on the reliability and variability of any measurement. If students can begin to understand these constraints, they are more likely to appreciate the complexity of, and care needed in, drawing conclusions on controversial socio-scientific issues.

FURTHER READING

Hunt, A. and Millar, R. (2000) *AS Science for Public Understanding*, Oxford: Heinemann.

Jarman, R. and McClune, B. (2007) *Developing Scientific Literacy: Using News Media in the Classroom*, Maidenhead: Open University Press.

Kolsto, S. (2004) Socio-scientific issues and the trustworthiness of science-based claims, *School Science Review* 86, 59–65.

Ratcliffe, M. and Grace, M. (2003) *Science Education for Citizenship*, Maidenhead: Open University Press.

Roth, W.-M. and Calabrese Barton, A. (2004) *Rethinking Scientific Literacy*, London: RoutledgeFalmer.

Solomon, J. (1993) *Teaching Science, Technology and Society*, Buckingham: Open University Press.

Ziman, J. (1980) *Teaching and Learning about Science and Society*, Cambridge: Cambridge University Press.

REFERENCES

Bauer, H. (1997) A consumer's guide to science punditry, in R. Levinson and J. Thomas (eds) *Science Today: Problem or Crisis?* London: Routledge.

BBC News. 'No doubt', sun beds cause cancer, 28 July 2009. Online. Available HTTP: <http://news.bbc.co.uk/1/hi/health/8172690.stm> (accessed 22 January 2010).

BBC World Service. World Agenda, Who says climate change matters? 23 December 2009. Online. Available HTTP: <www.bbc.co.uk/worldservice/worldagenda/2009/12/091222_worldagenda_copenhagen_poll.shtml> (accessed 21 January 2010).

Bridges, D. (1979) *Education, Democracy and Discussion*, Slough: NFER.

British Medical Association (2007) Online. Available HTTP: <http://www.bma.org.uk/health_promotion_ethics/environmental_health/hotpsunbeds.jsp?page=8 > (accessed 19 January 2010).

Bryce, T. and Gray, D. (2004) Tough acts to follow: the challenges to science teachers presented by biotechnological progress, *International Journal of Science Education* 26, 717–733.

Cancer Research UK. 'Sunbeds'. Online. Available HTTP: <www.sunsmart.org.uk/advice-and-prevention/sunbeds/index.htm> (accessed 21 January 2010).

Chalmers, A. (1999) *What Is This Thing Called Science?* Buckingham: Open University Press.

Crick, B. (1998) *Education for Citizenship and the Teaching of Democracy in Schools*, London: Qualifications and Curriculum Authority.

Dearden, R. F. (1981) Controversial issues in the curriculum, *Journal of Curriculum Studies* 13, 37–44.

Donnelly, J. (2004) Humanizing science education, *Science Education* 88, 762–784.

Irwin, A. and Michael, M. (2003) *Science, Social Theory and Public Knowledge*, Maidenhead: Open University Press.

Jarman, R. and McClune, B. (2007) *Developing Scientific Literacy: Using News Media in the Classroom*, Maidenhead: Open University Press.

Jeng, M. (1998) Can hot water freeze faster than cold water? Online. Available HTTP: <www.physics.adelaide.edu.au/~dkoks/Faq/General/hot_water.html> (accessed 21 January 2010).

Keogh, B. and Naylor, S. (1999) Concept cartoons, teaching and learning in science: an evaluation, *International Journal of Science Education* 21, 431–446.

Layton, D. (1986) Revaluing science education, in P. Tomlinson and M. Quinton (eds) *Values across the Curriculum*, London: Falmer Press.

Levinson, R. (2006) Towards a theoretical framework for teaching controversial socio-scientific issues, *International Journal of Science Education* 28, 1201–1224.

Levinson, R. and Turner, S. (2001) *Valuable Lessons*, London: Wellcome Trust.

McLaughlin, T. (2003) Teaching controversial issues in citizenship education in A. Lockyer, B. Crick and J. Annette (eds) *Education for Democratic Citizenship*, Aldershot: Ashgate.

Millar, R. and Osborne, J. (1998) *Beyond 2000: Science Education for the Future*, London: King's College London.

Osborne, J., Erduran, S., Simon, S. and Monk, M. (2001) Enhancing the quality of argument in school science, *School Science Review* 82 63–70.

Popper, K. R. (1972) *Conjectures and Refutations: The Growth of Scientific Knowledge*, London: Routledge & Kegan Paul.

Ryder, J. (2001) Identifying science understanding for functional scientific literacy, *Studies in Science Education* 36, 1–44.

Ryder, J. (2002) School science education for citizenship: strategies for teaching about the epistemology of science, *Journal of Curriculum Studies* 34, 637–658.

Sunbed Association 2010. Online. Available HTTP: <www.sunbedassociation.org.uk/> (accessed 5 February 2010).

Sutton, C. (1992) *Words, Science and Learning*, Buckingham: Open University Press.

Thomas, J. (2000) Using current controversies in the classroom: opportunities and concerns, *Melbourne Studies in Education* 41, 133–144.

Wellington, J. and Osborne, J. (2001) *Language and Literacy in Science Education*, Buckingham: Open University Press.

A useful activity on the effects of UV light on different types of skin can be found in SATIS Revisited. Online. Available HTTP: <www.satisrevisited.co.uk/> (accessed 5 February 2010).

6 ARGUMENTATION

Shirley Simon

INTRODUCTION

The focus of science teaching in the United Kingdom and worldwide has traditionally been on the content of science – that established body of scientific knowledge that forms the bedrock of the curriculum and of school science examinations. However, the requirement of the new GCSE science programme of study that one-half of the course should now address How Science Works (QCA 2005) signals a commitment that teaching science needs to accomplish more than detailing what we know. The change emphasizes the importance of educating students about *how* we know and why we believe in the scientific worldview, and to see science as a distinctive and valuable way of knowing (Driver *et al*. 1996; Millar and Osborne 1998). To appreciate the origins of scientific knowledge and thus develop an epistemological understanding of science, students need to explore reasons why accepted ideas have become established and why alternative theories are considered to be 'wrong'.

In foregrounding the epistemic basis of science, school science can now provide more opportunities for the development of scientific reasoning through the coordination of theory with evidence (Kuhn 1991), and of epistemological understanding through the evaluation of scientific knowledge claims (Sandoval and Reiser 2004). The goals of science education can thus be extended beyond the teaching of science content, to encompass cognitive, epistemic and social aims. By engaging collaboratively in argumentation activities that make reasoning public, students can gain experience of constructing arguments, justifying arguments with evidence, evaluating alternative arguments and reflecting on the outcomes of argumentation. Experience of argumentation in different contexts can equip students with the skills to make decisions about controversial issues in science, to understand how evidence is used to construct explanations and to understand the criteria that are used in science to evaluate evidence. Though the role of argumentation has become more highly valued in science education, research shows that only if it is specifically addressed in the curriculum and explicitly taught through task structuring and modelling will students gain the skills needed to explore its use in science and socio-scientific contexts (Osborne *et al*. 2004a; Jiménez-Aleixandre and Erduran 2008). In this chapter I draw on some of this research to discuss pedagogical strategies that have been developed to enhance the practice of argumentation in school science.

At this point it is worth saying a few words about the meaning of 'argument', as much attention has been paid to this issue in the literature (Jiménez-Aleixandre and Erduran 2008). Billig (1987) takes the view that argument encompasses both individual and social meaning, a perspective shared by Jiménez-Aleixandre and Erduran, who describe this dual meaning in terms of an inner chain of reasoned discourse (individual) and a dispute or debate between people holding contrasting positions (social). These authors also acknowledge that internal and social aspects are linked (Kuhn 1993) in that social dialogue offers a way to externalize internal thinking strategies embedded in argumentation.

In a research project undertaken by myself, Jonathan Osborne and Sibel Erduran to enhance the quality of argumentation in school science (EQUASS), we set out our theoretical perspective on argument by drawing a distinction between 'argument' and 'argumentation'. Argument refers to the claim, data, warrants and backings that form the substance or content of an argument. These are the components of Toulmin's (1958) model of argument, which we used as a basis for analysing the quality of argument (Erduran *et al.* 2004). Argumentation refers to the process of arguing, between two or more people, which involves the construction, justification and refutation of arguments. Our research focused on exploring the strategies that scaffold and support the argumentation process in groups of students, using activities in science or socio-scientific contexts. This chapter draws on the outcomes of this research in some detail.

ARGUMENTATION ACTIVITIES

To promote the use of argumentation requires activities that are designed to achieve the set of goals referred to above and an understanding of how these goals can be realized through student engagement. Much research has been undertaken on the development of students' epistemological reasoning and understanding – that is, how students come to recognize that a claim can be falsified, that evidence can be used to falsify or support a claim, and that theory and evidence are seen as distinct. Driver *et al.* (1996) found, for example, that students have difficulty determining the role of theories in science and the way that theories are evaluated against existing data by experimentation. Theories were viewed as simple descriptions of taken-for-granted facts, having lower status than facts. Hofer and Pintrich (1997) suggest that there are different stages that represent the sequence of epistemological understanding, and Kuhn and Franklin (2006), taking this work further, have identified a developmental pattern with four steps: Realist – where knowledge is seen to be copied from an external source; Absolutist – where knowledge consists of facts; Multiplist – where subjective opinions are equally right; and Evaluatist – where judgements are made on the basis of evaluating evidence. Students' personal epistemologies need to become evaluatist if they are to develop an understanding of the epistemology of science. Argumentation activities set in social contexts can be the vehicle for developing students' epistemological understanding as, with appropriate scaffolding, students can be encouraged to value the role of evidence in knowledge claims.

Garcia-Mila and Anderson (2008), in reviewing studies of student argumentation, ask 'What are the students' interactive argument skills in a classroom debate? How do they argue when they are organized in small groups or in pairs?' The conclusion they draw is that many students have difficulty engaging with another's statements; they tend to make their own claims without addressing opposing claims of others. In a study of a nineth-grade genetics class, Jiménez-Aleixandre *et al.* (2000) found that most of the claims offered in a discussion were unrelated to the rest of the elements in the argument. Further studies (see Garcia-Mila and Anderson 2008) show that a set of skills is needed for sound argumentative reasoning. Without these, students tend to select evidence to confirm prior theories, ignore evidence that does not fit, or jump to conclusions before enough evidence is available. An effective pedagogy of argumentation is needed to develop reasoning, including activities that are designed to enhance the use of interactive argument skills.

Thus, to optimize the opportunities for developing epistemological understanding and scientific reasoning, argumentation activities used in classroom contexts need to be carefully designed. Although we now have an established body of work on the value of argumentation and small-group discussion in science education, few studies have attempted to unpack the nuances of how argumentation activities are designed (Howe and Mercer 2007), as research has tended to focus on evaluating argumentation outcomes. Activities need to engage students' interest, stimulate discussion, provide resources that can be used as the basis of evidence in constructing and evaluating arguments, provide alternative choices or positions, involve a solution that is not obvious, and be manageable for teachers. In our EQUASS project (Osborne *et al.* 2004a), materials were developed by working together with teachers, according to the curriculum needs they identified and their interpretation of the theoretical perspective on argument we presented. We used frameworks for developing argumentation activities that involved the generation of differences – for example, presenting competing theories for students to examine, discuss and evaluate. In addition to providing such stimulus material, the activities we developed also included small-group discussion so that students would co-construct arguments justifying their case for one or other theory. As students require data to construct arguments, the activities also included information that could be used as evidence to support different theories. In this research we developed nine generic frameworks from literature sources (see Osborne *et al.* 2004a for the sources), summarized as follows. The choice of generic frameworks by teachers was essentially pragmatic, as topics being taught varied from school to school.

■ Table of statements: students are given a table of statements on a particular science topic; they are asked to say whether they agree or disagree with the statements and argue for their choices.

■ Concept map of student ideas: students are given a concept map of statements derived from student misconceptions; they discuss the concepts and links to decide if these are scientifically correct, providing reasons and arguments for their choice.

■ A report of a science experiment undertaken by students: the experiment is written in a way that could clearly be improved in order to stimulate disagreement; students have to discuss how improvements could be made.

■ Competing theories – cartoons: students are presented with two or more competing theories in the form of a cartoon; they are asked to show who they think is correct and why.

■ Competing theories – story: students are presented with competing theories in the form of an engaging story, and are asked to provide evidence and reasons for which theory they believe.

■ Competing theories – ideas and evidence: students are introduced to a physical phenomenon and offered competing explanations; they are asked to consider statements that can be used to support each theory, thus construct arguments with evidence.

■ Constructing an argument: students are given an explanation of a physical phenomenon, such as day and night being caused by a spinning Earth. They are presented with data statements and they have to discuss which statements provide the strongest explanation, providing an argument why.

- Predicting, observing and explaining: students are introduced to a phenomenon and have to predict what will happen when it is demonstrated, justifying their reasoning. Once it has been demonstrated, students are asked to re-evaluate their initial arguments. Discussion focuses on theory and evidence for their prediction.
- Designing an experiment: students are asked to work in pairs to design an experiment to test a hypothesis. They then meet with another pair to discuss their design, to propose alternatives and argue for their relative merits.

Building on this original research, we continued to work with teachers to develop a set of training materials called the IDEAS pack, which would help other teachers to practise the skills needed to implement argumentation (Osborne *et al.* 2004b). The pack includes a resource of fifteen lessons that incorporate a variety of frameworks, including examples based on the frameworks introduced in the original research. In a more recent analysis of the IDEAS lessons, Katherine Richardson and I explored how the activities do or do not address reasoning (Simon and Richardson 2009). We focused on a selection of lessons to examine the design framework, the science context used, lesson planning notes and the teacher's role. A summary of our analysis of a classification framework, which was not included in the original research, is presented in this chapter using the example from the IDEAS pack called *Euglena*. *Euglena* is a single-celled organism that shows some characteristics of both plant and animal cells: it has chlorophyll, which makes it plant-like, but it also moves in an animal-like way. In the *Euglena* activity, students are asked to use pieces of information about *Euglena* and their knowledge of plant and animal cells to decide how the information could provide evidence to support arguments that *Euglena* is a plant, an animal or neither (see Box 6.1).

The reasoning involved in classification activities can be analysed in terms of Piagetian operations, as was done by Shayer and Adey in describing and measuring cognitive development in the Cognitive Acceleration in Science Education (CASE) research (Shayer and Adey 1981; Adey and Shayer 1994). Simple classification that puts objects into groups according to a given criterion is indicative of concrete reasoning, but to see that this is only one of many possible ways in which classification might be carried out requires formal or more abstract reasoning. More complex classification systems use more than one criterion at a time to group objects into several categories. To be able to see whether a classification operation involves inclusion or exclusion and is part of a hierarchy requires formal operational thinking. Argumentation activities that use a classification framework would need to involve this level of complexity in order to create the differences required for categorization (Simon and Richardson 2009). A classification framework offers different opportunities for argumentation: at one level, choosing a category from various options requires the need to justify that choice when challenged; at another level, inclusion of controversial cases in which the object displays some characteristics of different categories can trigger counter-arguments. The *Euglena* activity uses different pieces of data which clearly relate to different categories (for example, *Euglena* has a cell wall like a plant, but feeds like an animal), which encourages students to select data to support a claim or mount a counter-claim, and to consider the relative importance of different pieces of evidence. If irrelevant data that do not help to discriminate between categories are included, then students are encouraged to recognize that not all information is evidence; it only becomes so when it is incorporated into an argument. The *Euglena* activity takes advantage of controversial cases and irrelevant evidence and challenges students because *Euglena* is different from typical plant and animal cells, providing an 'edge' case. Students have to consider which features of plant and animal cells are most important in classification.

Box 6.1 *Euglena*: plant or animal?

In this activity, students are required to use and evaluate statements presented on cards to argue whether *Euglena* is a plant, an animal or neither. The evidence is then summarized in a table format. The students work individually, then in discussion groups and finally they make presentations. The goals are that students will construct arguments and use statements from the cards as evidence in support of their arguments. They will also learn to evaluate the statements for relevance and ambiguity, and discuss with others the relative merits of each other's chosen evidence. They will also learn that there are organisms that are not classified as plants or animals (protists).

To introduce the activity, *Euglena* is demonstrated directly from a culture using a projection microscope or from an internet source. The demonstration stimulates engagement and discussion. A sheet with columns for decision-making (see below) and statement cards are distributed and the students work in groups of three or four. While the students discuss and sort the cards, the teacher moves around, encouraging argumentation and reasoning and providing more information about plant and animal characteristics, if needed. Writing frames can also be used to help present the final decision about *Euglena*.

A plenary is held to report on discussions and decisions, and further debate to evaluate arguments and the evidence used. Finally, the teacher confirms that *Euglena* is neither plant nor animal, and reiterates that the goal for them was to evaluate evidence and justify claims.

Headings for decision-making columns in which to place cards (laid out on A3 paper):

Evidence that suggests *Euglena* is a plant	Evidence that suggests *Euglena* is an animal	Evidence that suggests *Euglena* is either plant or animal	Evidence that suggests *Euglena* is neither

Statements that can be used as evidence (cut into cards)

Euglena does not have a cell wall	*Euglena* contains chloroplasts	*Euglena* has a nucleus	*Euglena* is a single-cell organism
Euglena can absorb food from its surroundings	*Euglena* is normally green	Chloroplasts enable a cell to photosynthesize	A vacuole controls the amount of liquid in a cell
Euglena swims through water	*Euglena* can make its own food	*Euglena* has a vacuole	*Euglena* is light sensitive
Euglena contains cytoplasm	*Euglena* lives in puddles and ponds	*Euglena* can reproduce	There are more than two classification groups

(adapted from IDEAS, Osborne *et al.* 2004b)

The IDEAS pack includes other frameworks for developing lesson plans. One popular resource is that of the aforementioned competing theories, which involve analysing and evaluating evidence to argue for a position. A popular source for competing theories lessons is concept cartoons (Naylor and Keogh 2000), where children express alternative explanations as speech bubbles for a phenomenon represented in pictures. A commonly used cartoon shows two snowmen, one with and one without a coat, and children who express different theories as to which snowman will melt first. The articulation of alternative ideas by 'other' children serves to stimulate different positions of students studying the cartoon, encouraging them to find reasons to justify alternative views. Concept cartoons were originally designed for use in primary schools, yet have been successfully used to stimulate discussion and argument about scientific ideas with much older children.

Jane Maloney also developed argumentation activities in her work with primary children in a research project to see how groups of children evaluated and used evidence in decision-making (Simon and Maloney 2007). Four activities were designed to reveal differences in opinion so that small groups of children could explore their reasoning and expose their thinking while working autonomously. In each activity, information was made available in different formats, for example pictures, written information, or data from a scientific investigation. The first activity, called 'Finding a home for gerbils', was adapted from a task in the Science and Technology in Society 8–14 materials (SATIS 1993). The children were given pictures and descriptions of three homes for small pets and were asked to select one of these homes for some gerbils that they could keep in their classroom. Home 1 was made for hamsters and consisted of a large plastic tank with a roof and an exercise wheel; Home 2 was made of plastic and had lots of tubes connecting different cylinders; Home 3 was made from an old aquarium and had layers of garden soil, sand and gravel with rocks and twigs (this is the most appropriate home). The children used a range of information about the homes as evidence for their decisions. For example, Home 2 was chosen as it had different rooms for sleeping in, Home 1 as it was plastic and easy to clean. The most successful activities were those like this one about gerbils that provided limited options, as children found it more difficult to construct well-supported arguments when the decision was more open-ended.

There are many other sources of activities that can be used directly or adapted for argumentation. Teachers have found resources produced by the Association for Science Education on their UPD8 site to be stimulating as appropriate. Activities have also been developed for the Teachers TV series, and guidance is available through the National Strategies.

TEACHERS SCAFFOLDING ARGUMENTATION

In our research with teachers to enhance the quality of argumentation in school science, we determined the extent to which their practice in the use of argumentation developed over a one-year period (Simon *et al.* 2006). Lesson transcripts from recordings made before and after a year of monthly argumentation lessons were analysed and compared. Results showed that for some teachers the complexity of argumentation in the classroom was enhanced, as the discourse was found to include more extended arguments incorporating backings and rebuttals (Toulmin 1958; Erduran *et al.* 2004). Some teachers also developed more effective ways of scaffolding the processes of argumentation (Simon *et al.* 2006). We identified how teachers' oral contributions demonstrated epistemic goals implicit in their interactions, in both whole-class and small-group settings. For example, the act of asking students to provide reasons for their claims reflected a teaching goal that students should show the process of justification with evidence. An analytical framework that focused on teachers' oral contributions resulted in the formation of a tentative hierarchy of teaching goals that facilitate argumentation processes. These processes included:

- talking and listening
- knowing the meaning of argument
- positioning
- justifying with evidence
- constructing arguments
- counter-arguing
- reflecting on the argumentation process.

The hierarchical nature of the processes meant that students needed to learn how to listen and talk, justify claims, etc. before they could counter-argue; and that teachers themselves needed to value and learn how to implement group discussion and prompt justification before they could orchestrate effective counter-argument within their teaching. In a subsequent project (Simon and Johnson 2008) we found that raising awareness of these argumentation processes in relation to teachers' own practice facilitated reflective practice in the use of argumentation and helped teachers to be more proactive in incorporating them into classroom discourse.

As mentioned previously, we developed a set of resources called the IDEAS pack (Osborne *et al*. 2004b) comprising fifteen lessons that included lessons aims, teaching procedures and student materials. In addition to the fifteen lessons, the pack includes six INSET sessions, informed by the research and in partnership with teachers, each focusing on a different area designed to enhance the teaching of argumentation. The six sessions include video clips of classroom practice that serve to promote discussion about the pedagogy of argumentation. The teachers in the video clips took part in the original research and in designing and implementing the resource lessons in the pack. The sessions are designed to promote teachers' own rationale for argumentation and pedagogic strategies for use in the classroom such as constructing arguments, group work, evaluating arguments, counter-argument and modelling argument. The following sections include some of the valuable messages and examples of argumentation pedagogy developed in these sessions.

INTRODUCING ARGUMENT

For effective implementation of argumentation activities, teachers need to develop a strong personal rationale for devoting lesson time to their use. The first IDEAS session aims to develop teachers' understanding that argument is an essential component of science. One activity aims to help teachers consider that the evidential basis for scientific ideas is not easily articulated and therefore may not be explored in science teaching. Teachers are asked to decide what evidence there might be for some common ideas, for example that day and night are caused by a spinning Earth, plants take in carbon dioxide and give out oxygen during photosynthesis, living matter is made of cells, and we live at the bottom of a 'sea of air'. This activity has helped teachers to think about the value of using argumentation activities to extend their teaching goals beyond a focus on content to include epistemic questioning about the evidential basis for scientific claims. Teachers also find it useful to construct arguments for themselves using student activities, as they can become immersed in the kind of thinking that these activities demand.

MANAGING SMALL-GROUP DISCUSSIONS

Activities in this session involve the use of group work strategies, such as listening triads, to enable teachers to experience how such strategies might work with students. Triads are often used to explore the ideas within a concept cartoon (Naylor and Keogh 2000), where students express alternative ideas about a phenomenon, such as the rate of melting of a snowman with or without a coat. In the triad, one participant takes on the role of explaining the ideas portrayed by the students in the cartoon, one takes on a questioning role and one a recording role. Professional development activities such as these, using the pedagogical strategies and IDEAS lesson plans together, not only enable teachers to think about their approach but also provide a basis for them to analyse and become familiar with resources they can use with students. Teachers have also found it useful to consider issues such as group size and composition, and how to tackle problems such as lack of contribution, limited discussion, boredom, and reluctance to feed back.

TEACHING ARGUMENT

In much of my work with teachers I have introduced how we used Toulmin's model of argument (Toulmin 1958) to analyse teachers' and students' arguments in the EQUASS project. When teachers are provided with Toulmin's model and asked to identify the components of an argument (claim, data, warrant, backings, rebuttals) in example arguments, they find this task quite difficult, but it serves to help them think about ways of modelling and evaluating students' argumentation (Simon 2008). The main focus of the third session in the IDEAS pack is on the pedagogy of introducing argument activities, sustaining engagement and managing plenary sessions. The video clips play a prominent part in this session, in particular the clips of a teacher, Alex, teaching the *Euglena* activity. Box 6.2 summarizes Alex's enactment (Simon and Richardson 2009) of the *Euglena* activity.

A particular feature from IDEAS on teaching argument is the use of argument prompts, or questions, that teachers can use to encourage reasoning and justification with evidence. These prompts include:

- Why do you think that?
- What is your reason for that?
- Can you think of another argument for your view?
- Can you think of an argument against your view?
- How do you know?
- What is your evidence?
- Is there another argument for what you believe?

These prompts, though simple, have proved useful for teachers as a means of focusing on the reasoning process instead of confirming or supplying the 'right answers' as students engage in argumentation.

RESOURCES FOR ARGUMENTATION

The IDEAS session on resources reviews the frameworks found in the resource lessons (as listed previously and including classification) and focuses on the identification of learning goals of argumentation tasks to include conceptual, cognitive, epistemic and

Box 6.2 *Euglena* enactment

Alex introduces the lesson by drawing students' attention to a flask of water (she holds it up) in which there are what she describes 'little friends called Eugene', and suggests to the students that they probably cannot see them. She then projects them on to a screen so that students can see them swimming around. This introduction captures students' attention to something living that they can see and be curious about. She then asks the students to describe what they can see, adding the question 'What is an observable piece of evidence about the Eugenes?' This statement not only invites the students to observe and make a contribution but also begins to introduce the language of scientific reasoning. As children make observations, Alex rephrases their answers but limits her evaluation of their responses, as she does not want to close down the discussion but rather to invite further contribution. As students become interested, they ask 'what is it?', and Alex describes it as a 'single cell called *Euglena*', being cautious not to pre-empt the classification process. She draws attention to *Euglena*'s movements, encouraging the students to observe more features, asking them again, 'What can we say about them?' As students observe 'green bits' and 'swim very fast', Alex praises them. These are the characteristics she hopes they will use in their decision-making about classification. When a student asks the question 'is it a plant?', Alex responds with 'well, there is a question', and asks the students why it might be a plant. Throughout this introductory episode she is aware of her goals that focus on argumentation about classification, and the discourse is therefore open and exploratory, rather than closed in search of the 'right answer'.

After a range of observations and questions, Alex introduces the students' task and resources. She holds up the decision-making template and reads some of the statement cards so that she can give them instructions about the procedures, and she organizes the students into groups of four. She models the process the students will undertake by reading some of the cards, discussing what the statements mean, and choosing where the cards should be placed on the template by deciding whether the statement supports a classification of plant, animal or neither. While the students carry out the task, Alex moves from group to group, supplying extra textual information about cells for those who struggle with understanding the meaning of the statements, for example, '*Euglena* contains cytoplasm'.

When the students have finished choosing where to place the cards, and have decided whether *Euglena* is plant, animal or neither, Alex conducts a whole-class plenary and asks for a class vote on their decision ('who thinks plant?' etc.). She then asks students to explain their decisions, drawing out the arguments that have been constructed on the basis of the evidence statements. She uses the students' answers to draw their attention to further features (represented on a diagram of *Euglena*), so that they question more deeply the evidence base for their decisions. She then asks if anyone has changed their mind, having heard all the arguments. This episode allows the students to express their decision in a concise but inclusive way (voting), to articulate their thinking and to listen to other ideas and reflect on their own arguments. Alex then introduces the idea that *Euglena* is neither plant nor animal, but a protista, so that students extend their understanding of biological classification through the cognitive conflict arising from this alternative position.

(adapted from Simon and Richardson 2009)

social goals. A substantial section on using written argument includes writing frames that can assist students' reasoning. Writing frames can take different formats, but essentially include prompts such as:

- My idea is …
- The evidence to support my idea is …
- This evidence supports my idea because …
- Arguments against my idea are …
- I would convince someone who doesn't believe me by …

Writing frames have helped students to construct arguments and provide teachers with extra resources to scaffold argumentation.

EVALUATING ARGUMENT

Teachers have been concerned to find ways of evaluating the outcomes of argumentation activities so that they can see whether learning goals are met and also assess students' progress in developing argumentation skills. Teachers are encouraged to develop their own set of criteria using examples of their students' work, but the IDEAS session on evaluation also provides examples of how written arguments can be analysed using Toulmin's model. One example is a student's argument from the snowman concept cartoon which gives reasons why one snowman (Fred) who is not wearing a coat will melt faster than another (Birt) who is wearing a coat. The following paragraph shows an annotated version of the students' argument (Osborne *et al.* 2004b).

He (Fred) is not wearing a coat [data] so the sun's rays will touch him directly [warrant]. This will make him melt faster [claim]. Birt will take longer to melt [claim] because the coat and hat he is wearing help to insulate him [warrant]. The sun takes longer to melt him. The coat is an insulator so it stops the heat getting to the snowman quickly [backing]. It is the reverse of a human wearing a coat to stop heat escaping from their bodies.

Arguments that include more warrants and backing are of better quality as claims are justified with evidence.

A major line of analysis in the EQUASS project was the use of a system of levels to evaluate the quality of oral argumentation. These levels were applied to episodes of oppositional discourse, which provide opportunities for extended argumentation through the use of counter-claim and rebuttal. A useful activity for teachers is to supply them with extracts from transcripts and ask them to assign these levels and hence evaluate the quality of argumentation (also see Erduran *et al.* 2004):

- Level 1 argumentation consists of arguments that are a simple claim versus a counter-claim or claim versus a claim.
- Level 2 argumentation has arguments consisting of claims with either data, warrants or backings but do not contain any rebuttals.
- Level 3 argumentation has arguments with a series of claims or counter-claims with either data, warrants or backings with the occasional weak rebuttal.
- Level 4 argumentation shows arguments with a claim with a clearly identifiable rebuttal. Such an argument may have several claims and counter-claims.
- Level 5 argumentation displays an extended argument with claims supported by data and warrants with more than one rebuttal.

To illustrate this level system, one example of a Level 4 argument that includes a rebuttal is taken from an activity where students have been given alternative theories to explain the phases of the moon that are on a numbered card, A, B, C or D, referred to in the dialogue:

- M   … A, the Moon spins around, so the part of the Moon that gives out light is not always facing us. Jamal, A?
- J   The Moon doesn't give out light.
- M   Right, so that's why A is wrong. That's true. How do you know that?
- J   Because the light that comes from the Moon is actually from the Sun.
- M   He is saying the light that we see from the Moon is actually a reflection from the Sun. How do we know that?
- J   Because the Moon is blocked by the …

The first student presents the claim that it is explanation A, supported by 'the part of the Moon that gives out light is not always facing us'. There is then a rebuttal supplied with supporting data that the 'light that comes from the Moon is actually from the Sun' and a warrant that is unfinished.

Teachers have not found it easy to use these forms of evaluation based on a Toulmin perspective, but the exercises in the IDEAS pack have enabled them to adapt the ideas to devise their own evaluation systems (Simon and Johnson 2008; Simon 2008).

MODELLING ARGUMENT

The idea of modelling argument for students becomes more relevant to teachers as they themselves develop their own resources and strategies for incorporating argumentation activities into their teaching. One way to help teachers see the importance of modelling is to show video clips of other teachers introducing model arguments and to discuss the relative merits of these. I have found that teachers often like to develop their own everyday examples that they believe will have relevance for their particular students. The example in IDEAS draws from a model argument developed for 12-year-olds where two students, Emma and Julie, are presenting arguments for why their mum's cakes are the best. Only by talking about the reasoning involved and its qualities will students begin to gain an insight into the argumentation process and its attributes.

CONCLUSION

In this chapter I have presented a rationale for the teaching of argumentation in science in schools, and have drawn on personal research to highlight some important aspects that I believe are relevant in the context of teaching about how science works. In particular, the design of appropriate activities and the components of teacher development that I have discussed can inform teachers and curriculum developers who are engaged in developing schemes of work that address the How Science Works agenda. The argumentation activities in the IDEAS resource pack have proved invaluable in helping teachers new to argumentation to 'get started', because the materials can be used as they are. They can also be adapted for use to match curriculum topics and classroom contexts, which our work with trainee teachers (Simon and Maloney 2006) and practising teachers (Simon and Johnson 2008) has demonstrated. For example, the classification framework used in this chapter as an exemplar activity (*Euglena*) has been used in other science topics that require the same kinds of reasoning. All that is needed to adapt this idea is an analysis of the reasoning involved in the particular classification example to identify alternative categories and produce the statement cards.

The IDEAS activities continue to provide a stimulus for ongoing work with teachers who are developing argumentation within whole departments in London schools; initial use of the actual materials has evolved to incorporate individual designs appropriate to curriculum needs and classroom contexts. However, the process of teaching argumentation involves more than choosing a framework and using it or adapting it for a different context: teaching argumentation requires careful consideration of the nature of the teaching goals and learning outcomes, choice of appropriate groupwork strategies and of how to introduce, sustain and round off an activity. Therefore, planning becomes a complex task that also requires the teacher to imagine the ways in which students will respond and engage, and what they will find interesting and challenging (but not too challenging). It involves thinking about how the lesson begins, how the students are organized, how the resources are used, what role to take as the activity proceeds, and how the activity will finish. Teaching argumentation, with new ways of thinking about science learning outcomes and of interacting with students to emphasize the process of constructing arguments with evidence rather than delivering a body of facts, provides a challenge to the How Science Works agenda. However, we have learnt much from 10 years of research and development in this area that should help to embed new thinking into science pedagogic practice.

FURTHER READING

S. Erduran and M. Jiménez-Aleixandre (eds) (2008) *Argumentation in Science Education*, Heidelberg: Springer.

Naylor, S. and Keogh, B. (2000) *Concept Cartoons in Science Education*, Sandbach, Millgate House.

Osborne, J., Erduran, S. and Simon, S. (2004) Enhancing the quality of argument in school science, *Journal of Research in Science Teaching* 41(10), 994–1020.

Osborne, J., Erduran, S. and Simon, S. (2004) *Ideas, Evidence and Argument in Science*. In-service Training Pack, Resource Pack and Video London: Nuffield Foundation.

Simon, S., Erduran, S., and Osborne, J (2006) Learning to teach argumentation: research and development in the science classroom, *International Journal of Science Education* 28(2–3), 235–260.

Simon, S. and Maloney, J. (2007) Activities for promoting small group discussion and argumentation, *School Science Review* 88(324), 49–57.

Simon, S. and Richardson, K. (2009) Argumentation in school science: breaking the tradition of authoritative exposition through a pedagogy that promotes discussion and reasoning, *Argumentation* 23, 469–493.

REFERENCES

Adey, P. and Shayer, M. (1994) *Really Raising Standards*, London: Routledge.

Billig, M. (1987) *Arguing and Thinking: A Rhetorical Approach to Social Psychology*, Cambridge: Cambridge University Press.

Driver, R., Leach, J., Millar, R. and Scott, P. (1996) *Young People's Images of Science*, Buckingham: Open University Press.

Erduran, S., Simon, S. and Osborne, J. (2004) TAPping into argumentation: developments in the application of Toulmin's Argument Pattern for studying science discourse, *Science Education* 88(6), 915–933.

Garcia-Mila, M. and Andersen, C. (2008) Cognitive foundations of learning argumentation, in S. Erduran and M. P. Jiménez-Aleixandre (eds) *Argumentation in Science Education: Perspectives from Classroom-Based Research*, Heidelberg:Springer.

Hofer, B. and Pintrich, P. (1997) The development of epistemological theories: Beliefs about knowledge and knowing and their relation to learning, *Review of Educational Research* 67, 88–140.

Howe, C. and Mercer, N. (2007) *Children's Social Development, Peer Interaction and Classroom Learning* (Primary Review Research Survey 2/1b), Cambridge: University of Cambridge.

Jiménez-Aleixandre, M. P. and Erduran, S. (2008) Argumentation in science education: an overview. In S. Erduran and M. Jiménez-Aleixandre (eds) *Argumentation in Science Education*, Heidelberg: Springer.

Jiménez-Aleixandre, M. P., Rodríguez, A. B. and Duschl, R. (2000) 'Doing the lesson' or 'doing science': argument in high school genetics, *Science Education* 84(6), 757–792.

Kuhn, D. (1991) *The Skills of Argument*, Cambridge: Cambridge University Press.

Kuhn, D. (1993) Thinking as argument, *Harvard Educational Review* 62, 155–178.

Kuhn, D. and Franklin, S. (2006) The second decade: what develops (and how)? In W. Damon and R. M. Lerner (series eds), D. Kuhn and R. Siegler (vol. eds), *Handbook of Child Psychology*: Vol. 2, *Cognition, Perception, and Language* (6th edition), Hoboken, NJ: Wiley.

Millar, R. and Osborne, J. F. (eds) (1998) *Beyond 2000: Science Education for the Future*, London: King's College London.

Naylor, S. and Keogh, B. (2000) *Concept Cartoons in Science Education*, Sandbach: Millgate House.

Osborne, J. Erduran, S. and Simon, S. (2004a) Enhancing the quality of argument in school science, *Journal of Research in Science Teaching* 41(10), 994–1020.

Osborne, J., Erduran, S. and Simon, S. (2004b) *Ideas, Evidence and Argument in Science*, In-service Training Pack, Resource Pack and Video, London: Nuffield Foundation.

QCA (2005) *Programme of Study for Key Stage 4 from 2006*, London: Qualifications and Curriculum Authority.

Sandoval, W. and Reiser, B. (2004) Explanation-driven inquiry: integrating conceptual and epistemic scaffolds for scientific inquiry, *Science Education* 88(3), 345–372.

SATIS (1993) *Science and Technology in Society 8–14*, Hatfield: Association for Science Education.

Shayer, M. and Adey, P. (1981) *Towards a Science of Science Teaching*, London: Heinemann Educational Books.

Simon, S. (2008) Using Toulmin's Argument Pattern in the evaluation of argumentation in school science *International Journal of Research and Method in Education*, 31(3), 277–289.

Simon, S., Erduran, S. and Osborne, J. (2006) Learning to teach argumentation: research and development in the science classroom, *International Journal of Science Education* 28(2–3), 235–260.

Simon, S. and Johnson, S. (2008) Professional learning portfolios for argumentation in school science, *International Journal of Science Education* 30(5), 669–688.

Simon, S. and Maloney, J. (2006) Learning to teach 'ideas and evidence' in science: a study of school mentors and trainee teachers, *School Science Review* 87(321), 75–82.

Simon, S. and Maloney, J. (2007) Activities for promoting small group discussion and argumentation, *School Science Review* 88(324), 49–57.

Simon, S. and Richardson, K. (2009) Argumentation in school science: breaking the tradition of authoritative exposition through a pedagogy that promotes discussion and reasoning, *Argumentation* 23, 469–496.

Teachers.tv. Online. Available HTTP: <www.teachers.tv/series/how-science-works> (accessed 5 February 2010).

Toulmin, S. (1958) *The Uses of Argument*, Cambridge. Cambridge University Press.

7 QUESTIONS AND SCIENCE

Mike Watts and Helena Pedrosa de Jesus

You can tell whether a man is clever by his answers. You can tell whether a man is wise by his questions.

Naguib Mahfouz (Nobel Prize Winner)

To raise new questions, new possibilities, to regard old problems from a new angle, requires creative imagination and marks real advance in science.

Albert Einstein (genius)

INTRODUCTION

More than a hundred years ago the French philosopher Auguste Comte argued that science was not actually best placed to answer certain questions. As an example, he posed the unanswerable question: 'What are stars made of?' Even before the nineteenth century was over, however, he was somewhat undone by astronomers who realized even then that the spectral colours of different substances provide telltale evidence of the composition of stellar matter. The asking of questions lies at the very heart of science and, while Comte may be right that there are many that lie outside its domains, this still leaves innumerable questions wherein science and scientists might be expected to arrive at some coherent response. The very essence of science is the asking of questions: that is exactly how science works.

This chapter develops a four-track approach to questions. First, we discuss the nature of questions, their power and purpose in science. Second, we explore the area of study that has become known as 'learners' classroom questioning'. We take issue with the central tendency of this work, which sees learners as being thoroughly deficient in the asking of scientific questions: 'Kids can't ask questions.' Our view is that the relationship between learners, science and questions is complex, and deserves exploration. We see, commonly, that 'kids *don't* ask questions', and speculate about why. The third track we take examines the questions that learners do ask when discussing issues in science. Our suggestion here is that questions can be highly indicative of people's levels of understanding, 'snapshots' of their thought processes at the point of asking. The use of the plural here is intentional – we see the range of 'learners' to be wide and diverse, and therefore to have multiple and differing understandings of science and its accomplishments. Finally, our fourth track is to consider how classroom teachers can develop learners' classroom questioning in a measured way. We give two case study examples of these along the way.

Notice, we have said nothing here about teachers' questions – there has much been written about those elsewhere. Socrates' idea was quite reasonable: to engage a learner in dialogic questioning as a means of drawing him or her towards greater understanding of life. The trouble was that Socrates filled the 'zone'; it was Socrates' questions that dominated, not the learner's. In this discussion we attempt a 'reverse Socrates', where it is the learner's questions that predominate and the teacher that responds. In this respect, we see the role of the teacher as being one of tutoring, fostering and enhancing learners' question-asking, rather than flooding – and controlling – the teaching space with their own.

So, to come clean at the start: we advocate very open forms of science education surrounding inquiry-based learning, in particular where the inquiry stems from the learner. We need to justify this, since most schooling is not built around learners' inquiry and because we need to make the case during this chapter for inquiry-based learning, and that it can actually be achieved.

A QUESTION OF QUESTIONS

If questions form the basis of science, then what exactly is a question? Dennett (1991) describes human beings as 'informavores', needing, feeding off data and input, constantly trying to make sense of observation and experiences. As Desmond Morris, the celebrated zoologist, said , 'We never stop investigating. We are never satisfied that we know enough to get by. Every question we answer leads on to another question. This has become the greatest survival trick of our species, (2002: 22).

One theory is that we form schema, general patterns of thought that seem to fit the experiences we have. These schema, or conceptions, enable us to go about our daily lives, predicting what will happen around us to a fair degree of accuracy. However, we are also frequently faced with disturbances: new events or situations that cannot be fully handled by existing understandings, our usual schema. This creates an imbalance between what is understood and what is encountered. So, a 'disjunct', or 'variance' (Marton and Booth 1997; Moon 2004), a conflict in knowledge, is something that jars between past experience and a new event or anomaly. There is a lineage (Watts and Pedrosa de Jesus 2006) that can be portrayed as a question-formation 'lineage' as in Figure 7.1.

Variance of this kind is an 'adult' form of Piagetian individual constructivism, the core of which is driven by the processes of equilibrium and disequilibrium (Piaget 1971). Awareness of these shortcomings in our existing thinking produces dissatisfaction so that 'dis-equilibration' happens, which is an uncomfortable state sometimes referred to as cognitive conflict. We then attempt to reduce such imbalances by focusing on the issues that cause the disequilibrium, and adapt the old ones – or develop new thoughts, ideas, understandings – until equilibrium is restored once more. Some mismatches in schema lead to incongruity, puzzlement, curiosity, perplexity, doubt, challenge, wonder. And so to questions.

Through these processes, of accommodation and assimilation, we adopt increasingly more sophisticated modes of thought that serve to eliminate the shortcomings of the old ones and, having done so, we are then considered to have developed ourselves and improved the quality of our thinking: we have provided an answer, or solution, or resolution to the puzzlement that has occurred because of the variation in schema. So, questions can arise from variance that engenders '*cognitive dissonance*' (Festinger 1957), from '*epistemic*

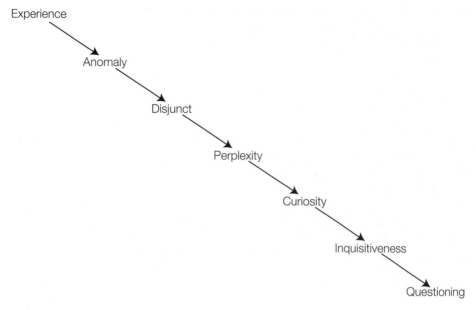

■ **Figure 7.1** A question formation lineage

hunger' (Berlyne 1954) or '*cognitive disequilibrium*' (Graesser and Olde 2003). The process of increasing the scope and scale of our schema is called conceptual development.

There is, though, a big difference between being aware of something puzzling, and then being able to articulate this as a clear and lucid question. Questions do not always arrive fully formed at the point of utterance, ready for the asking. Graesser and McMahen's (1993) study suggests, for example, that questions do not surface where this involves too much mental effort, or when it is socially awkward to ask them. Many people have had the experience of wanting to ask a question but of not doing so. This may well be because they feel the form of the question is inappropriate (it appears naïve or unduly complex), or they resist asking the question to avoid personal embarrassment or social ridicule. The upshot here is that even if there is awareness of disequilibrium, a knowledge gap, perplexity, doubt, wonder, etc., the learner may nevertheless override these feelings and resist 'verbal coding', the articulation of a question at that point.

EMPIRICAL QUESTIONS, THOUGHT EXPERIMENTS

In general, questions arise within a context or in response to particular situations; they do not simply materialize from the ether. Science questions often occur from within a specific discipline of science. They can arise, too, within everyday experience, where the response to the question is seen to be appropriate to the context of science. For example, O'Hare (2008) provides a compilation of questions contributed by readers of the popular *New Scientist* magazine. Some of these are:

■   How long could a person live on beer alone?
■   Why do people have eyebrows?

- How fat do you have to be to become bulletproof?
- What would happen if aliens stole the Moon?
- Why are there different shadings in the colour of earwax?
- Does anything eat wasps?

A similar book is 'Do bats have bollocks?' (Butler and Vincent 2008), and there are several more that are similar, listed in the bibliography below. It is clear these questioners have overcome any embarrassment or fear of ridicule to surface their puzzlements. Opinions might be divided as to whether they are 'good' questions (worthy of time and effort) or even science questions – although they do in general have a 'science slant'. Some of these questions might be seen to have answers – they are what Andrews (2003) calls 'answerable questions' – some clearly not, while others lie in the middle. So, it is quite probable that someone, no doubt an entomologist, would know the answer to the 'wasp' question, and, indeed, several answers are provided in O'Hare's book (birds, badgers, frogs and goldfish, apparently). Others are questions that could conceivably be put to experimental test, however grisly. So, it is faintly possible to give a person a diet simply of beer and watch to see how long it takes him or her to die.

'Why do people have eyebrows?' relies on a theoretical response from evolutionary theory: they may have developed over time as an effective signalling device to communicate emotions (surprise, anger, curiosity) and/or, as a way to keep water (sweat, rain) from running directly into the eyes. This is not an empirical question – the answer cannot be arrived at simply through direct observation or experimentation – and so the question is conjectural.

Other questions, like the consequences of aliens stealing the Moon, lie more fully in the realm of thought experiments. These are famous throughout science and the philosophy of science, and have received detailed attention, not least through Karl Popper's (1968) 'On the use and misuse of imaginary experiments, especially in quantum theory', and Thomas Kuhn's (1977) 'A function for thought experiments'. There is a long list of thought experiments: Borel's Monkeys; Einstein's Elevator; Einstein's Light-beam; Hawking's Turtles; Heisenberg's Gamma-ray microscope; Mach's 'Welcome to the edge of the universe'; Maxwell's Demon; Newton's Bucket; Schrödinger's Cat; Searle's Room; Parfit's Teleporter; Putnam's Twin-Earth, to note just a few.

One favourite is Galileo and the Tower of Pisa. Contrary to popular myth, Galileo Galilei did not drop balls from the Tower of Pisa; he asked the question and conducted the gravity experiment in the 'laboratory of his mind'. His sixteenth-century peers believed heavier objects fell faster than light ones. So Galileo imagined a heavy ball attached by a string to a light ball. His question was: 'Would the light ball create drag and slow the heavy one down?' No, he concluded, they would hit the ground simultaneously.

Our own research shows that young people, children, adolescents, university students, are all capable of asking a multitude of questions: given free rein, they can ask answerable, conjectural and unanswerable questions related to some, many, most, subjects. In science education, the subject and the session tend to give direction to the questions, such as: 'What is the pattern of movement of a given animal during the summer season?', 'How do various species interact in a given ecosystem?', 'What happens when certain environmental conditions occur?', etc.

KINDS OF CLASSROOM QUESTIONS

Our own work has studied classrooms of many kinds (Watts and Pedrosa de Jesus 2006), and has given rise to a hierarchy of learners' questions:

Acquisition questions

We define acquisition questions as questions dealing with relatively straightforward ideas. When asking acquisition questions, learners are attempting to deal with matters of information, fill in gaps, confirm explanations or clarify matters. In some instances, students may feel they have grasped an idea, or the structure of an argument, and are testing for reassurance that this is in fact the case. These are 'stick-to-the-facts' questions; for example, some from chemistry lessons are:

■ What are nano-materials?
■ What does disproportionation mean?
■ Is copper sulfate soluble in water?
■ What causes acid rain?

Acquisition questions are usually asked quickly within a class, are aimed at sorting out immediate issues and are usually fairly easy to deal with in the normal flow of a lesson.

Specialization questions

Specialization questions tend to go beyond an initial search for information; the student establishes relations and tries to understand and interpret the meaning of related issues. These kinds of questions try to generalize or relate specifics into meaningful patterns: the student has reached a sense of conviction in his or her understandings, and then uses the security of this 'base camp' to launch a few 'sorties' into the neighbouring terrain. For example:

■ What happens to the indicator that explains a colour change?
■ What might be the ways in which we could prevent acid rain?
■ Since one O_2 molecule can bind to each of the four haem groups of haemoglobin, why is it that the second and following O_2 molecules are more easily bound than the first one?

Questions like this are less easy to deal with because they require a more considered response – and this kind of consideration takes time. In the final section of this chapter we look at ways in which teachers can respond to questions of all kinds.

Integrative questions

One of the major characteristics of integrative questions is the reorganization of concepts into novel patterns and to hypothesize new or different applications of principles learned. Integrative questions are attempts to reconcile different understandings, resolve conflicts, test circumstances, force issues, track in and around complex ideas and their consequences.

Such questions may have some direct relevance to the classroom topic being taught, though questions may be triggered by tangential issues or be stimulated by something from outside the class entirely. Some examples of such questions are:

■ I wonder if it would make sense to design a H_2/O_2 fuel cell-based vehicle that would avoid carrying H_2 and O_2 in bottles by including an electrolytic cell, powered by solar panels, to decompose H_2O?

■ If the variation of entropy of the universe is always higher then zero – that is, if we are moving towards disorder – how do structures like planets, planetary systems and galaxies form?

■ Water has a high surface tension that allows, for instance, insects to rest on the water and not to sink. But there is a huge Australian lizard which runs over the water and never drowns. I can't understand this because that lizard is really quite heavy. How is this possible? Water cannot sustain a mouse or a squirrel, and yet can sustain the Australian lizard.

We see these kinds of questions being where the learners have the ability to elaborate different kinds of questions, according to their needs in diverse situations. The students in this case are asking integrative questions, and revealing understanding of the ways in which questions can work, and consciously designing questions through monitoring the question-asking process and organizing the nature and form of the question. They are also consciously alert to the impact of the question upon self-esteem and intend to have the highest possible impact on others. Students working in this way normally ask questions in a very spontaneous way.

We have two other categories of questions, somewhat different in intent:

Organizational questions

Organizational questions can be thought of as those questions that marshal, and lead to, procedural knowledge, the '*Knowing how to …?* rather than the '*Knowing what …?* of learn-ing. Holcomb's (1996) work shows that questions like these can be used as guides to the performance of individuals and groups in the preparation, focus, diagnosis, development, implementation and evaluation of their work. Specific questions can be used to guide these processes, so that, for example, in the 'focus' stage the question might be: *Where do we want to go?* While implementing, monitoring, and evaluating on the other hand, the questions might be: *How will we know we have got there?* Both Pearson (1999: 28) and Brockbank and McGill (2000: 62) suggest that some broad questions of this kind might be:

■ Where are we now?
■ Where do we want to get to?
■ How shall we get there?

Once in progress:

■ How well are we doing?
■ Are we keeping to time?
■ How do we move things along?

And, towards the end:

- Where have we got to?
- What have we gained?
- What happens next?

Reflective questions

A reflective question is where a clear amount of 'internal contemplation' has taken place – that is, where it is clear that the question has been consciously shaped by the asker, mindful of the process of questioning, the audience and the social/academic context. A reflective question shows some understanding of the ways in which questions can work, and can be designed through organizing the nature and form of the question. They usually express feelings, beliefs, values about some issue of personal importance and are revealing of self-esteem and the self-esteem of others, and show empathy with other people in the vicinity. Questions become reflective when emergent ideas are related to an existing sense of knowledge, self and the world, and as new understanding emerges. Brockbank and McGill (2000) suggest that examples of reflective questions might be:

- 'Something is happening that surprises me. It is not usual, but what is it about?'
- 'Is what I am doing appropriate at this moment?'
- 'Do I need to alter, amend, change what I am doing in order to adjust to changing circumstances to "get back into balance"?'
- 'If I am not on the right track, is there a better way of doing this?'

These four question types are not meant to be exhaustive and all-encompassing. However, we find them useful in working through ways in which to structure teaching and learning. Many questions lie inside each of these types, so that if a learner simply asks 'Why?' it could be for information, for something more specialized or as a way of integrating ideas. The intention behind such a deceptively simple question depends upon the context.

CLASSROOM CULTURES

This leads us to our next section, the notion of contextualization, or enculturalization. To enculturalize, or to become cultured in a particular field, is to engage with and become embedded within, in this case, the culture of science. As we said earlier, we believe that, at its heart, the scientific enterprise is driven by inquiry at both the individual and the group level. For the individual scientist, the quest for understanding is fostered by an insatiable curiosity about how things work and why things are the way that they are. For the discipline as a whole, developments in theory and practice are measured by the successful progression of responses to questions about the fundamental working of nature (Taber 2009). A scientist by definition is naturally an inquirer, and while much of the professional development that a scientist undergoes is seemingly about 'learning the lie of the land', in our view a key feature of science schooling should be apprenticing oneself to a master inquirer to learn how to ask good-quality questions – ones that lead to fruitful answers. That is, one purpose of science education is to help young people to 'get inside' science so that they learn to use the language, the ways of doing, the values and ways of working that are scientific. It entails growing into the patterns of language and thought, actions and behaviours, discussion and criticism, to ask the questions that are characteristic of science.

We want to focus our discussion here on two kinds of classroom culture: first, where questions are rare and inhibited; and second, where questions are frequent and encouraged. These two cultures are at opposite ends of a spectrum, of course, and there are many points in between, but polarizing like this serves to sharpen the debate. First, let us consider 'Learner production' of questions, and then move to 'Teacher reception'.

The key question here is 'Why do learners *not* ask questions out loud in class?' There are many answers that surround, for example, personality types (being reserved, anxious, disengaged), peer-group pressures (embarrassment in front of friends, looking foolish in front of the teacher), mode (easier after the lesson or in a small-group tutorial), and even in the framing of a question (sensing a puzzle or perplexity but not actually being able to put it into words). There may be other factors at play, such as gender issues, so that Li's (2002) study, for instance, found that in the classrooms he observed, boys were more likely to offer opinions and explanations, while girls were more likely to ask questions or ask for specific information. Many students do ask questions and overcome some of these issues, sometimes beginning a question by saying, 'I know this may sound daft, but why ...?', or 'Maybe I'm not asking this the right way, but what ...?'

In many instances, students' question-asking is shaped by the ways teachers respond, by 'teacher reception'. Imagine a classroom where any question is received with a 'put-down', where other people jeer or pass rude comments, where the teaching style is a strict lecture mode with no space for questions. Contrast this with a classroom where the teaching is based upon questions, where practical work and theory are driven by the questions the learners ask, where students are *required* to be actively questioning and inquisitive. The key question here is 'Why would teachers *not* encourage questions out loud in class?'

Again, there are many answers that surround personality types (reserved, anxious, lacking confidence), curriculum pressures (needing to 'get through' the syllabus, prepare for tests and exams), mode (easier to direct the lesson, keep its shape and 'flow'), and even feeling challenged (sensing a test of knowledge or authority, a criticism, a deliberate 'red-herring' to distract the lesson, take it off track).

We represent these contrasts in Table 7.1. The two polar contrasts are cell A and cell D. Throughout our research studies (some listed at the end of the chapter) we have sat and observed numerous examples of both.

■ **Table 7.1** Possible classroom cultures

	Teacher inhibited	**Teacher confident**
Learner inhibited	A	B
Learner confident	C	D

Cell A can be characterized by, say, a very didactic physics lesson given by a new or non-specialist teacher unsure of the broad sweep of the subject matter (say, Newton's Third Law of forces), where the class are required to copy notes from the board, complete a worksheet, do exercises from the textbook, where a shy hand may be raised but the likely questions are procedural ('Do we need to underline the title, Sir?'). We have sat in many of these classes.

Cell D can be characterized by other classes we have researched, where the topic is still about forces, but the class has been tutored in the asking of questions ('What exactly is a *good* question?'), have prepared questions in advance of the lesson, have been organized into groups around tackling selected questions, are asked to write down five more questions that their practical activities have raised ('If I push on a wall, and the wall pushes back on me, how does the wall know to stop pushing when I stop?')

In this second class, the teacher enjoys questions, both serious and 'wacky', has warned the class that while some questions have scientific answers, others lie outside science but in different fields of knowledge (such as sociology, politics or religion); some can only be answered way in the future, if at all. Moreover, not all questions are empirical questions; some questions need to be refined and 'flipped' to become susceptible to systematic investigation.

A culture of questioning means that in the learning context of a science classroom, the representation and deliberation of the science content knowledge, the social interactions among learners and the teacher, and the learning environment and classroom activities that are perceived and practised by students, all contribute to the context of students' question-asking. In other words, it is when students intuitively 'feel right' that they are more likely to ask questions, good science questions.

Questioning cultures

Pulling away from the extremes slightly, the other two cells in Table 7.1, B and C, occupy some of the middle ground. In cell B the teacher is confident, happy to engage in questioning, and it is the students, the class, that feel inhibited. Sometimes it is the general school culture that does not encourage dialogic teaching, where the science teacher is working against the trend. In other cases it is the 'chemistry' of that particular group. Part of our work has explored with individuals their disposition towards asking questions in class. One young person said, 'I don't worry about being seen as stupid by my teacher, I just hate looking daft in front of my friends.' That is, she accepted that the teacher would be receptive of her exploratory questions, her vulnerable gaps in knowledge; she was more concerned with the reaction of her peer group. In this respect, our research has shown that where the teaching conditions are right, one good questioner can show the way for others. We have called this the 'snowball effect'. It trades on peer role-modelling such that where one confident student leads, then other students on the edge, on the learning periphery, will then join in so that questioning snowballs and blossoms. This is particularly the case when the questioner is rewarded by the teacher's serious and encouraging responses. As mentioned earlier, this can depend on the learner's personality type (reserved, anxious, disengaged), peer group pressures (embarrassment in front of friends, looking foolish in front of the teacher), mode (easier after the lesson, in a small-group tutorial), and even the framing of a question (sensing a puzzle or perplexity but not actually being able to put it into words). In their classic text, Lave and Wenger say that 'Learning is a process of participation in communities of practice, participation that is at first legitimately peripheral but that increases gradually in engagement and complexity' (1991: 27). It is clear in the work we have done that, in all cases, the capacity to ask classroom questions, and to have them answered seriously, provides an enormous 'motivational hook' into science: it multiplies learners' engagement with science.

In cell C, it is the students that have confidence, it is the teacher who feels inhibited. As we noted earlier, this can be for a variety of reasons; it often takes experience, practice and surety to open up classroom space to learners' questions, to encourage them, let alone instigate full inquiry-based learning. Needless to say, we see ways to build towards this in smaller, incremental steps, and consider some of these towards the end of the chapter. In the next section we want to discuss some of the kinds of questions that learners ask.

ENCOURAGING 'QUOUGHTS'

Here we return to the notion of reflective, pensive questions. 'Quoughts' are thought questions, not a term original to us but one that has crept into the literature on learners questioning to capture 'thought puzzles', unspoken perplexities, internal moments of wonderment.

In discussing the 'lineage of question formation', we indicated that within the space between the first variation or anomaly and the eventual question there exists a 'conversation', one that moves between the 'shape' of the question and the agenda of the question-asker. Such conversations are not necessarily spoken aloud between two or more people: as Harri-Augstein and Thomas (1991) suggest, individuals can have conversations alone within their own heads, as well as – sometimes – their hands having a 'conversation' with the materials they may be using. One way of considering these conversations might be to look at common kinds of everyday quoughts:

■ Teaching new and unfamiliar material to a new and unfamiliar class tomorrow morning: What will it be like?
■ Preparing to start a new science class with a new teacher: What will it be like?
■ Using new materials, methods or strategies in the context of a science lesson: What is supposed to happen?
■ Getting down to doing a project and meeting agreed deadlines against the normal pressures of the group: What needs to be done, and by when?
■ Why won't this software package (apparatus, computer printer, data logger, tape deck, digital recorder) work?

As we have discussed, how individuals articulate a 'quought' will depend upon their confidence, their self-belief about their own capabilities and talents, the set of beliefs, mores and norms concerned with the issues involved, how well they have dealt with similar questions before and, therefore, their repertoire of past successes. It will depend, too, on past failures ('I'm not that good at writing'; 'I'm hopeless with electrical things'; 'I'm all fingers and thumbs when it comes to...'; 'I'm not particularly artistic/scientific/mathematical...'). The conversations had with ourselves, then, mean that people 'work through' the question, chew over fears and foibles, rehearse 'scenarios' in their head, struggle with what is involved, plan for the task and for wayward contingencies, imagine the very worst, dream for the very best, and so on.

Box 7.1 **Case study 1: Articulating 'quoughts'**

As a part of our project, one of our group devised an intranet system across the department and made it available to learners off-campus. This software system has been accessible through the use of an appropriate password, operating within the building, the resource areas and the computer suites. Computers with this software installed were available in the laboratories, in tutorial rooms and in the interconnecting corridors, in this way providing free access to students. The software enabled the students who had internet facilities outside to work at home and access the system. Throughout our research, the email system prompted a large number of questions, largely because these students had time and privacy in which to formulate and ask questions. It is clear, too, that although one student was the author, the question itself was often a product of several students working together ('We would like to know ...').

What were the outcomes? Some 30 per cent of the questions that students asked in one term were asked away from the classroom through this 'remote' use of the software system. At first glance this supports some of our discussion; it might be taken as unwillingness to ask questions in the give-and-take of a lesson or group situation. When we investigated further, however, we understood that the software system allows students to ruminate on their questions, to undertake reading and to tackle assignments and then to ask questions in 'downtime' when away from the formal situation. In this sense it is taken as an illustration of their willingness to engage in science in their own self-directed time, to articulate their 'quoughts'.

How did the teachers respond to these? First, the promise was that students would receive a reply within a week. The reply might be a mass-produced one ('I am working on your question') or a personalized one ('Have you thought about ...?'). Some questions were easily answered, and where there were many similar ones, the teachers quickly produced 'stock' answers to FAQs (frequently asked questions), for instance reference to a page in the textbook or a good website. Where there were a lot of FAQs, after a particular lesson for example, then it was clear that something had been unclear; some common misunderstanding had occurred and needed to be tackled. Some questions gave rise to empirical questions, and some of the 'mini-projects' that were inaugurated, are described in Case Study 2 (p.97)

But exploring the 'question space' means more than simply talking to oneself and worrying about the outcomes. 'Question space conversations' enable progress with an issue by allowing it to be explored to some depth. In our view, good questions are able to open up a problem, tease out core issues, require explanations, explore around the edges of an issue, force adequate answers. In some cases this concerns the articulation of the question itself. In Box 7.1 we outline a case study in which we enabled learners to ask open questions in a private way, to articulate 'quoughts' without fear of too much embarrassment. And as time went by, and they saw that their questions were treated sensitively and seriously, they were able to develop the kinds of questions they asked.

ENCOURAGING EMPIRICAL QUESTIONS

First-hand inquiry involves exploration; generating investigable questions and carrying out a planned study are more than that. The development of inquiry skills has two key tensions, between open-ended discovery on the one hand and structured investigation on the other. Both are important: the capacity to play, see what happens, employ guesswork and trial and error, is very much part of the learning process. So, though, is controlled and systematic experimentation. The practice of inquiry is a way of thinking, of processing, of operating in the world. For us, the key is having an initial curiosity about something and a framework within which to ask questions. Scientific inquiry, whether at school or in later studies, is personally driven and then involves the skills of directed observation, problem-solving, analysis and experimentation.

Using our discussion from earlier, scientific inquiry is shaped by dissatisfaction, some variation between a particular worldview and an anomalous event or observation, causing disequilibrium. Scientific inquiry occurs within an existing framework of previous knowledge alongside a desire to fit into the particular developing self-consistent picture that is the current scientific paradigm. A key feature of this paradigm is the repeatability of results and the use of mathematics as a tool for maintaining self-consistency.

So, what are some of the processes of developing empirical questions? At an initial level, students can be encouraged to ask the generic 'W' questions: Who? What? Where? When? Why? and How? In a study by King (1992), for example, she required students to use a series of generic question 'stems' such as: 'What is the main idea of ...?' 'How are ... and ... alike?' 'What are the strengths and weaknesses of ...?' 'How does ... affect ...?' 'Where would one find examples of ...?' 'Why is it important to ...?' These were used within each session and as the basis for written assignments to the point that students became adept at using the questions unbidden. Good questions can take time to develop but, in their review of such ways of working, Rosenshine *et al.* (1996) maintain that the regular use of such questions and prompts was very successful in developing inquiry.

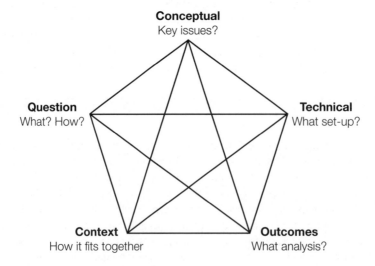

■ **Figure 7.2** The design decision pentagon
Source: adapted from Barlex (2007)

Small-group work is a popular way to prompt students to question each other, and to discern the levels of response needed. The teacher plays a crucial role in promoting the co-construction of knowledge in classrooms by designing effective tasks, guiding classroom discussions and encouraging students to contribute their ideas and engage in conversation (Palincsar and Herrenkohl 2002). Thus, the whole classroom is viewed as a series of small groups, part of a larger community of learners engaged in separate but related activities within a single discourse. In a learning community the goal is to advance the collective knowledge. So, members share their individual and small-group efforts towards a deeper understanding of the subject matter under study (Bielaczyc and Collins 1999).

The scale and size of any project or experiment will depend on the time to be had, the materials and tools available, the nature of the questions and topics. An empirical question is often constrained by what can be managed with the resources at hand. In Figure 7.2 we have

---

Box 7.2 **Case study 2: Empirical questions and mini-projects**

Needless to say, the stages we observed and report here are not rigid; rather, they were present to a smaller or larger degree in successive meetings as the groups met, discussed, recapped and then made progress towards their aims.

1   Team organization: At this case study, the participants (Amy, Bruno, Candida and Dino) were not necessarily part of a friendship group and so there was a period of 'getting to know each other'. It meant that the initial choice of question for the mini-project had to be explicitly, clearly articulated and judged between themselves, rather than the group moving forward quickly on more implicitly and tacitly understood assumptions.

2   Accumulation of ideas: Amy was the creative questioner in the group and generated a great number of ideas. The other three treated these very seriously and enlarged upon them with their own suggestions. The 'key' question: 'Why is the percentage of body's fat different during the course of a single day?' had been stimulated by the manual of a commercial weighing balance Amy had bought, to measure fat percentage through bio-impedance. The manual indicated that percentages of fat could vary along the course of a day.

3   The data-gathering was marked by a search for information through several sources, but mostly via the internet. This search brought a considerable number of additional ideas and sub-themes that, while they were linked to the main theme, could not all be treated in the same mini-project. The final experiments looked at data from each member of the group over a period of 24 hours (they each took the scales home in turn) as they recorded their results at regular intervals.

4   The report-writing was a joint effort involving much negotiation and to-ing and fro-ing as they compiled a common report, through emailing each other and compiling graphs, errors and limitations in class.

5   During the presentation, the group had to present their work to the assembled class. They had 5 minutes of presentation and a further 5 minutes for questions and discussion. All the members of the group participated in the presentation, and the distribution of the tasks was agreed between them.

---

adapted a successful 'decision pentagon' from the work of Barlex (2007) from the teaching of design and technology, giving general pointers to the decisions students might make to shape their experiment.

So, what would good empirical questions look like? Our 'shopping list' would be along the lines that learners' questions:

- are exploratory of the discipline through which they want to approach the topic – that is, they are answerable within a broad view of science and technology;
- are appropriately vague at the beginning but grow to be clear, concise and focused, honed within a small group and with teachers' help;
- lead to team organization in the choice of the theme and selection of a sub-theme, and in the organization of the project, with a strong harmony as personalities allow;
- are descriptive of components, aspects, variables in empirical terms, wherever appropriate, allowing for the empirical work, data-gathering, analysis, interpretation;
- are built on learners' experiences but shaped by reading available literature and sources, so that they are novel but could replicated; able to pass the 'So what?' test;
- are feasible and ethical in the environment and material circumstances;
- lead to intermediate writing, then a fuller report, oral presentation, exhibition of the poster and evaluation of the work.

We use a case study (Box 7.2 on the previous page) to illuminate this use of students' group questions because, as Wiederhold and Kagan (1992: 206) say: 'Students' question can be the focus of cooperative lessons, allowing time to think critically: first in constructing questions, second in asking them, third in responding, and again in paraphrasing, praising, and augmenting them.'

QUOUGHTS FOR TEACHERS

Inquiry-based learning is certainly a different classroom approach. Scientific inquiry is as much about asking good questions as getting good answers; it is concerned with gathering good evidence, and is developed in 'emergent scientists' through individual and group mentoring process over a considerable length of time. In the work described by Jones *et al.* (1992), teachers too are encouraged to ask themselves questions in order to evaluate this kind of classroom work; for example:

- 'Does this kind of open investigative work meet curriculum needs?'
- 'How much initiative am I prepared to give the students?'
- 'What changes are required to carry out this kind of work?'

Lemke argues that

[l]earning sciences means learn to talk science. It also means learning to use this specialized conceptual language in reading and writing, in reasoning and problem solving, and in guiding practical action in the laboratory and in daily life. It means learning to communicate in the language of science and to act as member of the community of people who do so.

(1993: 1)

Table 7.1, our four 'classroom cultures', could be summarized as:

- Cell A: Traditional teacher-directed classroom: the teacher is the main source of ideas, asking frequent, short questions, and learners – who are largely passive listeners with little or no peer interaction or 'science talk' – give short answers in return.
- Cell B: The teacher begins to pursue learners' thinking and questioning: he/she asks probing questions about issues, learners provide a brief description of their thinking. The teacher at this level still plays a central role in the science-talk community.
- Cell C: The teacher is held back from helping learners build new roles, where he or she could facilitate peer interaction by encouraging students to share their own thinking and evaluate the ideas of others.
- Cell D: The teacher as co-teacher and co-learner: he/she coaches and assists students as they take on leading roles in the science-talk learning community; students ask one another questions about their work and confidently justify their answers with little prompting from the teacher.

Some swift tips for 'Cell D teaching' might be as follows:

1   Document questions and inquiries (creating a rich portfolio of anecdotes, ideas, etc.). Note questions raised, indicating which ones can be answered and which ones cannot; collect materials, odd data and references (books, journals and notebooks).
2   Find time, make time, in the class (or outside it) to give inquiry experiences: give 'odd' demonstrations, pose a 'thought for the day', get students to make oral presentations of questions or investigations that have intrigued them; explore the public defence of inquiries, findings and news items, orally in discussions and also in writing. There is always a lot of science 'news' around.
3   Make time for, and encourage, 'quoughts' that – maybe – have no empirical outcomes. These questions are intended to provoke thought and inspire reflection. Strong questioning skills fuel and steer the inventive process required to 'cook up' something new.

Without such questioning skills, our students become prisoners of conventional wisdom and the trend or bandwagon of the day. Probing questioning explores the underlying principles, characteristics and possibilities of any given situation. In the popular series, Harry Potter is denied the right to ask questions by foster-parents who find his asking threatening and disrespectful. Our prompts for teacher 'quoughts' are as follows:

- What do I want to be known for in school, and what am I going to do to make this a reality? What do I care about enough in education to defend in conversation with people I respect?
- Am I working on my strengths? How can I best teach in ways that both allow me to express my own interests and strengths and contribute to my students/class/school/community?
- Where is my teaching going? What would I like to achieve with learners? How would I teach differently this year if I had no fear?
- Am I enjoying what I do on a daily basis? If not, can I figure out why? Then, what can I do to change that?

- Given that, while no single lesson is guaranteed to change the trajectory of a class, a particular student or a relationship, what is the 'teaching conversation' that has my name on it?
- Am I doing what matters right now? What is my theme for the coming year? How do I know when I've 'done enough'?

FINAL QUOUGHTS

There are many ways in which teachers can use learners' questions, but the first need is to collect them – to harvest questions. We have used a cardboard 'question box', like a ballot box, for quickly scribbled questions; email and online forums for sharing questions; 'Ask a Scientist' sessions where learners have had access to a guest expert for an hour (both 'live' and online); pinned-up classroom posters of questions; group presentations and questions as well as usual classroom questions. The key part has been to welcome questions from all directions. A second element is to signal the likelihood of (1) there being an answer, and (2) there being a quick answer.

This second part, answering questions, is not the exclusive domain of the teacher. There is no stigma attached to saying, 'Hmmm, not sure, I'll have to look that up.' An old Chinese proverb has it that 'one foolish man can ask more questions than ten wise men can answer'. Instead, questions become homework tasks, group work or, where appropriate, classroom activities. Over time, each teacher will compile a set of FAQs and will have a useful stock of 'frequently used answers' – even if that is a reference to page 17 of the classroom text.

The final suggestion is that the teacher becomes a powerful role model for the asking of questions – not as a means of classroom control, but as an entry into exactly how science works.

> Once you have learned how to ask relevant and appropriate questions, you have learned how to learn and no one can keep you from learning whatever you want or need to know.
>
> (Postman and Weingartner 1965)

> Knowing the answer may or may not indicate an understanding of the subject matter. However, being able to formulate a good question is always contingent upon such understanding
>
> (Schodell 1995).

A USEFUL 'QUESTIONS BIBLIOGRAPHY' AND FURTHER READING

Moore, P. (2008) *Can You Play Cricket on Mars?* Stroud: The History Press.

Will the universe ever come to an end?

Do all stars have their own names?

Is there an owl in the sky?

Was the moon ever part of the earth?

O'Hare, M. (Ed.) (2008) *Do Polar Bears get Lonely?* London: Profile Books.

Why does garlic make your breath smell?

Does it matter what lottery numbers you choose?

Can you harm your hands by cracking your knuckles? Does a dog know it is a dog?

Do pigeons sweat?

Heiney, P. (2008) (Ed.) *Do Cats Have Belly Buttons?* Stroud: The History Press.

Can cows walk downstairs?

Do people with sticky-out ears have better balance?

Can stress make you sick?

Do birds have earwax?

How does heat make things rise?

Is AC more dangerous than DC?

How big is the earth?

Pedrosa de Jesus, H., Almeida, P. and Watts, D. M. (2004) Questioning styles and students' learning: four case studies, *Educational Psychology* 24 (4), 531–548.

Pedrosa de Jesus, H., Almeida, P. and Watts, D. M. (2005) Orchestrating learning and teaching in inter-disciplinary chemistry, *Canadian Journal for Science, Technology and Mathematics Education* 5 (1), 71–84.

Pedrosa de Jesus, M. H., Neri de Souza, F., Teixeira-Dias, J. J. C. and Watts, D. M. (2005) Organising the chemistry of question-based learning: a case study, *Journal of Research in Science and Technological Education* 23 (2), 179–193.

Teixeira-Dias, J. J. C., Pedrosa de Jesus, M. H., Neri de Souza, F. and Watts, D. M. (2005) Teaching for quality learning in chemistry, *International Journal of Science Education* 27(9), 1123–1137.

Watts, M. and Pedrosa de Jesus, H. (2005) The cause and affect of asking questions: reflective case studies from undergraduate sciences, *Canadian Journal of Science Mathematics and Technology Education* (CJSMTE/ RCESMT) 5(4), 437–452.

REFERENCES

Andrews, R. (2003) *Research questions,* London: Continuum Press.

Barlex, D. (2007) Assessing capability in design & technology: the case for a minimally invasive approach, *Design and Technology Education: An International Journal*, 12.2, 9 – 56

Berlyne, D. E. (1954) A theory of human curiosity, *British Journal of Psychology*, 45, 180–191.

Bielaczyc, K. and Collins, A. (1999) Learning communities in classrooms: A Reconceptualization of educational practice, in C.M. Reigeluth (ed.) *Instructional-Design Theories and Models: A New Paradigm of Instructional Theory* (Vol. 2), London: Lawrence Erlbaum Associates.

Brockbank, A. and McGill, I. (2000*) Facilitating Reflective Learning in Higher Education*, Milton Keynes: Open University Press.

Butler, J. and Vincent, B. (2008) *Do Bats Have Bollocks?* London: Sphere Books.

Dennett, D. C. (1991) *Consciousness Explained*, London: Penguin Books.

Festinger, L. (1957) *A Theory of Cognitive Dissonance*, Stanford, CA: Stanford University Press.

Graesser, A. C. and McMahen, C. L. (1993) Anomalous information triggers questions when adults solve quantitative problems and comprehend stories, *Journal of Educational Psychology* 85, 136–151.

Graesser, A. C. and Olde, B. A. (2003) How does one know whether a person understands a device? The quality of the questions the person asks when the device breaks down, *Journal of Educational Psychology* 95, 524–536.

Harri-Augstein, E. S. and Thomas, L. (1991) *Learning Conversations: The Self-Organised Way to Personal and Organisational Growth*, London: Routledge.

Holcomb, E. L. (1996) *Asking the Right Question,* Thousand Oaks, CA: Corwin Press.

Jones, A. T., Simon, S. A., Black, P. J., Fairbrother, R. W. and Watson J. R. (1992) *Open Work in Science. Development of Investigations in Schools*, Hatfield: Association for Science Education.

King, A. (1992) Comparison of self-questioning, summarizing and note-taking-review as strategies for learning from lectures, *American Educational Research Journal* 29 (2), 303–323.

Kuhn, T. (1977) A function for thought experiments, reprinted in T. Kuhn, *The Essential Tension*, Chicago: University of Chicago Press. First published 1964.

Lave, J. and Wenger, E. (1991) Situated Learning: Legitimate Peripheral Participation, Cambridge: Cambridge University Press.

Lemke, J. L. (1993) *Talking Science: Language, Learning and Values*, Norwood, NJ: Ablex.

Li, Q. (2002) Gender and computer-mediated communication: an exploration of elementary students' mathematics and science learning, *Journal of Computers in Mathematics and Science Teaching* 21(4), 341–359.

Marton, F. and Booth, S. A. (1997) *Learning and Awareness*, Hillsdale, NJ: Lawrence Erlbaum Associates.

Moon, J. A. (2004) *A Handbook of Reflective and Experiential Learning*, London: Routledge.

Morris, D. (2002) *Peoplewatching: The Desmond Morris Guide to Body Language*, London: Vintage Press.

Palincsar, A. S. and Herrenkohl, L. R. (2002) Designing collaborative contexts, *Theory into Practice* 41, 26–32.

Pearson, G. (1999). *Strategy in Action: Strategic Understanding and Practice*, Harlow: Pearson Education.

Piaget, J. (1971). *Biology and Knowledge*, Chicago: University of Chicago Press.

Popper, K. (1968) On the use and misuse of imaginary experiments, especially in quantum theory, In K. Popper, *The Logic of Scientific Discovery*, London: Routledge.

Postman, N. and Weingartner, C. (1969) *Teaching as a Subversive Activity*, New York: Dell.

Rosenshine, B., Meister, C. and Chapman, L. (1996) Teaching students to generate questions: a review of intervention studies, *Review of Educational Research* 66(2), 181–221.

Schodell, M. (1995) The question-driven classroom, *The American Biology Teacher* 57 (5), 278–281

Taber, K. S. (2009) *Progressing Science Education: Constructing the Scientific Research Programme into Contingent Nature of Learning Science*, Dordrecht, the Netherlands: Springer.

Watts, D. M. and Pedrosa de Jesus, M. H. (2006) 'Questioning', London: Staff Education and Development Association (SEDA) paper.

Wiederhold, C. and Kagan, S. (1992). Cooperative questioning and critical thinking, in N. Davidson and T. Worsham (eds) *Enhancing Thinking Through Cooperative Learning*, New York: Teachers College Press.

ENHANCING INVESTIGATIVE SCIENCE

Alan West

One thing that helps to make science real for students is the practical dimension; laboratory work is a unique feature of science education and one that provides opportunity for students to engage with authentic activity.

In this chapter we will:

- look at a range of authentic investigations;
- suggest development strategies for investigations which address the How Science Works dynamic; and
- consider ways in which such investigations may be developed as creative opportunities for learners.

The contexts for my comments and observations are drawn from a number of professional experiences from which I will provide examples. These experiences are based on the development of investigative contexts for the CREST Awards (Awards for CREativity in Science and Technology), a scheme designed to encourage investigative work in science and technology coupled with an accreditation for work accomplished; on developing contexts and opportunities for extended problem-solving experiences; and on addressing the needs of specific groups of learners through laboratory investigations.

How Science Works is intended to expose students to the concepts of science through meaningful contexts and to cause them to act as scientists in the way that they approach a wide range of relevant tasks. The Science National Strategy (2009) notes that:

> *How science works* is more than just scientific enquiry. It provides a wonderful opportunity for pupils to develop as critical and creative thinkers and to become flexible problem-solvers. The How Science Works strand has been split into two significant areas of skills development:
>
> - Explanations, argument and decisions
> - Practical and enquiry skills.
>
> Developing ideas and theories to explain the world is at the heart of science. *How science works* focuses on the critical analysis and linking of evidence to support or refute ideas and theories. Effective enquiry work involves exploring questions and finding answers through the gathering and evaluation of evidence. Pupils need to

understand how evidence comes from the collection and critical interpretation of both primary and secondary data and how evidence may be influenced by contexts such as culture, politics or ethics.

(National Strategies 2009)

Programmes developed for the CREST Awards and for university outreach through summer schools and master classes have drawn extensively on a constructivist approach to problem-solving activity. In the early 1980s the Assessment of Performance Unit (APU) conducted research into the ways in which young people conducted scientific investigations. Part of the outcome of this work was a model for problem-solving investigations, which subsequently became a template for much of what is now seen in guidance for scientific inquiry. The APU model has given rise to pedagogical approaches for CREST and, more recently, problem-solving work undertaken within the context of university outreach activity and summer schools. The development of CREST and a raft of other activities involving members of the scientific community acting as mentors have won support as interventions that can enrich and enhance the science experiences of students by making them more meaningful and relevant. How Science Works should provide the stimulus to embed such contextualized approaches into teaching and learning in science within the experience of all learners in secondary education. However, timing issues frequently mean that the opportunity for students to experience whole investigations rather than carry out a set of prescribed experiments is the challenge for teaching professionals. So what does school science now have to do to show How Science Works for the majority? It is important to review the cycle of investigation and to audit it in terms of the teaching models advocated through the National Strategy for teaching How Science Works and practical approaches for achieving these.

The iterative problem-solving model informed by the APU (Murphy and Gott 1984) contains a number of key phases, which form part of an investigation cycle (Figure 8.1). Ideas and pedagogical processes associated with the APU model were at the core of the

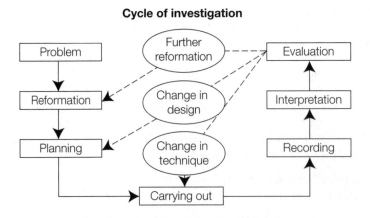

Cycle of investigation

■ **Figure 8.1** Cycle of investigation, informed by the Assessment of Performance Unit
Source: Murphy and Gott (1984)

CREST Award development, which encouraged students to tackle science- and technology-based problem-solving challenges, either provided through contextualized stimulus material or those which had been identified by the students themselves as something they wished to investigate.

Pedagogical approaches that place students in the role of genuine investigators exposed to the whole of the problem-solving cycle have also been at the heart of our development work for summer school activity and a wide range of university outreach such as the STEM World Summer School offered by Imperial College London, or the University of Leicester Space School. Indeed, one of the drivers for such programmes was the desire to expose students to more of the process of scientific investigation.

The National Strategy identifies a variety of approaches to teaching at Key Stage 4 (ages 14 to 16 years) and encourages teachers to explore different teaching approaches, which 'may be new or relatively infrequently used in current General Certificate of Secondary Education GCSE science teaching'. Figure 8.2 points to what I see as a relationship between the problem-solving cycle and the various teaching strategies proposed to support How Science Works. Different teaching approaches illuminate different parts of the problem-solving process. The opportunity for whole investigation requires students to integrate learning achieved over time through all of the suggested How Science Works teaching approaches recommended within the strategy.

The National Strategy teaching approaches are described as follows:

- Constructing Meaning
- Enquiry (Deductive)
- Direct Interactive
- Inductive Enquiry
- Modelling and Visualizing.

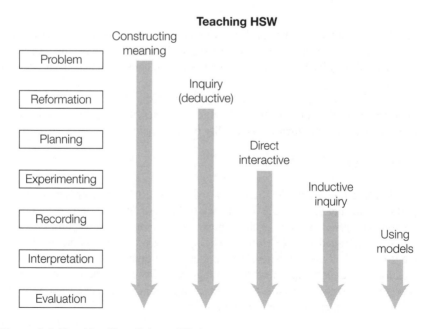

■ **Figure 8.2** Teaching How Science Works

CONSTRUCTING MEANING: THE PROBLEM

Based on a constructivist approach, this teaching model starts with the ideas the students have – their view of the world. Students' ideas are compared, with students then reformulating ideas into a problem or challenge which can be investigated experimentally and which addresses cognitive conflict that may have arisen. So, for example, when using a simple kinetic model to explain states of matter, the behaviour of water molecules can give rise to cognitive conflict when students attempt to explain the arrangement in particles within a solid compared to a liquid and are then asked, 'So why does ice float on water?' Discrepant or unexpected behaviour of this kind can be the starting point for investigations, which can then cause students to restructure their ideas according to the outcomes of the investigations, thereby reinforcing learning. Students are able to review the information they have gathered to test their hypothesis; testing may result in further investigation as well as providing opportunities for students to share or communicate their ideas. Constructing meaning in this way draws in all aspects of the problem solving cycle.

Identifying an appropriate problem is a critical factor for all students and their teachers. A useful source of starting points for investigations is unusual phenomena that are demonstrated, described in the literature or experienced in some way by the students. So, for example, the fact that blue jeans fade is something that students are likely to have observed and may prompt questions about cause. If problems or observations of this type are made by students and brought to the learning environment by them, they will be more motivated and more inclined to seek answers to the questions they have raised. The problem for teachers is the classroom management issue of dealing with such observations when they do not conform to the planned progression through the subject. Problems become given rather than owned, and therefore devalued by learners.

The National Strategy now talks about students' 'learning journeys' with four key elements:

■ developing a range of practical skills which are fit for purpose in terms of students being able to gather data and evidence from which they can make conclusions;
■ acquiring the skills necessary to gather and evaluate evidence from secondary sources;
■ using evidence to hypothesize and test explanations;
■ understanding the processes through which the scientific community shares information, thereby strengthening the quality of explanations.

The National Strategy notes that:

The learning journey in *How science works* is multi-faceted, complete in itself yet part of an intriguing whole. It is not easy to understand without a context, yet has a value that transcends that of the context. It is important not to build the curriculum on a restricted view of *How science works* based simply on practical work or enquiry skills. In a world where we are faced with dilemmas rooted in science and technology, young people need a full range of skills to be able to look critically at issues from a range of perspectives, and to understand the strengths and limitations of science in generating responses and solutions.

(National Strategies 2009)

INQUIRY (DEDUCTIVE): REFORMULATION

The inquiry model requires that students gather information in response to a given stimulus. This information is classified and sorted by the student as a prequel to making a hypothesis. Students then re-sort the information to test the hypothesis and, once this testing process is completed, form a conclusion through deductive reasoning. Reformulation involves taking the phenomena identified as a problem and building around this a causal question, which incorporates the variables that are to be investigated. This is the hypothesis that students over the decades have written at the start of their practical work – but to what extent do they own the hypothesis? The key to this learning approach is the selection of an appropriate stimulus or challenge for the investigation and the 'selling' of this starting point to the students. So, in the early CREST example of the 'Causes of Fading Blue Jeans', students might hypothesize that this is due to the amount of washing, the type of washing powder used, exposure to sunlight, etc. and suggest investigations to explore this. The reformulation step of the problem-solving process provides genuine opportunities for students to shape an investigation and establish some ownership for what will take place. Teachers need to be able to take the risk of allowing these students the freedom to do this if the work is to become a valid thinking skill activity for learners.

Since its launch in 1986 the CREST Award programme has provided students with an opportunity to develop context-based problem-solving activities in science and technology. One of the key strengths of the programme rests in the progression in problem-solving opportunity provided by the different award levels, with students at the early stages being prompted towards investigation through a diverse range of starter ideas. At the latter stages, associated with the 14–19 curriculum, students are expected to conduct their investigation over a longer period and to gather information and evidence from a wider range of sources. Significantly, the scheme also presents opportunity for students to work with science mentors and also to develop a range of communication skills with which to share the outcomes of their work with others. This national scheme is supported by a regional network of coordinators able to build links between schools and industry or higher education, where 'through the mentoring process students will learn about the way science and scientists work within society' (British Science Association 2009).

CREST supports How Science Works by providing a wide range of potential starting points for project work for which the entry point is the formulation of a hypothesis. A series of themed approaches lead students to areas of potential investigation in a non-prescriptive way. Themed areas of potential investigation are shown in Table 8.1.

Drilling down through these themes, for example travel, students might be encouraged to give consideration to problems encountered with bird migration (Box 8.1).

■ **Table 8.1** Themed areas of potential investigation

Fashion	Health and hygiene	Life at the edge
Environment	Detective work	Space
Food and drink	Entertainment	Sport
Travel		

Box 8.1 **Migrating birds**

The pied flycatcher, willow warbler and garden warbler now fly south almost a week earlier than formerly, according to researchers from the Swiss Ornithological Institute. These long-distance migrant birds have had to alter their flight times because of the climate change due to global warming. Short-haul migrational birds, on the other hand, are benefiting from the climate changes; it seems they have a longer breeding season and will migrate shorter distances in the future.

Have you ever wondered how far a bird can migrate? You might like to:

- compare the migration patterns of different birds;
- find out what devices are used to track the migration of birds and animals;
- research the effect of global warming on migration;
- examine the theories about homing pigeons; try to work out how you could test them.

Further links:

http://www.birdwatchireland.ie/
http://birding.about.com/
http://www.britishscienceassociation.org/web/ccaf/CREST/FreeProject Ideas/MoreProjectIdeas/Travel/SpeedandDistance/Migratingbirds.htm (accessed 2 September 2010)

Exposing students to the whole cyclical investigation clearly provides an opportunity for them to demonstrate creativity and for this reason it was taken as a baseline for activity within the CREST Awards programme. In Qualifications and Curriculum Authority (QCA) terms this is indicative of imagination and purpose. The reformulation of problems into something that can be tackled with the available resources gives rise to opportunities again for imagination but also originality. The iterative process gives a result or product that can be valued by the student. Students gain an appreciation of how science works and are further motivated in their learning of science concepts. Within the CREST Awards programme, students are required to review the progress they have made in relation to the problem-solving taxonomy. Such self-assessment can provide teachers with important evidence of effective learning. However, investigations of this type still fall outside the experience of many students, and the lack of such opportunity, or the fact that students cannot readily understand the purpose for undertaking a segment of an investigation, can be demotivating.

Consider also as an example of an inductive inquiry approach the case of a recent summer school, where more time was made available for students to develop their own ideas. Students working in small teams were presented with a scenario for science problem-solving based on an enterprise activity. Students were cast in the role of experts needing to pitch for a contract on the basis of their techniques and estimates of cost and benefit for the processes they developed. The students were provided with a project brief and were also taught specific laboratory techniques required for the activity. They were placed in a situation where they could make real choices as part of their research and development of a product. The scenario is set out in Box 8.2, 'A juicy problem – a clear solution'.

Box 8.2 **A juicy problem – a clear solution**

The brief

The company Crystal Clear manufactures high-quality carbonated drinks. It wishes to extend its range of fizzy waters to include one flavoured with pure apple juice. Crystal Clear has put out to tender a lucrative contract to supply the company with the high-grade apple juice. You represent a company that is bidding for this contract. Your team, as expert apple specialists, will research a range of juices and select one for flavouring the carbonated water.

In selecting a suitable apple juice, Crystal Clear has contacted Brogdale, home to the National Fruit Collections. Brogdale has the largest collection of varieties of fruit trees and plants in the world, including over 2,300 different varieties of apples grown in 150 acres of orchards. As such, Brogdale is the leading specialist in the area of fruit production and has a range of juices that is being made available for your company to investigate.

In developing this product, Crystal Clear has conducted a consumer survey. This survey showed that customers prefer flavoured water that:

1   Should taste sweet.
2   Is free from artificial flavourings and colourings. The water should therefore only be flavoured with pure apple juice and, importantly, should be clear in appearance.
3   Should have a tangy, acidic after-taste.
4   Should be healthy to drink, containing a significant proportion of an individual's Recommended Daily Allowance of vitamin C.

Science

Your company will have to ensure that your chosen juice meets the criteria outlined above. In the course of your research, therefore, you will have to scientifically assess the following:

1   The sweet taste of the drink.
    In attempting to detect, describe and standardize different aspects of food-stuffs, the food industry employs people who critically compare characteristics such as aroma, texture and flavour. This process of assessment is a scientific discipline in itself and one you will use to assess not only the sweetness of the different juices, but many other aspects as well. You will produce scientific data as a group, which you will present to the Board of Crystal Clear in trying to win the contract.
2   How to clarify the cloudy apple juice.
    The juices produced by Brogdale are pure and have little intermediate process-ing. As a result, all are cloudy. However, you will need to clarify the juice to fulfil the contract for Crystal Clear. It is suggested that the molecules responsible for the cloudiness of the apple juice can be broken down by enzymes. In your group, you will be given a choice of enzymes that may, or may not, assist in clarifying the juice. You will investigate the optimum conditions to clear the juice and go on to measure how clear the juice really is.

3 The pH of the drink.
   Acidity and alkalinity can be assessed in many different ways. Some are more accurate than others and require more or less technical and expensive equipment. You will have to decide which is the best, most cost-effective way to measure the pH of the drink, given the criteria outlined above.
4 Calculate the level of vitamin C in the drink.
   From known data, you will calculate the concentration of vitamin C in the final drink. This should reach a minimum percentage of the Recommended Daily Amount and these data should be presented to the Board of Crystal Clear.

(Adapted from Exscitec and NCBE 2006)

Students working on this challenge were required to make a presentation of their science and business plan associated with the production of the clarified juice. The idea was that they were competing for a contract to produce the product. They were also required to suggest how the product could be promoted and marketed within the code of practice of the Advertising Standards Authority.

What was clear from this activity was that when allowed to plan in an open context, students generate greater ownership for the activity and derive motivation from this. Planning is a high-level thinking skill and as such will be a key activity for learners who have the ability to think through the implications of their activity and its relationship to the outcomes being sought. Planning also offers scope for learners to demonstrate their creativity in terms of finding 'novel' [for them] ways of approaching an investigation. In the case of Crystal Clear, this might translate into agreeing a 'fair test' protocol for comparing the sweetness of different fruit juices or the selection of a cost-effective enzyme system for clarifying the selected juices.

DIRECT INTERACTIVE: EXPERIMENTING – CARRYING OUT

Carrying out the investigation effectively means following the plan that has been made. The ability to do this in a consistent and reproducible way will require students to have or develop the skills required for the practical context – that is, they will have the ability and the dexterity to manipulate equipment, read instruments and to make appropriate observations within the dynamic of the laboratory or field context. Expert leadership, such as that provided by the National Centre for Biotechnology Education (NCBE), can introduce students to experimental techniques and protocols, which help make accessible exciting new areas of science. For example, within a Year 11 summer school context, students were challenged with this question:

Some medicinally important proteins, e.g. insulin, are now produced using genetically modified bacteria – a cheap and rapid method. But how do you clone the gene that encodes the protein, and how is the gene then introduced into bacteria where it is expressed?

(NCBE and Exscitec 2007)

Under direct instruction, students were able to learn how to cut DNA sequences (using restriction enzymes) and paste them into DNA carrier molecules called plasmids (using the enzyme DNA ligase). The different forms of the plasmid were then separated and visualized by gel electrophoresis. Through the process of transformation, students then introduce a plasmid into bacteria. After incubation, successfully transformed bacterial colonies were selected by their ability to grow in the presence of an antibiotic and by a colour change – characteristics encoded by the plasmid.

Participants in this workshop therefore gained hands-on experience of molecular genetics by working with scientists skilled in using techniques such as handling bacteria safely under aseptic conditions. The opportunity to work with experts adds a new dimension to work in science, especially when this might also expose students to university or other research facilities. Some university outreach programmes support this level and type of activity, particularly where this might also provide an opportunity for researchers to deliver public engagement activities, which may be a requisite part of their research grants.

Links of this kind can also help to develop the How Science Works contexts for examination work. For example, this summer school activity provided clear links to examination topics from a number of awarding bodies:

- What other useful substances can we make using micro-organisms?
- How can we be sure we are using micro-organisms safely?
- Inheritance and evolution
- Manipulating genes
- Biotechnology
- Gene technology
- Inheritance and survival
- Genetically modified organisms.

INDUCTIVE INQUIRY

Inductive teaching is a model that encourages students to categorise the subject knowledge, skills and understanding that they are learning, and to test and use those categories in challenging their levels of understanding.

(Learning and Skills Network 2007a)

This pedagogy requires students to gather information in response to a stimulus and then to sort and classify it so that they are able to form a hypothesis based on the information they have assembled. The potential exists for the hypothesis to be tested through future work. In terms of the problem-solving cycle this approach reflects the opportunity to further reformulate, change experimental design or modify techniques in preparing for further work of the Inquiry (Deductive) model, where a revised hypothesis can be tested through the accumulation of new data.

An example of this type of activity might be that of students working with molecular models representing alcohols and carboxylic acids, then comparing data about physical properties such as boiling point, looking for similarities, differences and trends. The activity might extend to the formation of esters between the alcohols and acids, again with consideration of their properties in relation to the molecular structures encountered. The use of these molecules in flavourings and fragrances might be a useful additional context for the work.

Given more time, the Inductive Inquiry approach can also prove to be a powerful motivator and an opportunity to explore the concepts that underpin subject knowledge. Within a summer school context, the Generating Genius programme provided students with a series of short lectures from university experts on the devastating impact of malaria on an African village, alongside some information about malaria control measures. Students were provided with information on the geographical location of a village impacted by malaria and a description of the local environment in terms of climate, the proximity to rivers and lakes, and details about the existing infrastructure. They were introduced to information on the cycle of malarial infection and possible techniques for controlling this. The students' challenge was to develop a scientific case for addressing the problem in different ways and to assess the financial implications of these processes for preventing death from malaria. The students were highly motivated by this topic, with some of them having family members who had suffered from or fallen victim to the disease. Working in small teams, they gathered information that allowed cost/benefit to be compared for different methodologies. The teams considered things such as chemical control of mosquitoes using pesticides; engineering control through the drainage of mosquito breeding sites; medical control through vaccination programmes; biological control through genetic manipulation, which might affect the breeding population of mosquitoes; and technological control through solutions such as mosquito nets. Their research included finding data about the cost of such interventions and using this information together with the science case for recommending or comparing different courses of action for poor communities (Exscitec and Generating Genius 2005).

USING MODELS, INTERPRETATION AND EVALUATION

The interpretation phase of the problem-solving cycle requires the investigator to relate the results to the experiment and to evaluate these in the context of the hypothesis and the experimental design. Such evaluation may cause further reformulation of the problem or highlight the need for a change in experimental design that will impact on the planning phase of the cycle. It might also be the case that interpretation and evaluation point to a need to change technique in carrying out the investigation. The interpretation of results or observations allows students to question and possibly to develop their own models for further testing or evaluation by others. The latter stages of the cycle of investigation provide a valuable opportunity for learners to demonstrate their high-level thinking skills and also their creativity in terms of their overcoming what might be perceived to be failure in the early iterations of this cyclical process. Too frequently, students in general are exposed to only segments of this cycle, with little time or opportunity being available for iteration that might cause activity to be repeated and refined. Students may be taught a model or idea, which might help them to visualize an abstract idea; models help students make sense of observations. However, for this teaching strategy to be effective, students need opportunities to use the model to explain related phenomena and through experimentation be presented with opportunities to change models, or possibly generate their own models and analogies. The Learning and Skills Network Triple Science guidance materials (2007b) observe that:

> Teachers may just use a 'good enough' teaching model and neglect to allow students the opportunity to explore the limitations of models or analogies and develop them further. Allowing students to question, restructure and develop their own models to explain other phenomena helps reinforce understanding.

The use of models requires teachers to be aware of the progression in learning of their students in respect of the concepts that will provide the scaffolding for the model to be developed. Difficulties may arise for learners as a consequence of mixing models. A scientific concept is usually first explained to the students using a simple, often older, model. Later, the students are introduced to more sophisticated, often newer models. Justi and Gilbert (2002) reported that students might be confused when a new model is introduced, and thus combine attributes from different models. It is, therefore, important to discuss the differences between the models presented, and to explain clearly why a new model is introduced. Knowledge of models and their uses, and recognition of their limitations in science, would allow students to gain a better understanding of both the scientific facts and the nature of science – that is, how scientific knowledge is achieved (Kinnear 1991; Boulter and Gilbert 2000). This process can be illustrated with the approaches to teaching about acids and bases and is highlighted in detail within teachers' perceptions of the teaching of acids and bases in Swedish upper secondary schools (Drechsler and Van Driel 2009).

Historically, the model used to describe acids, the Boyle model, was one in which acids are defined in terms of phenomenological properties such as sour taste, ability to neutralize bases, turning blue litmus red. Much later in historical terms, and later in terms of students' ability to develop the concept of an acid, comes the Arrhenius model of 1890, which describes acids as substances that form hydrogen ions in water; bases dissolve in water to form hydroxide ions. Arrhenius defined acids as substances that are ionised by water to produce hydrogen ions in aqueous solution. This model, however, requires students to be able to understand and use a particulate model within which molecules dissociate to form ions. It is therefore important for teachers to identify the content knowledge required by learners in advance of introducing a model that relies on other models for its assimilation and use. It is also important for teachers to be aware of this issue when students are gathering information from secondary sources.

CONCLUSION

In preparing university outreach courses for learners in the context of both short and long intervention periods, we have found it valuable to blend teaching models when introducing practical activity and sustaining the work once it is initiated. We have adopted a common pattern across a number of courses designed to provide students with support for understanding how science works. The provision includes:

■   background and range finding through demonstration lectures;
■   problem analysis and question-raising using mentors;
■   team working and discussion to reformulate and plan possible investigations;
■   time to carry out a meaningful investigation and establish a body of results data;
■   interpretation and opportunity for model testing and reformulation for further investigation;
■   presentation of outcomes to peers and those who introduced the topic area;
■   ongoing support and discussion through a closed-community managed learning environment (MLE) and the potential for publication of outcomes via this medium.

It is also valuable within this short overview to reflect on the comments of a small group of learners who have experienced outreach intervention based on developing and understanding How Science Works and who have subsequently entered the scientific community. Although this is a small sample, there are some interesting common features that emerge about making science practical work meaningful for these learners.

> Science teaching across Curriculum in school was not stimulating; we really didn't get taught very much that was stimulating. KS 3 and GCSE was basic stuff; the chance to do project work and do my own research was a good motivation. Until Yr 10 we would dabble in interesting areas and we went quite fast but by Yr 11 we had to refocus our learning and just do what was on the curriculum and so we took 10 steps back and did things that we did in Yr 8 and this undermined the whole system. Practical work is massively important. Whilst theory is good, practical application is so important; practical clarifies many things. Newton's laws [1st 2nd and 3rd laws of motion] are an excellent example and this illustrates how they [scientists] determine these equations – where you are proving a concept through a demonstration. Anything happening in front of you is a proof of how it all works. It bridges the gaps between the text books and science to the real world. How could you learn if you don't have a practical? It's not enough just to read about it! Seeing it in practice and doing it yourself you can alter and see what happens [if you are] just watching you don't have that control.
>
> (Steven, who is now conducting research in astrophysics)

> In secondary school we started more formal science. It was early on with the red cabbage experiment that I really started to latch on to science; it was fun and through good teaching and practical work, like the experiments in Biology, it was stimulating. I enjoyed the idea of tests on your own body, so biology was more fun in the beginning because it was more relevant to me. Flash bang chemistry – magnesium burning was also fun. Copper sulfate blue, add zinc and then the zinc displaces the copper – displacement reactions were fun! Putting a scenario around the experiment, like a murder investigation – who killed who? – through a chemical test also inspired me. There was a purpose to it all and you were doing real science. Without realising it, you have used knowledge to get to a solution. Practical work was good because lessons passed much quicker. I quite often found that lessons were going too slowly and theory in lessons was boring and tiresome.
>
> (Jad, now a research scientist in CERN)

> There were more practicals in Year 9 than in GCSE when there was just more course work. The topic you could choose yourself but maybe no variations; whatever the topics were, we all seemed to do the same thing in the same way. No clear progress was seen here and it made it quite dull. Too often problems given to us were trivial and did not really involve problem solving at all. We were simply expected to regurgitate what we could have read about more quickly
>
> (Florencia, now undertaking postgraduate research)

> I find school science immensely frustrating to teach. I don't feel that it is a subject that can be examined effectively and attempts to do so strike me as having produced a curriculum that is prescriptive in a field where students need the independence to think freely above all else. I found, in particular, that Physics is taught with a great deal of analogies that are not only misleading but also only necessary because topics

must be moved through quickly. This leaves a superficial approach where students are not really encouraged to question; even in practical work there is always an answer the students are expected to produce. How Science Works should provide opportunities to recreate the original conditions of discovery around a particular bit of Science or, give students opportunities to consider many answers, not just one, and the freedom to choose between them – like a real engineering problem. When we offer an activity, it doesn't matter if a student knows the particular interpretation of a concept that will appear in their exam; what matters is that they get the idea of what is going on and, most importantly, understands and shares the motivation for investigation in the first place.

(Neil, now working in Outreach)

The Nuffield Bursary scheme places students within science or engineering research environments. Usually undertaken halfway through a course of post-16 study, the scheme involves students spending between four and six weeks working as members of a research team. Saranja participated in the programme during the summer of 2009 and made observations which again highlight a dislocation between her experience of school science and work within a science/engineering research environment.

Certainly, a Nuffield student starts from scratch, and will inevitably hit a brick wall several times during the placement, as I did. This experience improved my lateral thinking as I quickly learnt to approach the same problem from different angles, as scientists have done so in the past – every scientist will try to find a way to resolve any issue that offends their solution. By doing a Nuffield Project, a student can briefly undergo the thought processes of famous scientists – they will look at an issue and consider how and why it is occurring and produce innovative solutions/discoveries – this is how science develops and it is easier to understand the process once you have tried it yourself.

As I carried out an engineering project in a high security organisation, data collection was impossible – hence, this made me think about how I could justify my choices (i.e. which structural and scientific concept I selected). So, I had to think of qualitative (diagrams) and quantitative (trade-off studies/spreadsheets) techniques, which I had not used before. This was new to me, especially because I was used to the classroom environment where practical activities are pre-determined and designed such that they produce the perfect set of results. Real science is not like that, and relationships between the different variables are not easy to spot in real life – the Nuffield project emphasized this, and allowed me to learn new methods of analysis and interpretation. Finally, the Nuffield Project also enables you to display your work to a whole variety of audiences, I for one explained my project to numerous curious engineers at EADS Astrium (and suffered much interrogation as a result). Having to answer questions from a professional engineer in itself forces you to consider your project to great depth, but even the differing views of scientists and engineers with backgrounds in different disciplines was also very interesting.

Also, when carrying out a project in industry, you learn to look at how other factors influence the quality of your solution – for example, money is important, and in my case, the reason I investigated aerobots and not satellites was because aerobots were a much cheaper option.

(Saranja, 2009 A level student)

What do we take from these personal statements? Students interviewed place a high level of importance on a stimulating science intervention or experience, coupled with owning the science taking place within an investigation. Working with large numbers of learners through CREST and in the context of summer school and master class activity makes it clear that problem-solving approaches, embodying students' own investigations, provide an excellent vehicle for enriching the science experience for learners. The challenge facing teachers through How Science Works is to develop provision that exposes many more students to holistic science experiences rather than relying on intervention. It seems to remain the case for too many that this type of enhancement is only made through intervention that causes students to be removed from the usual teaching environment and placed in some kind of specialist arena. What, therefore, makes a school laboratory a special place? Is it somewhere for students to take notes, watch a DVD, listen to a teacher or is it a place for scientific investigation, discussion and review of scientific work? Schools benefit from different levels of investment in terms of their laboratory facilities, but how much time is actually used by students for laboratory work and does this reflect the investment that has been made in terms of the infrastructure? Hopefully, the drive to provide all students with experience of how science works will mean that school laboratories are viewed with the same degree of excitement and anticipation as visiting research spaces outside of the school environment.

FURTHER READING

TRIPLE SCIENCE COMMUNITY PAGES

http://community.triplescience.org.uk/Pages/Default.aspx
(This offers a free registration service and subsequent access to a host of downloadable resources and references.)

QUICK GUIDES

http://community.triplescience.org.uk/News/Pages/QuickGuidesdevelopedwithRC-UKnowav ailabletodownloadfromtheTripleScienceSupportProgrammeWebsite.aspx

REFERENCES

Boulter, C. and Gilbert, J. K. (2000) Challenges and opportunities of developing models in science education, in J. K. Gilbert and C. Boulter (eds), *Developing Models in Science Education*, Dordrecht, the Netherlands: Kluwer Academic Publishers.

British Science Association (2009) CREST. Online. Available HTTP: <http://www. britishscienceassociation.org/web/ccaf/CREST/> (accessed 3 December 2009).

Drechsler, M. and Van Driel, J. (2009) Teachers' perceptions of the teaching of acids and bases in Swedish upper secondary schools, *Chemistry Education Research and Practice* 10(86), 86–96.

Exscitec and NCBE (2006) Entrepreneurial Bioscience Course, Imperial College London, Exscitec Limited and National Centre for Biotechnology Education, unpublished course materials.

Exscitec and Generating Genius 2005, unpublished course materials.

Justi, R. and Gilbert, J. K. (2002) Modelling, teachers' views on the nature of modelling, and implications for the education of modellers, *International Journal of Science Education* 24(4), 369–387.

Kinnear, J. (1991) Using an historical perspective to enrich the teaching of linkage in genetics, *Science Education* 75, 69–85.

Learning and Skills Network (2007a) *Teaching Triple Science: GCSE Physics*, London: Learning and Skills Network.

Learning and Skills Network (2007b) *Teaching Triple Science: GCSE Biology*, London: Learning and Skills Network.

Murphy, P. and Gott, R. (1984) Assessment of Performance Unit. Science report for teachers: 2. Science Assessment Framework Age 13 and 15. London: Department of Education and Science, Welsh Office, Department of Education for Northern Ireland.

National Centre for Biotechnology Education and Exscitec (2007) HEFCE Year 11 Summer School, Imperial College London, unpublished course materials.

National Strategies (2009) *How Science Works*. Online. Available HTTP: <http://nationalstrategies.standards.dcsf.gov.uk/node/102668> (accessed 3 December 2009).

THE ROLE OF INFORMATION AND COMMUNICATIONS TECHNOLOGY

Jocelyn Wishart

INTRODUCTION

Electronic computers and other information and communications technologies (ICTs) have been important to scientists in their work since their invention (by scientists) in the 1950s. Without powerful machines able to carry out many thousands of calculations in seconds it is unlikely that man would have ventured far into space, let alone landed on the Moon or devised spacecraft such as the Cassini Explorer and the Hubble Telescope that are currently mapping the universe. We would not have been able to start decoding the human genome without the ability to share huge databases of genetic information, or design drugs to target specific interactions within the human body without sophisticated three-dimensional computer modelling systems. In fact, it would be difficult to identify a scientific development in the past 30 years that did not rely on the use of computers for data processing and storage. The World Wide Web itself was developed by Tim Berners-Lee to facilitate sharing of information among scientists, in this case, particle physicists working at CERN in the 1980s.

Following a similar meteoric rise, the use of ICT now plays a major role within science education. In its summary review of the importance of ICT to UK schools, Ofsted (2009) commends a range of activities found in school science departments, including the use of digital video cameras to record experiments and employing the video in subsequent presentations, and the use of data logged from environmental sensors within the school building to learn about heat loss and sustainability. It also highlights the use of handheld personal digital assistants (PDAs) to collect data and images by students working collaboratively in class and on field trips. In all, there appear to be five forms of ICT used within school science which are relevant to teaching and learning (Osborne and Hennessy 2003). These include:

- tools for data capture, processing and interpretation, including data logging systems, data analysis software (e.g. Insight), databases and spreadsheets (e.g. Excel);
- multimedia software for simulation of processes and carrying out 'virtual experiments' (e.g. Science Investigations 1, Chemistry Set, Multimedia Science School);

- information systems such as CD-ROM encyclopedias, the World Wide Web and school-based learning platforms;
- publishing and presentation tools (e.g. Word, PowerPoint);
- digital recording equipment – still and video cameras;
- computer projection technology – interactive whiteboards or data projectors plus screens.

Of these, by far the most relevant to the everyday work of professional scientists working in industry, research and manufacture today are the tools for data capture, processing (including modelling) and interpretation. Scientists also rely on information systems such as electronic databases and journals to support them in their research in addition to presentation tools to publish their work. McFarlane and Sakellariou (2002) point out the iterative nature of this process; their model (Figure 9.1) shows how scientists' work with ICT can be used to structure students' experience of science at the school level.

However, developments in ICT are characterized by the speed with which things change, and recent advances in computing such as the development of social networking (web 2.0) tools, grid computing and PDAs have now further changed the way scientists can work. This chapter focuses on these relatively new developments in ICTs that have enabled scientists to change the way they collect, record, analyse and share information as part of their work. It is therefore organized into four sections that acknowledge the key roles played by data, including their collection, storage and processing, and communication (of the information derived from the data) in teaching How Science Works with ICT.

The first section of the chapter focuses on data collection and includes an acknowledgement of the central role electronic monitoring devices play in logging the data from

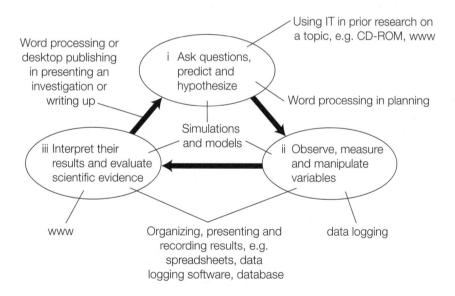

■ **Figure 9.1** Model of the iterative process of science that can be used to structure experience of science at the school level with some examples of uses of ICT
Source: Adapted from McFarlane (2000)

experiments in locations as diverse as a centrally heated, climate-controlled university laboratory and the permanently frozen, windswept Antarctic wastes. Real-time data logging has been central to scientists' understanding of many processes, and now, new handheld devices mean that both scientists and students studying science, young and old, can collect and analyse data, on the spot, wherever they happen to be. It includes a vignette from a research project investigating how science teacher trainees explored the potential of PDAs for supporting science teaching and learning.

One aspect then springs to mind: what are the scientists going to do with all the data now being collected and how can these data be stored safely and responsibly? The latest mainframe computer installed at the University of Bristol, Blue Crystal 2, has 73 terabytes of storage. That's 73 million megabytes, enough to store the complete genome sequences of over 24,000 individuals or over 14 million copies of the complete works of Shakespeare. Thus, the next section of the chapter addresses the storage and sharing of scientific data. Parallels are drawn for the science teacher attempting to manage good practice in the classroom environment.

The third section of the chapter focuses on the role of ICT in processing large quantities of data. Many of today's scientists work on projects such as modelling protein folding, weather forecasting and brain imaging. Computer-based modelling is also common in schools, where it has been found that encouraging students to build models enables them to develop an understanding both of modelling as a process in science investigation and of the scientific ideas that they are attempting to model (Brodie *et al*.1994; Webb 1993). The most complex models, such as those used for weather forecasting and climate change predictions, are run on networks of powerful computers such as Blue Crystal 2 forming distributed, computer power-sharing grids. In addition to producing complex visualizations that aid scientists in interpreting patterns in their data, the grids can also enable collaborative data analysis. There are a number of international projects where scientists, across the globe, are sharing their data with school students to engage them in conducting real science experiments.

Scientists do not necessarily need powerful research or industry-sponsored computing facilities; many are finding that web 2.0 tools such as wikis and blogs enable them to engage in necessary debate with their peers over social, ethical and environmental impact of their findings. The final section of this chapter considers how the internet has changed the way scientists publish their work and enabled new avenues for professional discourse. This is being mirrored in secondary schools, where Ofsted (2009) report, that students make the best use of ICT in communicating their ideas and presenting their work. This section includes a vignette of a research project investigating the use of online discussion for teaching about ethical issues in science. Lastly, it addresses the need for science teachers to teach their students how to check online publications for reliability and validity.

DATA COLLECTION

Collecting data through observation is central to scientists' work. They use a wide range of electronic sensors to detect and record physical and chemical changes in their investigations. Similarly, much use of ICT in school science lessons has centred on data logging, where software running on a laptop or desktop PC is used to display recordings from simple sensors measuring temperature, light, pH levels, etc. While such experiments can seem complex to set up, for sensors need first to be plugged into an interface that must be connected to the computer; they are generally thought to provide valuable learning opportunities. Frost (2010) hosts details of over forty data logging experiments taken from UK science classrooms on his Dataloggerama website. Using such tools for data capture and display frees students from laborious processes (Osborne and Hennessy 2003) that include the need to regularly take readings and to plot the relevant points on a graph of their data. This freedom allows students working together to discuss the shape of a graph as it emerges in real time on the computer screen. Newton (1997) found that such talk can help develop students' appreciation of the meaning of patterns in their data and their skills in communicating about it.

Data logging sensors can also be connected to handheld computers or PDAs and taken outside the classroom to collect data in the real-world environment. This allows students to collect authentic data and enables them to see 'on the spot' how their recordings relate to the processes being observed. From his experience of the Science Learning in Context project, Krajcik (2001) describes this learning in real-world environments and enabled through the use of handheld devices as contextualized, active and constructed through interaction with others. The project itself involved students from schools in Michigan and Washington using handheld Palm Pilots with probeware for a range of data-logging activities outside the classroom. In a typical example a class of grade 7 students monitored the quality of water in a nearby stream with pH, temperature, conductivity and dissolved oxygen probes (sensors). Their teachers reported that the students showed enhanced understanding and motivation for learning in this way (Novak and Gleason 2001). In particular, the teachers were impressed by the growth they observed in their students' ability to analyse and synthesize collected data.

More recently, the inclusion of Global Positioning System (GPS) receivers in handheld devices such as mobile phones has enabled locations as well as data to be recorded. In the Participate project (Woodgate *et al.* 2007), Year 10 students at a school in Bath logged carbon monoxide levels and GPS coordinates on their routes to and from school. These were then displayed for the class on Google Earth. Woodgate *et al.* (ibid*.)* report that such visualizations not only made previously invisible information more concrete and more understandable to the students but also supported them in reflecting on and discussing their findings. The pupils themselves indicated that participating in the project had helped them learn that environmental issues were part and parcel of their everyday lives. In another GPS-enabled project, WildKey, researchers worked with 937 children aged from 6 to 14 using PDAs with integrated GPS running digital species identification keys to identify wildlife and record its location (Hughes 2007). The data collected could be uploaded to a desktop computer back in the classroom and maps or graphs produced, for example by using a Google Earth mash-up (a mash-up is the combination of data from two or more digital sources to create a new service). The children's teachers agreed that using WildKey on handheld computers provided a worthwhile learning experience and motivated their students. They also agreed that it provided an improvement on paper-based keys and that having access to such a resource would enhance their own confidence in leading wildlife identification sessions with their pupils.

Data logging has recently received an unanticipated boost from the Apple iPhone, released in the United Kingdom in 2007, which has become the latest 'must have' gadget for school physics teachers. Its internal accelerometers sense angular rotation and acceleration. This has led to teachers showing off apps such as Dynolicious to their classes. This displays recordings of the teacher's car's speed and charts its acceleration. Roller Coaster Physics, which will graph how the acceleration and velocity of an individual change as the person carrying it rides a roller coaster or simply gets in a lift, is also becoming popular.

Thus, handheld computers, PDAs and similar mobile devices can be seen to offer contextualized, constructive, authentic opportunities for science learning. Sharples *et al.* (2005) propose a theory of learning for the mobile age that highlights interaction between learner and context, as well as between learners, and between learners and their devices. Teachers need to be aware of the importance of concepts of control, context and communication to interactions involving learning via mobile devices both outside the science classroom and when the students return to it.

Box 9.1 **Can PDAs support science teaching as well as learning?**

Handheld computers or PDAs are becoming popular in professions such as medicine and law where access to an extensive body of knowledge is needed at varying locations. It is clear that trainee science teachers too need access to information such as course documentation, timetables, emails from their tutor or mentor, pupil attendance records and grades, science constants and formulae exactly when and where it is needed to support their teaching or learning. This information may come from applications on the PDA, dedicated science software or the web, especially via a course-linked virtual learning environment (VLE), or from previously recorded pupil data or via communications with peers and tutors.

Science teachers in a secondary school and small group of teacher trainees were loaned internet-enabled PDAs in a small-scale study (Wishart 2009) set up to investigate whether such devices could support student science teachers in their teaching and learning. Results were varied; however, both teachers and trainee teachers recognized the potential of the PDA for learning and teaching support as described by Naismith *et al.* (2004) and identified the same three software applications as central to this potential as had been identified in an earlier study (Wishart *et al.* 2007b). These were the calendar or diary scheduler for organizing yourself (shown in Figure 9.2), the spreadsheet of attendance or mark book for organizing your students, and the use of a word processor to make notes on information and events immediately after they are encountered (shown in Figure 9.3). This latter activity was particularly supportive of trainees' learning; on teaching placement they would make notes in separate files on their PDAs, as shown in Figure 9.3, and later, through a process linked to further research and reflection, reconstruct those notes into a reflective essay demonstrating their learning.

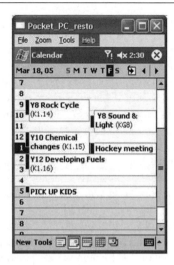

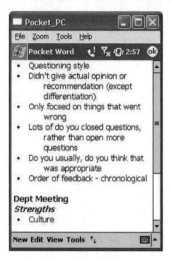

■ **Figure 9.2** A teacher's timetable   ■ **Figure 9.3** A student teacher's notes

The effectiveness of these kinds of activities is reinforced by this student's report:

> During teaching practice I have found myself constantly bombarded with new and noteworthy information (e.g. scientific facts, ideas for teaching approaches, school procedures, evidence for QTS standards etc.). The PDA has allowed me to keep meaningful notes of this information, and structure the information in a way that allows me to access it easily.

Teachers also found note-taking on the PDA useful, for example when meeting colleagues by chance in the corridor between lessons. Other activities had individual champions. One member of staff was very emphatic about how useful it was to set up a class administration system in Excel on a desktop computer and synchronize it to the PDA so that it could be quickly and easily updated during lessons. He used multiple worksheets for attendance, grades, practical science skills achieved and commendations. Another teacher was particularly positive about his use of the camera, taking photos and video clips of lesson activities to later play back to his students in revision classes.

Lastly, several of the trainee teachers reported a feeling of confidence about their use of the PDA, especially being able to access the internet wherever they happened to be, for both personal and professional information. Also, the ability to use and then hide the PDA back in a pocket or bag led to its being perceived as an educational technology that was more manageable in front of students than a desktop computer.

STORING AND SHARING DATA

Data logging implies both recording and storage of data. It is important that scientists and teachers understand how setting up initial parameters such as sample rate can affect the amount of data that needs to be stored. Data logging equipment now found in schools can check, say, the temperature of a liquid, up to 50,000 times a second. Two sensors accidentally set at this rate are going to produce 360 Mb of data per hour. Video data too produce files of huge sizes sufficient to overload a school network in seconds if stored without due care and attention. Researchers in a recent project, Bioethics Live! (BEEP 2010), that involved pupils producing video clips as part of learning about ethical debates in science, observed the students lose their work as they saved their edited video to the default network drive rather than to the computers' hard drives as they had been instructed. However, once safely stored in electronic format on World Wide Web servers, data resulting from scientific experiments can readily be widely shared.

The potential for increasing the scope and scale of research by globally sharing digital research data from publicly funded projects was formally recognized by ministers for science from the thirty-four countries of the Organisation for Economic Co-operation and Development's Committee for Scientific and Technological Policy in 2004 (OECD 2004). Scientists across the world have agreed to support the creation of research data archives that can promote scientific progress through underpinning future investigations, encouraging scientific inquiry and providing resources for education and training. Additionally, scientific journals such *Science* and *Nature* now support the need to archive and collate published data for the use of the scientific community. This policy of open access reaches beyond the research community. Currently, many ongoing scientific endeavours such as NASA, BBC Springwatch and the British Antarctic Survey are making their data available in a form accessible to science teachers for use with their pupils directly as they are captured. Other science projects or resources such as the Faulkes telescope (2010) and Jason Science (2010) have been set up specifically to share data between scientists, teachers and school pupils.

Data-sharing between schools is also easily achieved via the internet. In the Sense project (Woodgate *et al.* 2007a), a forerunner to the Participate project described earlier, children aged between 9 and 14 in Nottingham and Sussex shared and compared their environmental monitoring data. They also discussed their data with a pollution expert remotely. It was found that, as well engaging in authentic scientific inquiry, the pupils from different schools who had engaged in similar processes came to understand new perspectives on their own and others' data. A much larger project, Kids as Global Scientists, involved 3,500 schoolchildren in collecting weather data across the United States. The students measured and shared their observations on wind speed, temperature, air pressure and precipitation as well as engaging in online communication about their results with professional meteorologists (Mistler-Jackson and Songer 2000). An in-depth investigation of one Grade 6 class participating in this project concluded that the authentic nature of the project, communication with professionals, and collaboration among students supported science content knowledge gains and opportunities for the development of self-efficacy. Such projects do not have to involve creating complex websites and online data repositories. Jarvis *et al.* (1997) found that primary school children from six different primary schools collaborated successfully by email to log varieties of moths found in their different local habitats.

This use of ICT in education, to enable local and remote communication and collaboration on scientific topics and with scientific data, has been defined as eScience (Woodgate and Stanton Fraser 2005). Underwood *et al.* (2008) point out the need for considerable preparation on the part of the teacher for planning on engaging in eScience in the classroom. They note the bulk of the teachers' time spent on eScience activities (46 per cent) involved locating and/or creating materials such as multimedia, worksheets, lesson plans and data recording proformas that were intended to make the activity accessible, appropriate, relevant and engaging for specific learners. Other key activities involved matching the science activity to curricular requirements, coordinating collaboration and communication (global time zones can be a particular issue), manipulating data into a format suitable for pupils, managing equipment and, last but not least, testing equipment and fixing breakdowns. This final activity comprised 25 per cent of time spent and remains a significant challenge to educators. Issues noted included the need to check that the 'chat' or videoconferencing software is allowed on school networks, to check that batteries are charged, to learn how to 'wake up' the PDA and to wait for an initial GPS fix. As with the storing of video noted earlier, these technical issues that bedevil pioneering teachers and educational researchers should diminish with practice.

Internationally, areas where collaboration and sharing of previously recorded data between scientists are proving fruitful include the study of climate change and the mapping of the human genome. In particular, the study of climate and environment is ideal for collecting and sharing data, and a good starting point for a simple eScience project in school. On a more global scale, the World Data Center system comprises fifty-two centres across twelve countries which store baseline information for research by international scientists, especially for monitoring changes in the geosphere and biosphere. The Globe Program (2010), set up in 1995 to engage schools with authentic science inquiry projects supporting research scientists, is now established as one of the leading international eScience projects. Having involved more than 7,000 schools in 100 countries at the time of writing, it is now planning a two-year student research campaign on climate change, starting in 2011. The project team expects to recruit more than a million students, empowering them and their teachers to engage in meaningful and relevant research to enhance climate literacy and understanding. Evaluation of the Globe Program (Penuel *et al*. 2006) suggests that for effective student learning and engagement in eScience, teachers must make time for teaching subject matter content and considering practical implementation issues in their planning. Additionally, teachers may need support in setting up equipment and in 'localizing' the project aims within their classroom context.

One of the best-known examples of a collaboratively built data resource is the Human Genome Project (HGP). Started in 1990 at an estimated cost of $3 billion, it aimed to sequence the human genome to find out the exact structure of the entire DNA in a human cell. Therefore, the project needed to identify all the 20,000-plus genes in human DNA and to determine the sequences of the base pairs in each gene (approximately 3 billion). To do this, scientists had to devise new software for data analysis and to create vast databases. About two-thirds of the HGP was completed in the United States; other scientists around the world, including the United Kingdom, Germany, France, Japan and Canada, were allocated individual chromosomes to sequence. The project, originally planned to last for 15 years, was actually completed in 2003 because scientists developed improved techniques for sequencing the genes. It has resulted in shared understanding of the human genome, inherited disorders and a variety of gene therapies across the world. However, scientists and science teachers need to be aware of ethical considerations over the storing of such data. Many scientific data, like the DNA sequences collected from individuals by the HGP, have impact beyond their intended purpose. In particular, there are issues with privacy and confidentiality. Scientists and health professionals gaining access to genetic data must keep them confidential and store them safely. For example, insurance companies would be particularly interested in discovering whether an individual has inherited a tendency to develop a particular disorder. In the United Kingdom the storing of personal data is regulated by the Data Protection Act (1998), which contains specific data protection principles that require that data are processed only for the purposes for which they were acquired, kept up to date and stored securely.

PROCESSING DATA: ANALYSING AND MODELLING

One key aspect of ICT that has proved immensely useful to scientists is the speed with which data can be processed. Many science investigations involve recording observations, usually repeatedly to ensure reliability, and then using them in further calculation. In both science laboratories and schools the use of computer software such as spreadsheets to do this has freed up time which can be used by researchers and learners to focus on the underpinning science concepts – though it should be noted that pupils need to be specifically directed to make the best use of this time (Newton 2000). Creative ways in which teachers used this 'time bonus' include sharing results, prompting analysis and discussion, and generally emphasizing the interpretation of results with associated thinking about the underpinning science (Rogers and Finlayson 2003).

The vastly increased speeds of data analysis now available have led to the popularity of modelling as a process for developing science knowledge. Scientists developing new drugs or attempting to predict the behaviour of weather systems, for example, can build digital three-dimensional images of possible interactions and try out many possible scenarios. In schools, spreadsheets enable speedy, multiple calculations, allowing pupils to practise 'what if?' scenarios where they change the parameters of a theory-based mathematical model and engage with the underpinning science as they review the outcomes. Spreadsheet models commonly seen in school science classrooms include predator–prey relationships, projectile motion and dietary analysis. In their analysis of English science teachers' use of ICT in a range of lessons resulting from a national training programme, Rogers and Finlayson (2003) found that more able pupils in particular were extended by the opportunities that spreadsheet modelling enabled for prompt reflection on the results and further exploratory thinking. Teachers also frequently recognized that while using an ICT model that engaged the more able, they had more time to give attention to the lower-achieving pupils.

However, Sins et al. (2005) point out that students do not always find modelling easy. In an in-depth investigation of eleventh grade students modelling how friction affects an ice skater, they found that students working on building their own model tended to focus only on adjusting the model parameters to fit the empirical data they had been given. Sins et al. (2005) concluded that teachers need to scaffold this kind of task carefully to focus their pupils' attention on relevant prior knowledge.

Moving beyond mathematical models and use of spreadsheets, Osborne and Hennessy (2003) note that specially designed modelling tools can provide dynamic, visual representations of data collected electronically or otherwise. Use of these tools in the classroom offers immediate feedback to pupils, and introduces a more experimental, inquiring style in which 'what if?' trends are investigated and pupils' ideas are tested and refined. Such models used to visualize and simulate underpinning science processes support children's learning through immediate feedback and through making the invisible (the movement of particles in a sound wave or during evaporation, for example) visible. These types of simulations are now widely available from science teaching resource websites. Teachers in Rogers and Finlayson's

(2003) survey often cited their use in an investigative approach to task design, where pupils are encouraged to make predictions and then use the software to test them, as a successful teaching strategy. Other teachers and researchers have created specialist computer-based simulations that model the processes of scientific inquiry in order to investigate the potential role for ICT in teaching How Science Works. In particular, these generate simulated data, often accompanied by context-relevant images and animations for students to analyse. Some successful examples include the Euroturtle Virtual Field Station (Poland *et al.* 2003) and Blast – a simulated gene sequencing tool (Gelbert and Yarden 2006). However, it is important to note that a theoretical science model underpins any simulation of this kind. Hennessy *et al.* (2007) highlight one teacher's concerns about the predictability of the dataset programmed into the simulation of a school laboratory experiment that he was using to study the effect of temperature upon enzymes. The teacher also disclosed his pleasure that a number of his more able students realized this limitation of computer models. Tinker (1993) suggests that the study of modelling itself should be part of the science curriculum so that pupils understand how models are constructed, their utility and their limitations.

Computer visualization tools can be used with data as well as models. Colours are used to indicate subtle differences in observations of temperature, pressure, density, conductivity and depth, and it is now common to see brightly coloured satellite images, body scans, weather charts and digital micrographs. With the processing power of grid computers working in parallel it is now possible for scientists to work collaboratively in global teams on visualizations shared over the internet. Recent research highlights from the Open Science Grid (2010) include DNA sequence analysis to identify new viruses, analysis of laser interferometry data to detect gravitational waves, and the study of elementary particles through analysis of nuclear decay. The CoVis Project (Pea 2002) was set up to understand how science education could take advantage of these technologies. It brought together teams of researchers from two universities, a science centre, a telecomms provider, teachers from over fifty middle and high schools in the United States, and thousands of pupils. Pupils were provided with a range of collaboration and communication tools. These included desktop videoconferencing, shared software environments for remote real-time collaboration, access to the resources of the internet, a multimedia scientist's 'notebook' and scientific visualization software. The project aimed to develop new curricula and new pedagogical approaches that could take advantage of project-enhanced science learning via collaborative visualization supported by high-performance computing and communications tools. The researchers found such project-enhanced science with its model of science learning via cognitive apprenticeship (with pupils guided, both by their teachers and by remote mentors, to think about science in many of the ways that scientists do) to be a fundamental pedagogy for achieving deeper learner understanding and distributed intelligence among the science learning community. In contrast to the common 'course delivery' models of instruction and distance learning, the advantage of such communities is that learning is situated with respect to community-based goals and activities in which knowledge is developed and used.

SHARING RESULTS AND MAKING DECISIONS

The final stage in McFarlane and Sakellariou's (2002) iterative model of the process of science that can be used to structure the use of ICT in school science (Figure 9.1) comprises the use of ICT tools such as word processors and desktop publishing software for sharing experimental results. Publication of findings is important to the development of shared scientific understandings both in school and internationally. It has already been noted that the World Wide Web itself arose from the need for scientists to share the results of their research. Students in school are expected to write up their experimental work. The use of a word processor, especially with teacher-generated templates to scaffold their work, can be supportive here. Also, students are often encouraged to present their findings to the class. Typically, a PowerPoint slide show is created, though this has led to concerns in some classrooms that children can engage more with choosing a font than with explaining the underpinning science. The web itself offers many opportunities for publication and can be used in schools to provide an authentic context for children's writing. For example, in the final phase of the Kids as Global Scientists project mentioned earlier (Mistler-Jackson and Songer 2000), children produced an online newspaper to share their personal stories and expertise. Additionally, features of word processors such as grammar and spelling checkers, text to speech and word prediction can be used to support the writing processes of children with learning disabilities (MacArthur 1996). Nor are students restricted to reporting in text-based media. In the Bioethics Live! project (BEEP 2010) mentioned previously, teachers reported students showing their videos on the BEEP website to both friends and family; and at the time of writing there are nearly 3,000 video clips of school science projects on YouTube.

Research scientists in universities and industry aim to publish their work in academic and professional journals. Their publication record is tremendously important to a scientist, for the quality of their work is often judged by it. Before a paper can be published in an international academic journal it is subjected to the process of peer review. This is where other scientists with expertise in the relevant field read through and check that the work is of sufficient quality and worthy of publication. Many key journals such as *Science*, *Nature* and the *BMJ* have online versions. However, the World Wide Web has also enabled those scientists who are concerned that the peer review process takes too long, or that journals cost too much, to publish their results for open debate. The Directory of Open Access Journals (2010), started by a Swedish university, now has links to over 1,700 academic journals, many of which are peer-reviewed.

In fact, ICT has supported online sharing and debate since the first bulletin boards were developed in the 1990s. Today scientists are quick to take advantage of new technologies such as web 2.0 to help them disseminate their findings. For example, NASA publishes more than twenty blogs, the Large Hadron Collider runs its own blog (US/LHC blog 2010) that people can also follow via Twitter, and a group of international climate scientists have set up RealClimate (RealClimate 2010), a commentary site with a blog and a wiki. Many teachers too have created blogs in order to provide their pupils with science resources and news that can be accessed any time from outside school. Examples include teachers from North Chadderton School (PlanetScience Support 2010) who provide support and resources for Key Stage 3 and 4 science teachers in England, and The Frog Blog (St Columba's College 2010), a more personal look at science in the news, from St Columba's College in Ireland. Richardson (2006) points out that this explosion in blogging means teachers need to be literate in the ways of web publishing. This means knowing how to check a web source for authenticity, bias, reliability and validity, knowing how to manage information in quantity and knowing how to model being a producer, editor and consumer of web-based information.

Box 9.2 **Using online discussion to teach about ethical issues in science**

Online discussion between scientists has developed from the rather stilted internet relay chat and bulletin boards to instant messaging via Facebook or MSN. Threaded discussion boards were set up by a team based at the University of Bristol to investigate whether online discussion could provide science students with a realistic context where they could practise dialogue and develop their arguments before having to produce them in an examination. The boards were linked to two websites containing background information on ethical issues to support students and their teachers with their discussions.

■ **Figure 9.4** Screen-shot of an online discussion board

It was found (Wishart et al. 2007a) in a survey of eight schools using the biology site the Bioethics Education Project (http://www.beep.ac.uk) that students and their teachers really liked the design and ease of use of the main site. However, most were unwilling or unable to take the time necessary to find out how to make the most of the opportunities for online discussion. However, the two teachers who did use the online discussion were very positive about the results of the activity. Their students' feedback was also positive. Topics that they had discussed included abortion, euthanasia, human reproduction, when life begins, hedgerows, the human genome and global warming. In fact, five students cited the discussion opportunities as being the best thing about using BEEP. These two schools' students also displayed the greatest skills in developing arguments; their schools were clearly those where practice of skills in argument was an overt part of their science learning experience.

In a second study comparing the use of online discussion with face-to-face discussion, Wishart et al. (2009) found that teachers still appeared reluctant to let their students experiment with online discussion unsupervised. However, within their somewhat smaller than expected sample of ten discussions, the students' dialogue in online discussions clearly demonstrated higher levels of argumentation than that in face-to-face discussions. Online discussion regularly reached Level 5, the highest in the framework put forward by Erduran et al. (2004) for assessing the quality of argument in students' work in science. Students reported that they learned slightly more from online discussion than from face-to-face discussion, a result that was confirmed by their teachers. Wishart et al. (2009) proposed that the asynchronous nature of online discussion is particularly important to developing an evidence-based argument as it enables longer, more thoughtful contributions than were found in the face-to-face discussions.

CONCLUSION

In summary, this chapter has shown that teaching How Science Works in school through ICT can engage pupils and enhance learning in many ways. Different software packages and applications can be deployed effectively by science teachers to scaffold their pupils' learning as they move through the investigative science inquiry cycle. It helps if teachers plan for the key roles played by data (including their collection, storage and processing) and communication (of the information derived from the data) in their teaching of investigative science through ICT.

Additionally, schools may well see more software available to scaffold science inquiry. For instance, the Web-based Inquiry Science Environment (WISE) is designed specifically to harness opportunities offered by the use of ICT to support students' learning through science inquiry (Slotta 2004). Researchers focused on using multimedia and online collaboration to support the process of knowledge integration across scientific activities of observation, analysis, interpretation, reflection and evaluation. They aimed to make the processes of scientific thinking visible with inquiry maps, evidence pages, models, pop-up prompts and hints for analysis and reflection, argument representation and peer review tools. The resulting WISE project's library of investigatory science projects and activities has been well received in hundreds of North American schools.

New ICT tools such as handheld computers and mobile phones, too, are now having an observable impact in schools. In the United Kingdom, the PI (personal inquiry) project (Anastopolou *et al.* 2009) is currently examining the opportunities for science inquiry learning supported by personal mobile devices such as netbooks and hand-held data loggers. The associated online toolkit comprises a scripted set of activities for secondary school children that follow through the complete scientific inquiry process of setting out a research question, data collection, data analysis, presenting conclusions and evaluation. The personal aspect is highlighted with activities investigating fitness and healthy eating coming under the topic of 'Myself' and different environmental investigations brought together under 'My Community'. Early results show that using personal technologies to support personally relevant activities that bridge home and school contexts was very engaging for most students but care needed to be taken with the 'Myself' activities to ensure they were not too personally revealing.

Thus, it appears that, as Osborne and Hennessy (2003) foresaw, the new school science curricula are beginning to enable a stronger link between science-as-it-is-taught and science-as-it-is-practised. As seen in this chapter, researchers in science education and teachers are seizing this opportunity for the integration of ICT within the science curriculum to access information and data and to support their interpretation and critical evaluation. This is necessarily accompanied by a change in pedagogy that focuses on the inclusion of the interactive use of ICT to support and develop school students' scientific observation, reasoning and analytic skills.

FURTHER READING

Barton, R. (ed.) (2004) *Teaching Secondary Science with ICT*, London: McGraw-Hill.

Holliman, R. and Scanlon, E. (2004) *Mediating Science Learning through Information and Communications Technology*, London: RoutledgeFalmer.

Newton, L. R. and Rogers, L. (2001) *Teaching Science with ICT*, London: Continuum.

Osborne, J. and Hennessy, S. (2003) Science education and the role of ICT. Bristol: FutureLab. Online. Available at http://www.futurelab.org.uk/resources/publications-reports-articles/literature-reviews/Literature-Review380.

Sang, D. and Frost, R. (eds) (2005) *Teaching Secondary Science using ICT*, London: Hodder Murray.

REFERENCES

Anastopoulou, S., Sharples, M., Ainsworth, S., Crook, C., Norton, B. and O'Malley, C. (2009) Personal inquiry: lessons learned. Paper presented at MLearn 2009, Orlando, Florida, 28 October.

BEEP (BioEthics Education Project) (2010) Bioethics live! Online. Available HTTP: <http://www.beep.ac.uk/content/1505.0.html> (accessed 17 February 2010).

Brodie, T., Gilbert, J., Hollins, M., Raper, G., Robson, K., Webb, M. and Williams, J. (1994). *Models and Modelling in Science Education*, London: Association for Science Education.

Directory of Open Access Journals (2010) Online. Available HTTP: <http://www.doaj.org/> (accessed 17 February 2010).

Erduran, S., Simon, S. and Osborne, J. (2004) TAPping into argumentation: developments in the use of Toulmin's Argument Pattern in studying science discourse, *Science Education* 88(6), 915–933.

Faulkes Telescope Project (2010) Online. Available HTTP: <http://faulkes-telescope.com/> (accessed 2 January 2010).

Frost, R. (2010) Roger Frost's Dataloggerama. Online. Available HTTP: <http://www.rogerfrost.com/> (accessed 17 February 2010).

Gelbart, H. and Yarden, A. (2006) Learning genetics through an authentic research simulation in bioinformatics, *Journal of Biological Education* 40(3), 107–112.

Globe Program (2010) Online. Available HTTP: <http://www.globe.gov> (accessed 17 February 2010).

Hennessy, S., Wishart, J., Whitelock, D., Deaney, R., Brawn, R., la Velle, L., McFarlane, A., Ruthven, K. and Winterbottom, M. (2007) Pedagogical approaches for technology-integrated science teaching, *Computers and Education* 48, 137–152.

Hughes, L. (2007) Engendering a new generation of wildlife recorders. Oxford: WildKnowledge. Online. Available HTTP: <http://www.wildknowledge.co.uk/media_client/docs/final_report.pdf> (accessed 22 October 2009).

Jarvis, T., Hargreaves, L. and Comber, C. (1997) An evaluation of the role of email in promoting science investigative skills in primary rural schools in England, *Research in Science Education* 27(1), 223–236.

Jason Science (2010) Online. Available HTTP: <http://www.jason.org/> (accessed 2 January 2010).

Krajcik, J. (2001) Supporting science learning in context: project based learning, in R. Tinker and J. S. Krajcik, (eds) *Portable Technologies: Science Learning in Context*, Dordrecht, the Netherlands: Kluwer.

MacArthur, C. A. (1996) Using technology to enhance the writing processes of students with learning disabilities, *Journal of Learning Disabilities* 29(4), 344–354.

McFarlane, A. (2000) The impact of education technology, in P. Warwick and R. Sparks Linfield, (eds) *Science 3–13: The Past, The Present and Possible Futures*, London: RoutledgeFalmer.

McFarlane, A. and Sakellariou, S. (2002) The role of ICT in science education, *Cambridge Journal of Education* 32,(2), 220–232.

Mistler-Jackson, M. and Songer, N. (2000) Student motivation and internet technology: are students empowered to learn science? *Journal of Research in Science Teaching* 37(5), 459–47.

Naismith, L., Lonsdale, P., Vavoula, G. and Sharples, M. (2004) Mobile technologies and learning, Bristol: Futurelab. Online. Available HTTP: <http://www.futurelab.org.uk/resources/publications-reports-articles/literature-reviews/Literature-Review203> (accessed 14 November 2009).

Newton, L. R. (1997) Graph Talk: some observations and reflections on students data-logging, *School Science Review* 79(287), 49–54.

Newton, L. R., (2000) Data-logging in practical science: research and reality, *International Journal of Science Education* 22(12), 1247–1260.

Novak, A. M. and Gleason, C. I. (2001). 'Incorporating portable technology to enhance an inquiry, project-based middle school science classroom', in R. F. Tinker and J. S. Krajcik, (eds) *Portable Technologies: Science Learning in Context*, Dordrecht, the Netherlands: Kluwer.

OECD (Organisation for Economic Co-operation and Development) (2004) Committee for Scientific and Technological Policy, *Science, Technology and Innovation for the 21st Century*, Meeting of the OECD Committee for Scientific and Technological Policy at Ministerial Level, 29–30 January – Final Communique. Online. Available HTTP: <http://www.oecd.org/document/0,2340,en_2649_34487_25998799_1_1_1_1,00.html> (accessed 4 March 2010).

Ofsted (2009) *The Importance of ICT: Information and Communication Technology in Primary and Secondary Schools, 2005/2008*, London: Ofsted Reference: 070035.

Open Science Grid (2010) Online. Available HTTP: <http://www.opensciencegrid.org> (accessed 2 January 2010).

Osborne, J. and Hennessy, S. (2003). *Literature Review in Science Education and the Role of ICT: Promise, Problems and Future Directions*, Bristol: NESTA Futurelab.

Pea, R. D. (2002) 'Learning science through collaborative visualization over the internet', paper presented at Nobel Foundation Virtual Museums Symposium, Stockholm, 26–29 May.

Penuel, W. R., Bienkowski, M., Gallagher, L., Korbak, C., Sussex, W., Yamaguchi, R. and Fishman, B. J. (2006) GLOBE year 10 evaluation: into the next generation. *SRI International*. Online. Available HTTP: <http://www.globe.gov/fsl/evals/y10full.pdf> (accessed 1 November 2009).

PlanetScience Support (North Chadderton School) (2010). On-line. Available HTTP: <http://planetscience.org> (accessed 17 February 2010).

Poland, R., la Velle, L. and Nichol, J. (2003) The virtual field station (VFS): using a virtual reality environment for ecological fieldwork in A-level biological studies – case study 3, *British Journal of Educational Technology* 34(2), 215–231.

RealClimate (2010) Online. Available HTTP: <http://www.realclimate.org/> (accessed 17 February 2010).

Richardson, W. (2006) *Blogs, Wikis, Podcasts, and Other Powerful Web Tools for Classrooms*, Thousand Oaks, CA: Corwin Press.

Rogers, L. and Finlayson, H. (2003) Does ICT in science really work in the classroom? Part 1, The individual teacher experience, *School Science Review* 84(309), 105–111.

St Columba's College (2010) Frog Blog. Online. Available HTTP: <http://blog.sccscience.com/> (accessed 17 February 2010).

Sharples, M., Taylor, J. and Vavoula, G. (2005) Towards a theory of mobile learning *Proceedings of MLearn 2005*. Online. Available HTTP: <http://www.mlearn.org.za/CD/papers/Sharples-%20Theory%20of%20Mobile.pdf> (accessed 20 October 2009).

Sins, P. H. M., Savelsbergha, E. R. and van Joolingen, W. R. (2005) The difficult process of scientific modelling: an analysis of novices' reasoning during computer-based modelling, *International Journal of Science Education* 27(14), 1695–1721.

Slotta, J. D. (2004) The Web-based Inquiry Science Environment (WISE): scaffolding knowledge integration in the science classroom, in M. Linn, E. A. Davis and P. Bell (eds) *Internet Environments for Science Education*, Mahwah, NJ: Lawrence Erlbaum Associates.

Tinker, R. (1993) Modelling and theory building: technology in support of student theorizing, in D. L. Ferguson, (ed.) *Advanced Educational Technologies for Mathematics and Science*, Berlin: Springer.

Underwood, J., Smith, H., Luckin, R. and Fitzpatrick, G. (2008) E-Science in the classroom: towards viability, *Computers and Education* 50, 535–546.

US/LHC blog (2010) Large Hadron Collider blog. Online. Available HTTP: <http://blogs.uslhc.us/> (accessed 17 February 2010).

Webb, M. E. (1993) Computer based modelling in school science, *School Science Review* 74(269), 33–47.

Wishart, J. (2009) Use of Mobile Technology for Teacher Training, in M. Ally, (ed.) *Mobile Learning: Transforming the Delivery of Education and Training*, Edmonton, Canada: AU Press.

Wishart, J., la Velle, L., Green, D. and McFarlane, A. (2007a) Using on-line discussion in the teaching of bioethics: the views of teachers and students, *School Science Review* 88(324), 59–65.

Wishart, J., Ramsden, A. and McFarlane, A. (2007b) PDAs and handhelds: ICT at your side and not in your face, *Technology, Pedagogy and Education* 16(1), 95–110.

Wishart, J., Green, D., Joubert, M. and Triggs, P. (2009) Discussion and Argument in Science (DAIS): comparing online and face to face discussions in bioethics teaching, paper presented at ESERA 2009, Istanbul.

Woodgate, D. and Stanton Fraser, D. (2005) *eScience and Education 2005: A Review:* JISC. Online. Available HTTP: <http://www.jisc.ac.uk/uploaded_documents/ACF2B4.pdf> (accessed 31 August 2010).

Woodgate, D., Stanton Fraser, D. and Crellin, D. (2007) Providing an 'authentic' scientific experience: technology, motivation and learning, in *Proceedings of the Workshop on 'Emerging Technologies for Inquiry-Based Learning in Science*, Thirteenth International Conference on Artificial Intelligence in Education, Marina Del Rey, CA, July.

TEACHING SCIENCE OUTSIDE THE CLASSROOM

Justin Dillon

INTRODUCTION

My own science education was rather traditional and took place almost exclusively in laboratories and classrooms. It was only when I started teaching science and, in particular, A level chemistry that I began to realize the enormous potential offered by, for want of a better phrase, 'the outdoor classroom'. In the 1980s, Nuffield O level and A level courses offered teachers a range of options, many of which focused on the application of science or on some of its historical dimensions. After teaching food science and bio-chemistry options that were interesting, though rather staid, for some years, I went on a weekend course which challenged the way that I saw science teaching and changed the direction of my career for ever.

The course focused on a new A level Chemistry Special Study, Mineral Process Chemistry. Sponsored by the Mineral Industry Manpower Careers Unit, the course involved students extracting metals from two samples of ore. A unique dimension of the option was that it was possible for students to visit an old mine beneath Ecton Hill on the Staffordshire/Derbyshire border. Spoil from the mine provided a source of copper, lead and zinc minerals which, as one's eyes tuned in, became progressively easier to find and identify. Access to the mine was possible through one of the adits – horizontal tunnels that allowed ore to be removed from the mine which operated during the seventeenth, eighteenth and nineteenth centuries. For my students, used to working in anonymous school laboratories in inner London, the opportunities to collect mineral specimens from a hill-top in the Peak District, to feel what it must have been like to have been a copper miner deep beneath the 370-metre hill, and to test the nearby Manifold River water for metal ions were unforgettable and more authentic than anything that they could experience in school. For them, and for me, it was as close as we got to appreciating how science works during the two years of their A-level course.

This chapter, then, examines the potential for teaching science outside the class-room, whether it be fieldwork as described above; visits to museums, science centres, zoos and botanical gardens; or activities in the school grounds. Given the focus of the book on How Science Works, the chapter will concentrate on the affordances such activities, done well, can offer teachers in terms of learning how scientists carry out their activities and on the nature of science.

THE BENEFITS OF OUTDOOR SCIENCE EDUCATION

We have known for some time about the benefits of teaching science outside the classroom (Rickinson *et al.* 2004). A substantial amount of research has been carried out looking at residential and non-residential fieldwork, school visits to museums, aquariums, farms, etc. and at strategies to maximize the learning that takes place. That said, only a limited amount of research has looked at the impact of such experiences on students' views of how science works. So, in order to make the case for teaching science outside the classroom, I will draw not only on research findings but on my own observations carried out during evaluations of projects and initiatives in the United Kingdom and elsewhere.

Taking students into the outdoors has a long history in the United Kingdom (HMI 1985). As well as the physical and mental benefits of outward-bound experiences, the outdoor classroom has offered a range of activities and contexts across the curriculum, including fieldwork opportunities for geographers and biologists, and plays and exhibitions for English teachers and historians. In terms of enriching the science curriculum, every year huge numbers of school students visit the national museums such as the Science Museum and the Natural History Museum or local institutions including the Eden Project, at-Bristol and the newly opened Centre of the Cell in London's East End. The situation in other countries varies, but a recent survey by Phillips *et al.* (2007) found that

> more than 70% of science-rich cultural institutions in the United States have programs specifically designed for school audiences. These programs include supplementary classroom experiences; integrated core academic curricula; student science learning communities located in afterschool, summer, and weekend programs; teacher professional development programs and communities; and even district infrastructure efforts around issues such as standards and assessment development or teacher preparation.
>
> (Bevan *et al.* 2010: 11)

The United Kingdom's provision of science-based visitor attractions is the envy of educators in many countries around the world. That said, there has been some concern in recent years that the numbers of students going on educational trips and visits as part of their science education has fallen. While compelling evidence to support that finding is limited, reasons why it might be the case are not hard to find. Increasing costs (particularly of transport), and worries over risk and litigation (fuelled by occasional statements by some teacher unions), are seen as being behind the perceived fall in visitor numbers (Rickinson *et al.* 2004). In 2002, the Field Studies Council found that only 10 per cent of schools surveyed reported that 14- to 16-year-old students had undertaken some form of science fieldwork activity (Barker *et al.* 2002) – a sharp drop on previous years.

The sector responded strategically to these concerns, commissioning research and lobbying effectively for government action. The success of the Real World Learning Campaign can be judged partly by the fact that in the run-up to the 2005 UK general election, all the major political parties referred to the importance of outdoor learning. One explanation for this political consensus was that earlier in the same year the House of Commons Education Select Committee had published a report summarizing the findings of its inquiry into education outside the classroom. The report's authors were clear that despite some legitimate concerns for students' safety, the case for increasing access to the outside classroom was overwhelming. The committee noted critically, however, that 'neither the DfES or local authorities have done enough to publicise the benefits of education outside the classroom, or to provide strategic leadership or direction in this area' (House of Commons 2005: 5). The committee recommended that there should be a Manifesto for Outdoor Learning, an idea that had its roots in the success of the earlier Music Manifesto. In November 2006 the *Learning outside the Classroom Manifesto* was launched at the Natural History Museum in London. Signatories to the manifesto committed themselves to the statement that 'We believe that every young person should experience the world beyond the classroom as an essential part of learning and personal development, whatever their age, ability or circumstances' (DfES 2006: 1). So, the political support for learning outside the classroom is well established, at least in England and Wales.

As part of the campaign for outdoor learning, a review of research was carried out which critically examined 150 pieces of research on outdoor learning published between 1993 and 2003 (Rickinson *et al*. 2004). The authors summarized their key finding as follows:

> Substantial evidence exists to indicate that fieldwork, properly conceived, adequately planned, well taught and effectively followed up, offers learners opportunities to develop their knowledge and skills in ways that add value to their everyday experiences in the classroom.
>
> (Rickinson *et al*. 2004: 5)

Much of the literature reviewed focused on knowledge and attitudes rather than on aspects of how science works, which is the focus of this book. Nevertheless, many findings that have emerged from the research are relevant to out-of-the-classroom activities that focus on the nature of science and scientists. In particular, the value of preparatory work prior to the activity is well supported by research. Ballantyne and Packer (2002), for example, reported that students who had been prepared for an out-of-the-classroom activity both looked forward to and enjoyed their visit more than students who had not been prepared. A study in Israel by Orion and Hofstein (1994) recommends activities that prepare students for the cognitive (field trip concepts and skills), geographic (field trip setting) and psychological (field trip processes) aspects of fieldwork. In terms of what to do during visits or trips, Ballantyne and Packer warn against over-structuring learning activities, noting that 'the use of worksheets, note-taking and reports were all unpopular with students, and did not appear to contribute greatly to [their] environmental learning' (2002: 228). The value of follow-up activities, completed after returning to school, has been identified by several authors, including Orion and Hofstein (1994) and Uzzell *et al*. (1995). We know enough to make science beyond the classroom effective; the question is, how might it help students to appreciate how science works?

WHAT DOES LEARNING HOW SCIENCE WORKS INVOLVE?

For many teachers, the most familiar outdoor science activities include biological field-work and visits to museums. The traditional canon of outdoor ecological activities includes pond dipping for invertebrates; sampling using quadrats; and measuring the pH, nitrate level and turbidity of river or stream water. Such activities have been the staple diet of hundreds of thousands of students on day-long or residential visits. To some extent they provide an authentic opportunity for students to apply their scientific knowledge, to practise a range of skills and to use equipment that professional scientists would recognize from their own day-to-day work. However, as the curriculum contains more than content, the focus of beyond-the-classroom activities is shifting towards a consideration of what it means to learn about the nature and processes of science.

In 2009 the Qualifications and Curriculum Development Agency drew up a revised set of level descriptions for the subjects in the National Curriculum, which were published for consultation in January 2010 (the consultation is now closed so that the documents are no longer available). Included in the proposals were the nine level descriptions (Levels 1–8 plus 'Exceptional Performance') for How Science Works. These descriptions will be used to illustrate the value of learning science outside the classroom in a range of contexts ranging from school grounds to museums and science centres.

The level descriptions, which are very similar to the existing National Curriculum (QCDA undated), focus on the progressive development of a range of skills such as making observations and taking measurements. For example, at Level 1, students 'make observations about features of objects, living things and events', whereas at Level 3 they 'make relevant observations and measure quantities, such as length or mass, selecting and using a range of simple equipment'. At Level 5, students 'make a series of observations and measurements and vary one factor while keeping others the same'. At level 7, they 'select and use methods to obtain reliable data, including making systematic observations and measurements with precision, using a range of apparatus'.

There is, however, more to How Science Works in the revised descriptions than observing and measuring. Other strands that are developed include designing investigations, recognizing and controlling risks, recording and communicating findings, and suggesting improvements in experimental design. Those students who attain Level 8 should be able to 'recognize that different strategies are required to investigate different kinds of scientific questions, and use scientific knowledge and understanding to select an appropriate strategy'. Implicit in this description is a recognition that there is more than one 'scientific method'. The scientific approach that John Snow used to identify the cause of the cholera outbreak in Victorian England is quite different from the approach used by Jocelyn Bell Burnell and her colleagues in discovering pulsars. It is true to say that both interpreted data in a logical and systematic way, but that, perhaps, is about as close as they come to sharing a 'method'.

The skills which the descriptions identify can be taught in different ways and it is quite possible that they can all be taught in standard school laboratories. But why would anyone choose to take that approach when there are so many opportunities to enrich science teaching using the resources beyond the classroom? In the next section, some of the opportunities for developing students' awareness of the world of science and of how science works are described.

TEACHING HOW SCIENCE WORKS OUTSIDE THE CLASSROOM

Science in the school grounds and in local open spaces

Numerous organizations support science learning in the school grounds. Unsurprisingly, most of them promote the growing of plants, or, more specifically, vegetables for consumption. Towards the end of 2003, Learning through Landscapes and the Federation of City Farms and Community Gardens were contracted to develop and deliver the Growing Clubs element of the Food in Schools (FiS) programme. FiS was a joint venture involving the Department of Health and the Department for Education and Skills. Growing Clubs was designed to offer children practical, hands-on activities that motivated and enhanced their learning and built self-esteem. The wider benefits potentially included developing a deeper understanding of farming and growing and the interdependence between urban and rural communities, and the opportunity to stimulate children to make links between food production, healthy eating and sustainable development.

When I evaluated the pilot programme in 2004, it became clear that schools which appeared to be more likely to sustain growing clubs displayed one or more of four factors, including a core of committed and enthusiastic parents, ideally with some knowledge of gardening or agriculture in the United Kingdom or from their country of origin. Such projects provide a legitimate opportunity to see that what is taught in school science can be applied to growing food in the outside world. Done well, such projects allow students to see that adults in the community possess scientific knowledge and skills that have been passed down from generation to generation. Perhaps the premier example of this approach in the Garden Mosaics project organized by Cornell University in the United States, which involved young people finding out about how to grow and garden from ethnic minorities and recent immigrants in the context of local community gardens (Doyle and Krasny 2003).

More recently, we have been involved in a curriculum development project, Thinking Beyond the Urban Classroom, which has developed science activities for use in school grounds and in local open spaces that have more of a focus on physics and chemistry topics than on traditional biological and ecological themes. The activities are underpinned by a pedagogy that recognizes what we know about group work, assessment for learning, and cognitive acceleration. Many of the activities, which are aimed at the lower secondary (Key Stage 3) age range, involve using observational skills to consider how scientists work.

One of the ten activities developed by Melissa Glackin and colleagues, 'Seeing the world through rose-tinted spectacles', involves pairs of students comparing what colours they perceive when they wear red- and green-tinted glasses. The activity addresses aspects of the curriculum such as colour and how we see, as well as giving teachers the opportunity to discuss questions about the validity and reliability of observations in science. The activities, the development of which was funded by the AstraZeneca Science Teaching Trust, can be found at http://www.field-studies-council.org/projects/bordercrossings/index.aspx. A second year of funding facilitated the integration of a mathematics dimension into the activities under the aegis of the Border Crossings project. These activities complement the range of ecological fieldwork resources, which continues to expand (see, for example, Glackin 2007). They provide opportunities for students to appreciate how science works as well as to develop their understanding of science concepts – it is not an either/or approach.

Learning how science works in science centres, museums, zoos and botanic gardens

Countless opportunities exist within the museum sector (a rather unsatisfactory term in common use to describe the plethora of science centres, museums, zoos, aquariums and zoos in the United Kingdom and elsewhere) for teaching about how science works. The museum sector and the school sector appear to be increasingly aware of the needs and strengths of each other. Museums continue to expand their provision of curriculum-focused courses and resources, and schools are aware of the potential of museums to add value to students' appreciation of science in the outside world.

The major London-based institutions such as the Science Museum, London Zoo, the Natural History Museum and the Royal Botanic Gardens, Kew, now treat education as a core activity rather than as something of low status to be bolted on to conservation or preservation of specimens. The rise in popularity of specialist centres such as at-Bristol, the London Wetlands Centre, Techniquest (Cardiff), ThinkTank (Birmingham), the Centre for Life (Newcastle), the Eden Project (Cornwall) and many others have resulted in more students and teachers being aware of what they have to offer. The Newcastle Life Science Centre's website provides a typical description of the approach that the sector is using to attract visitors:

> Life's schools' programme aims to provide hands-on, minds-on, hearts-on science education that cannot be replicated in the classroom. A key part of the education programme is Lifelab – the largest provider of formal taught science workshops in Europe, providing over 40,000 educational experiences to school students every year. Lifelab offers curriculum enrichment and enhancement by providing access to equipment and expertise that is not normally available in schools.
>
> (Life Science Centre, undated)

Such institutions now understand that they can offer unique opportunities to teach about how science works. They can offer access to scientists through, for example, live on-line broadcasts, opportunities to see actual specimens not simply photographs, and the chance to use techniques and apparatus unavailable in schools (see Case Study 1).

Box 10.1 **Case study 1: The Natural History Museum**

The Natural History Museum's 'How Science Works at the Museum' workshop is aimed at students aged 14–16. The 75-minute workshop is designed to help students to appreciate that the museum has around 350 scientists working with its 70 million specimens. The museum's learning team worked with the Micropalaeontology Department to produce an authentic scientific procedure that consistently produces results in a short space of time.

The topic chosen for the workshop is micropalaeontology, and once inside the laboratory, students watch a video of one of the museum's researchers at work. The students are given 75 grams of Gault Clay from Folkestone in Kent. The challenge that they are presented with is to work out the age of the clay by seeing if there are any microfossil species present in it. The grey clay looks homogeneous

---

but successive washing and filtration – speeded up by microwave-assisted drying – reduces the sample to a small collection of material which, under a powerful microscope, reveals itself as a collection of diverse micro-fossils. With the help of a professional identification key, students are able to work out that the fossils, and therefore the clay, appear to be from the late Jurassic or early Cretaceous periods, which means that they could be 150 million years old.

The plenary activity begins with a comparison of the students' results to reinforce the ideas that they will have covered in school about reliability. Finally, the students are asked how the Natural History Museum's scientists might tell other scientists about the novel aspects of their experimental methods. The museum's education staff outline the value of conferences in disseminating ideas and describe the role of journals and the editorial and peer review process. By chance, on the day that I observed the workshop at first hand – watching students from Boswells School in Chelmsford, Essex, taking part – the BBC reported that fourteen leading stem cell researchers had written an open letter to journal editors in order to highlight their dissatisfaction with the peer review process (BBC, 2 February 2010). This ongoing debate provides interesting material for a post-visit activity.

The workshop is popular with students and, because it has a clear curriculum link, appeals to those teachers who have to work hard to justify why they plan to take students out of lessons. The workshop, which is aimed at secondary school students complements the activities in the museum's Investigate gallery, which are aimed at primary-school-aged children. Shortly after I visited the workshop, one student from a Pupil Referral Unit who had taken part in the workshop wrote on their evaluation form, 'this is cool I have never enjoyed science until now' (Sally Collins, personal communication).

Though the majority of out-of-the-classroom experiences might last for a lesson or a day, many students are fortunate enough to take part in longer visits. For many students, their first experience of residential fieldwork will be as part of a GCSE or A level course in either geography or biology. Some element of fieldwork is compulsory in geography, but that has not been the case in science subjects. The new GCSE specifications suggest that this situation might change and that fieldwork might become more common. However, there will no doubt be little by way of compulsion for residential experience and it will be up to individual schools to decide what use they make of the many opportunities available around the United Kingdom.

Enterprising institutions are beginning to see opportunities for attracting visitors by focusing specifically on their ability to teach about how science works. Case study 2 describes how the newly opened Life Science Centre (Cumbria) has found a way to integrate the benefits of residential experience, outdoor activities and industrial quality science investigations.

Box 10.2 **Case Study 2: The Life Science Centre**

The Life Science Centre (www.thelifesciencecentre.org.uk), based at Field Studies Council (FSC), Castle Head, opened in the summer of 2009. In late September of the same year it hosted its first 4–day residential course for a group of twelve Year 12 students from Wallasey School. During the course, students used a range of techniques aimed at developing their understanding of A level modules in genetics, gene technology and biotechnology. The course was designed to inspire the pursuit of science subjects in school in order to increase participation in higher education and scientific careers. As well as aiming to increase motivation in science subjects, through engagement with scientific project work, hands-on practical experience and enjoyment of a positive residential experience, including outdoor adventure, the centre staff aimed to develop the participants' scientific skills such as team work, communication, problem-solving and the How Science Works agenda.

During the course the students worked in teams to identify a bacterial clone able to produce human insulin for diabetic patients. They cultured the potential clones, isolated DNA and carried out restriction mapping and analysis by gel electrophoresis. The students collected their data on laptop computers.

The students worked in three teams of four students. Each group represented a small biotechnology research team keen to find a solution for diabetic patients. There was an element of competition between the teams, but the importance of collaboration between teams to achieve the ultimate goal was also stressed. Outdoor adventure activities were run by an FSC tutor alongside the scientific activities to further develop skills in problem-solving, communication, teamwork, competition and collaboration. The course concluded with presentations of the teams' findings and a scientific discussion of the results and implications for the scientists and the patients.

The course was evaluated using a pre/post questionnaire, informal discussions with tutors and the accompanying teacher, and by observations of the students' presentations at the end of the course. The students were asked to rate how good they thought they were at ten scientific skills, such as 'Considering validity and reliability of data as evidence', immediately before the course started and after it had ended. Ten of the eleven students who completed both the pre and the post tests indicated that their rating of their competence had increased. Generally, the students who had scored themselves lowest at the beginning of the course showed the greatest gains. There are several explanations for the changes in the scores. One explanation is that participation in the course gave students an opportunity to realize that they were better at science than they had previously thought. Another explanation is that the students were generally feeling more positive at the end of a three-day residential experience than they were at the beginning.

A delayed post test carried out two months after the course showed that several of the students were slightly less positive about their skill levels than they had been immediately following the course, but all but one appeared to have levels greater than at the start of the course. There is some cause for optimism that such courses can make a difference to students' skill development in an authentic, research-focused context.

PUBLIC PARTICIPATION IN SCIENTIFIC RESEARCH (PPSR)

Increasingly, the museum sector is finding ways to involve the public in science through large-scale research. The potential of these activities for teaching people about how science works is substantial, as a recent report noted:

> Participants in many PPSR projects also gain knowledge of the process of science. Indeed, this is one area where PPSR projects have the potential to yield major impacts, particularly Collaborative and Co-created projects, which engage participants in project design and data interpretation to a significant degree.
>
> (Bonney *et al*. 2009: 12)

The report notes that public involvement in research dates back to at least 1880, when lighthouse keepers began collecting data about bird strikes. Most people will be familiar with annual garden bird censuses organized by bodies such as the British Trust for Ornithology which involve thousands of members of the public collecting data. Again, these studies are not new: the US National Audubon Society started its Christmas Bird Count in 1900.

More recent projects include The Birdhouse Network (TBN), developed and operated by the Cornell Lab of Ornithology, which was set up in 1996 and ran until it was absorbed into NestWatch 11 years later. Participating members of the public set up nest boxes close to their homes and monitored bird activity during the spring and the summer. The project 'aimed to enhance volunteer appreciation and understanding of the biology and ecology of breeding birds along with an understanding of the process by which scientific research is conducted' (Bonney *et al*. 2009: 24). At a more basic level, in the What on Earth? project, set up as part of the National Science and Engineering Week 2010, members of the public and school students are encouraged to photograph plants and animals that they do not recognize and upload them to the project website. A panel of scientists will help to identify the specimens, although anyone can have a go at working out what has been photographed (see http://www.whatonearth.org.uk).

Many schools take part in such projects, but many do not. The cost of taking part in such projects is low and it seems as though they capture the interest of the public. Given the ease of access to the internet in schools and the interest in developing international school links, the possibilities for schools to take part in national and global experiments would seem almost limitless. Not only would students be taking part in authentic science research, they would also be learning about the value of multinational scientific collaborations. In many cases it is teachers who decide whether or not their schools and their students will take part in any public engagement with science.

DEVELOPING TEACHERS' PRACTICE IN TEACHING BEYOND THE CLASSROOM

So far we have looked at the wide range of opportunities that exist for teaching outside the classroom. However, the existence of case studies of good practice and the availability of resources and institutions will not necessarily result in a change in teachers' practices. Teachers can point to a number of barriers, mentioned above, that might hinder them in making optimal use of the opportunities. The answer to the question 'How do we make sure that students get the maximum opportunity to realize their full potential through learning science beyond the classroom?' has to lie in improvements in teachers' initial training and in the opportunities provided for continuing professional development.

Learning to teach science beyond the classroom during initial teacher education and training

> The early-career training and development of science teachers in teaching outside the classroom and laboratory is critical to meeting the needs of contemporary science education and yet the provision for fieldwork training is very variable. This variability weakens attempts to develop and promote fieldwork teaching in our secondary schools.
>
> (Tilling and Dillon 2007: 1)

These opening words of the report *Initial Teacher Education and the Outdoor Classroom* highlighted the serious disparity evident in terms of pre-service teachers' access to training for teaching beyond the classroom. The report made several recommendations aimed at rebuilding the capacity to teach outdoor secondary science through the initial training and development of teachers, beginning with a call for all institutions to meet or exceed the training and development standards specified in the Malham Protocol – a set of minimum requirements for teaching science outdoors within initial teacher education (ITE). Another recommendation noted that 'ITE fieldwork training should be seen as the entry point to a developmental progression which formally recognizes the value of building experience of teaching science outside the classroom throughout teaching careers' (ibid.: 1).

Though the focus of the report was on science education generally, rather than on teaching about how science works, the authors noted that

> [t]here are many opportunities for fieldwork activities which link all areas of science, and such synergies can do much to promote a deeper understanding of, and meaningful access to, enquiry processes – how science works – and their role in present-day society. Involvement in practical activities – including those outside the classroom and laboratory – is known to aid recruitment to science.
>
> (Tilling and Dillon 2007: 5)

The report provided case studies from three institutions which showed that a range of strategies were adopted, involving working with schools on investigations, following urban trails and residential fieldwork. The campaign to promote the Malham Protocol included a parliamentary briefing in the House of Commons in November 2009.

Learning to teach science beyond the classroom during continuing professional development (CPD)

Teachers' opportunities to develop their abilities to teach about how science works through CPD appear to be rather limited. Few teachers are able to go on courses more than, say, once each year, and often these are to meetings organized by examination boards. In the short term the internet seems to offer the most likely route through which to access new ideas about teaching about how science works beyond the classroom (see, for example, Teachers tv 2007). A limiting factor, though, is the extent to which teachers appreciate what is meant by the nature of science (Osborne and Dillon 2010). Without such an understanding, teachers might not be able to utilize all the resources and opportunities that are available to them.

MEASURING IMPACT

Underlying this chapter is an assumption that learning about how science works in out-of-the-classroom contexts has an impact of some sort on participating students. The issue of impact measurement is one that has become increasingly vexatious in recent years. In 2008 the micro-economics company Frontier Economics was commissioned to measure the impact of science centres in England. Specifically, the researchers were asked 'to assess whether science centres represent "good value for money" in comparison with other STEM [science, technology, engineering and mathematics]-related organisations' (Frontier Economics 2009: 1). Four organizations were selected for the comparison: the British Science Association, STEMNET, RCUK and the Royal Academy of Engineering. The report concluded:

> We have not been able to assess whether science centres are good value for money relative to other comparator programmes. This is because there is insufficient evidence on the long term outcomes of science centres or comparator programmes.
>
> (Frontier Economics 2009: 2)

The researchers were able to identify a range of qualitative and quantitative data such as visitor numbers, participation costs and types of activities organized. On the basis of those data, the report notes that

> [i]t appears that science centres' activities and outputs map reasonably well to the Science and Society agenda. The science centres offer educational workshops for children at all stages of the National Curriculum and outreach. Some science centres offer continuing professional development (CPD) resources for teachers and organise public dialogue events.
>
> (Frontier Economics 2009: 2)

Nevertheless, while evidence for the impact of visits to museums and science centres continues to grow (see, for example, Dewitt and Osborne 2007), more research is needed into how learning outside school about how science works compares with learning about it solely in school.

CONCLUSION

I am a firm believer in the value of science beyond the classroom. Done well, fieldwork works. It improves knowledge; it improves skills; it improves motivation. Denying students fieldwork is like denying them books, or pens, or computers. Denying some students fieldwork while allowing others to benefit from it is intellectually bankrupt and morally indefensible. And yet that is the position that we find ourselves in now, in schools throughout the United Kingdom and elsewhere.

Education staff in museums, science centres, botanical gardens and other institutions that provide access to science in everyday contexts are developing increasingly appealing and effective ways to engage students in learning about how science works. Students in many schools have unrivalled access to working scientists, impressive and authentic specimens, and up-to-date data to enrich their understanding of science concepts and of how science works. What the future holds depends, to some extent, on whether teaching outside becomes the norm for school science education or whether the momentum that is building up is dissipated by a new series of externally imposed change in curriculum and assessment regimes. The last word, though not the final word, rests with the authors of the most recent report on school–museum partnerships as they address the impact of activities designed to help students 'to engage deeply in scientific inquiry processes of learning' (Bevan *et al.* 2010:11):

These experiences—with an array of real-life settings, animals, professional science communities, objects, scientific instrumentation, and current research and data—have been shown to spark curiosity, generate questions, and lead to a depth of understanding and commitment in ways that are often less possible when the same material is encountered in books or on screens. These formal–informal collaborations have rejuvenated the curriculum, the school-week, teachers' passions and commitments to their work, and in many cases have contributed to students' development of lifelong interests and career pathways.

(ibid.)

FURTHER READING

Bekerman, Z., Burbules, N. C. and Silberman-Keller, D. (eds) (2006) *Learning in Places: The Informal Education Reader*, New York: Peter Lang Press.

Dillon, J., Morris, M., O'Donnell, L., Reid, A., Rickinson, M. and Scott, W. (2005) *Engaging and Learning with the Outdoors: The Final Report of the Outdoor Classroom in a Rural Context Action Research Project*, Slough: National Foundation for Educational Research.

Glackin, M. (2007) Using urban green space to teach science, *School Science Review* 89(327), 29–36.

Griffin, J. and Symington, S. (1997) Moving from task-oriented to learning-oriented strategies on school excursions to museums, *Science Education,* 81(6) 763–779.

King, H. and Glackin, M. (2010) Supporting science learning in out-of-school contexts, in J. Osborne and J. Dillon (eds) *Good Practice in Science Education: What Research has to Say* (2nd edition), Maidenhead: Open University Press.

National Academy of Sciences (2009) *Learning Science in Informal Environments,* Washington, DC: National Academies Press.

Rennie, L. (2006) Learning science outside of school, in S. Abell and N. G. Lederman (eds) *Handbook of Research on Science Education*, Mahwah, NJ: Lawrence Erlbaum Associates.

REFERENCES

Ballantyne, R. and Packer, J. (2002) Nature-based excursions: school students' perceptions of learning in natural environments, *International Research in Geographical and Environmental Education* 11(3) 218–236.

Barker, S., Slingsby, D. and Tilling, S. (2002) *Teaching Biology outside the Classroom: Is It Heading for Extinction?* A Report on Biology Fieldwork in the 14–19 Curriculum, Shrewsbury: Field Studies Council/British Ecological Society.

Bevan, B., Dillon, J., Hein, G. E., MacDonald, M., Michalchik, V., Miller, D., Rauch, N., Root, D., Rudder, L., Scannel, S., Watson, B., Xanthoudaki, M. and Yoon, S. (2010) *Expanding Access, Enriching Science Learning: Developing Systemic Relationships between Formal and Informal Institutions* Washington, DC: Center for Advancement of Informal Science Education (CAISE).

Bonney, R., Ballard, H., Jordan, R., McCallie, E., Phillips, T., Shirk, J. and Wilderman, C. C. (2009) *Public Participation in Scientific Research: Defining the Field and Assessing Its Potential for Informal Science Education.* A CAISE Inquiry Group Report, Washington, DC: Center for Advancement of Informal Science Education (CAISE).

British Broadcasting Corporation (BBC) (2010) Journal stem cell work 'blocked', 2 February. Online. Available HTTP: <http://news.bbc.co.uk/1/hi/sci/tech/8490291.stm> (accessed 7 February 2010).

Department for Education and Skills (DfES) (2006) *Learning Outside the Classroom Manifesto*, London: DfES.

Dewitt, J. and Osborne, J. (2007) Supporting teachers on science-focused school trips: Towards an integrated framework of theory and practice, *International Journal of Science Education* 29(6) 685–710.

Doyle, R. and Krasny, M. E. (2003) Participatory Rural Appraisal as an approach to environmental education in urban community gardens, *Environmental Education Research* 9(1) 91–115.

Frontier Economics (2009) *Assessing the Impact of Science Centres in England* A report prepared for BIS, London: Frontier Economics.

Glackin, M. (2007) Using urban green space to teach science, *School Science Review* 89(327), 29–36.

Her Majesty's Inspectorate (HMI) (1985) *Learning Out of Doors: An HMI Survey of Outdoor Education and Short Stay Residential Experience*, London: HMSO.

House of Commons (2005) *Education outside the Classroom: Select Committee on Education and Skills Second Report*, London: HMSO.

Life Science Centre (undated) About the Life Science Centre. Online. Available HTTP: <http://www.life.org.uk/life-science-centre/about> (accessed 13 February 2010).

Orion, N. and Hofstein, A. (1994) Factors that influence learning during a scientific field trip in a natural environment, *Journal of Research in Science Teaching* 31(10),1097–1119.

Osborne, J. and Dillon, J. (2010) How science works: what is the nature of scientific reasoning and what do we know about students' understanding? in J. Osborne and J. Dillon (eds) *Good Practice in Science Education: What Research Has to Say* (2nd edition), Maidenhead: Open University Press.

Phillips, M., Finkelstein, D. and Wever-Frerichs, S. (2007) School site to museum floor: How informal science institutions work with schools, *International Journal of Science Education,* 29(12), 1489–1507.

Qualifications and Curriculum Development Authority (QCDA) (undated) *Level descriptions for Science.* Online. Available HTTP: <http://curriculum.qcda.gov.uk/key-stages-3-and-4/subjects/key-stage-3/science/Level-descriptions/index.aspx> (accessed 24 August 2010).

Rickinson, M., Dillon, J., Teamey, K., Morris, M., Choi, M.Y., Sanders, D. and Benefield, P. (2004) *A Review of Research on Outdoor Learning*, Preston Montford: Field Studies Council.

Teachers tv (2007) Online. Available HTTP: <http://www.teachers.tv/video/22614> (accessed 19 February 2010).

Tilling, S. and Dillon, J. (2007) *Initial Teacher Education and the Outdoor Classroom: Standards for the Future*, Preston Montford, Shropshire: Field Studies Council/Association for Science Education.

Uzzell, D. L., Rutland, A., and Whistance, D. (1995) Questioning values in environmental education, in Y. Guerrier, N. Alexander, J. Chase and M. O'Brien (eds) *Values and the Environment: A Social Science Perspective*, Chichester: John Wiley.

FINAL THOUGHTS

A book of this kind that provides an introduction to the background, rationale, pedagogy and practice of How Science Works in the secondary school science curriculum covers, of necessity, a wide and diverse range of topics. It is therefore a difficult task to provide a final section that both does justice to this diversity and avoids a glib summary of the contributors' expertise in their particular fields. What is important, if this subject is to become a persuasive, imaginative and engaging part of the school curriculum, is that the suggested approaches, the arguments for them, and the case studies and vignettes that support them become integrated into the teaching of science in schools.

Exactly how this integration and implementation of How Science Works into the school curriculum will be fully achieved in the future is something we can only guess at. Many science teachers – and student science teachers – are already working on imaginative and engaging approaches. I am reminded of two examples shown by student teachers (trainees) in the very recent past; both involve creative approaches to the use of ICT in science classrooms. The first was a data logging demonstration, where temperature and light probe results from average and energy-saving light bulbs were compared. In the second, a set of digital cameras were used because there was no access to a computer: a novel activity was created where pupils made stills and sequenced them for an animated presentation of tectonic plate subduction.

In order to innovate and develop new pedagogies there has to be a high degree of freedom and trust about what teachers do in the classroom. They need to be freed from interference and the burden of testing. There also needs to be an end to teachers working in isolation; they will require genuine professional development that allows them to share and evaluate new ideas, projects and expertise. New technology may help here, but only if harnessed so that it enhances communication and professional interactivity, rather than merely becoming a collection of depositories of information.

As with all curriculum initiatives, How Science Works will take time to bed down in order for teachers to develop further the approaches they already use, and to gain new ones. They will need the time and opportunity to share their wealth of ideas and imagination with each other. We can only hope that these ambitions are realized, not only to promote a relevant and meaningful science education for all students, but to reaffirm the professional importance of science educators.

INDEX